In Plato's Cave

In Plato's Cave

Alvin Kernan

Yale University Press ◆ New Haven and London

Published with assistance from the Kingsley Trust Association
Publication Fund established by the Scroll and Key Society
of Yale College.

Designed by Sonia L. Scanlon
Set in Joanna type by Tseng Information Systems.
Printed in the United States of America.
Library of Congress Cataloging-in-Publication Data
Kernan, Alvin B.
In Plato's cave / Alvin Kernan.
p.   cm.
Includes index.
ISBN 0-300-07589-8 (hardcover : alk. paper)
1. Education, Higher—Aims and objectives—United States.
2. Kernan, Alvin B.   3. Educators—United States—Biography.
I. Title.
LA227.4.K468   1999
378.73—dc21   98-34286

A catalogue record for this book is available from the British Library.
The paper in this book meets the guidelines for permanence and
durability of the Committee on Production Guidelines for Book
Longevity of the Council on Library Resources.
10 9 8 7 6 5 4 3 2 1

To the colleges and universities that educated me

Picture men dwelling in a sort of subterranean cavern with a long

entrance open to the light its entire width. Conceive them as having

their legs and necks fettered from childhood, so that they remain in

the same spot, able to look forward only, and prevented by the fetters

from turning their heads. Picture further the light from a fire

burning higher up and at a distance behind them, and between the

fire and the prisoners and above them a road along which a low

wall has been built, as the exhibitors of puppet shows have parti-

tions before the men themselves, above which they show the

puppets. . . .

See also, then, men carrying past the wall implements of all

kinds that rise above the wall, and human images and shapes of

animals as well, wrought in stone and wood and every material,

some of these bearers presumably speaking and others silent.

A strange image you speak of, he said, and strange prisoners.

Like to us, I said. For, to begin with, tell me do you think

that these men would have seen anything of themselves or of one

another except the shadows cast from the fire on the wall of the cave

that fronted them?

How could they, he said, if they were compelled to hold their

heads unmoved through life?

And again, would not the same be true of the objects carried

past them?

Surely.

If then they were able to talk to one another, do you not

think that they would suppose that in naming the things that they

saw they were naming the passing objects?

Necessarily.

—Plato, The Republic, VII, 514–515, trans. Paul Shorey

Contents

Acknowledgments

My gratitude is due to William G. Bowen and Charles
Cannon, both old friends and colleagues, for reading the manuscript
and making many helpful comments and corrections. The support of
the Andrew W. Mellon Foundation is also gratefully acknowledged.
Dorothy Westgate has done her usual fine work on the text and the
illustrations, and I thank her once again.

Illustrations are printed with thanks to the libraries of
Williams College, Yale University, and Princeton University.

Introduction

shifting educational plates

E very fall brings a "hungry generation" of new students, eternally young, to the colleges, and on a bright winter night Yale's Old Campus looks and feels just the same as it did when I first saw it fifty years ago. The lights in the Victorian brownstone dormitories, Nathan Hale still giving his one life for his country, "Hanc Statuam," Harkness Tower facing Phelps Gate; over in the shadows by Yale Station a new carved marble bench dedicated to Bart Giamatti, barely visible. But I know almost no one there any longer; and it is much the same at Princeton, where (except for a few months when it was stolen) my portrait hangs in Procter Hall in the graduate college among two long rows of graduate deans in bright red, orange, and blue academic gowns, staring defiantly at one another night and day, their names all unknown to the students who gulp down their food on the way to class. Old Dean West, who fought with

Woodrow Wilson to build his neo-Gothic college "above the golf links," understood that it is institutional stone that lasts, not people.

These are familiar images of the passage of time, common in some form to everyone who has played a part in the life of great institutions, and they are so powerful that, in colleges and universities particularly, they dull any sense that institutions in the long run are like people, subject to time. Presidents and trustees like to proclaim that the torch of scientific humanism has passed without a flicker from the Greeks to the present, and conservatives and liberals alike, even the younger ones who worked an educational revolution in the 1960s and 1970s, are now happy to applaud this view on sunny May and June days when Latin is spoken from cue cards and academic caps are thrown in the air.

But colleges and universities do have histories — they change from time to time, not only surface rattles and shakes, which are always taking place, but tectonic shifts that change the purpose of higher education, revise its organization and governance, and redefine the kind of knowledge it produces and teaches. Deep educational changes like this took place in the earlier transformation of the medieval universities, centered on debate and theology, to the classical and rhetorical schooling of the Renaissance. At the beginning of the nineteenth century, the scientific research university appeared in Germany; its positivist, elitist, meritocratic model, in turn, is in our time being displaced by a type of higher education that is institutionalizing the democratic values of American society.

Demographic changes make the democratic tendencies obvious. A vast popularization of American higher education, largely state financed, has made it possible for almost any American graduating from high school to attend college. To attract and accommodate the new students, between 1960 and 1995 the number of accredited institutions of higher education increased from 2,000 to 3,700 (all figures are rounded and taken from the *Chronicle of Higher Education*, August 29, 1997). Enrollments soared from 3.5 million to 12.25 million in the same period. Women's share of the total number of enrolled students increased from 37 percent to 55.5 percent, and minorities from 12 percent to 25 percent. To support this growth, federal aid to students jumped from $300 million to $12 billion a year, in constant dollars, and the states, which had spent $4 billion on higher education in 1960, poured in $46.5 billion by 1996. To provide teachers for the new colleges, doctoral degrees awarded went from 10,000 to 44,000 a year, and total faculty increased from 235,000 to more than 900,000. Comparable increases occurred in income, endowments, annual giving, tuition, faculty salaries, and the size of the support staff. By 1996 the total budget expenditures for American institutions of higher education had reached $183 billion, and institutions that had been bastions of scholarship standing apart from the worlds of commerce and politics—ivory towers, in the old phrasing—had taken a place at the center of society, holding the keys to good jobs and high incomes, serving as national research institutes, and raising huge amounts of money every year.

This expansion of the campus to accommodate all who wanted to attend college was accompanied by a social revolution moving in the same democratic direction. Not only did many more go to college, when they did they rejected the upper-middle-class social ethos that had governed the older educational institutions. The smell of marijuana mingled with that of tobacco on campus, and free speech movements helped coarsen the language and broaden the discourse heard in the groves of academe. Student protests, strikes, and sit-ins were only the most visible challenges to traditional authority. Sex of all kinds came out of the closet. Affirmative action brought increased numbers of minorities into the classrooms, and a militant feminist movement established itself in university affairs. Where the old university had been Eurocentric in what Robert Nisbet called its "faith in the Western tradition: in the ideas, values, systems, and languages that belong to the tiny part of the world that is the promontory of the Eurasian continent known as Western Europe," arguments were now made that education should encompass all cultures and should value all equally; and where the old university had tried to be an ivory tower of unbiased knowledge, outside and above politics, teaching and research now were politicized and treated as instruments of popular reform.

There was a technological as well as a demographic and social revolution. This same period marked the end, or at least the beginning of the end, of the Gutenberg era. Knowledge in earlier universities had been defined largely as reading and writing, and the library had been the academic ziggurat. Science had already moved one large part of the educational scene from the library to the laboratory during the nineteenth century, but in the latter twentieth century an electronic revolution challenged the primacy of the printed book in all educational areas. Computers, virtual libraries, hypertext, databases, freely available materials on the Internet, direct downloading, photocopy machines: electronic technology ran in the same popularizing direction as the other forces working to change higher education. Where print fostered such limiting concepts as copyright, canonical works, textual fixity, originality, and uniqueness, which the university had assumed were given and fundamental, the new technologies worked against these Gutenberg institutions. Cheap copies of everything became available, the computer made it possible to move information about in ever new combinations, and unlimited information was now to be had, almost gratis, via the database and the Internet. Students and scholars sitting in the backwoods now were able to participate in on-line study groups, and they had access to the bibliographies and, in increasing numbers, to virtual texts in major research collections.

The shifts of these huge tectonic plates—demographic, cultural, technological—inevitably affected older conceptions of the primary product of higher education: knowledge. We have, therefore, to speak of a fourth major shift, an epistemological one, which tended like the other revolutions in a democratic direction by questioning established authority and "empowering" a much wider intellectual competence. Absolute knowledge, "essentialism," and traditional concepts of what we can know and who can know it were questioned at all levels. Science set the scene with relativity theory, fractals, and the uncertainty principle, but in the latter half of the century deconstruction—the most descriptive name for a much broader "postmodernist" movement in theory—took uncertainty to its nihilistic extremes in the humanities and social sciences, "demystifying" traditional knowledge, replacing positivism with relativism, substituting interpretation for facts, and discrediting objectivity in the name of subjectivity.

In Plato's Cave is about these seismic changes in American higher education since World War II. This book directly challenges the standard view that though there has been a lot of activity, nothing fundamental has *really* changed in the colleges and universities. Instead, I argue that without quite knowing what was happening, the academy during the latter twentieth century experienced structural changes, still in process, that laid down the foundations of a new kind of democratic university. Though my heart is with the old academic order in which I was trained, my argument is not that this radical change is, as many of my contemporaries believe, an educational catastrophe. The new democratic universities will in time make necessary compromises and settle into their own institutional forms to educate people to their own ends. But things will not be the same, ever again, as they once were, and this entails loss as well as gain.

By humanistic training as well as by experience, I do not, really do not, believe that we can understand historical events without having some sense of how they felt to the human beings who lived them and how those people responded. To go a bit further, I believe that you do not know a theory or attitude until you see it at work in the world. In accordance with these beliefs, my book is not an abstract history of education in the latter twentieth century, nor a sociological study of educational trends, but an intellectual autobiography. My method is narrative, that of the storyteller more than of the historian or the polemicist. You will even find that I am not much of a moralist, though where I stand on things is seldom in doubt. You are also advised not to take my story as a strict chronology or an explicit account of each and every detail. I believe that it is important to be accurate, and I have strenuously tried to get my facts right, but I have not hesitated in the manner of the novelist to conflate and move events about, giving a bit of shading here and there, in order to bring out what was really going on. I should perhaps add that in these memoirs you will not find a map of where the bodies are buried or a tragedy about a personal struggle with the angels of angst—though inevitably a few skulls turn up here and there, and there is enough angst to remind us how familiar it has been in our time. Nor will you hear much about my family—not because they were incidental to my life (quite the contrary) but because this is primarily a story about what happened to the university, not to the Kernans. This emphasis is also very much my wife's wish, as is the fact that in the one picture here that includes her she is turned away from the camera. My own life is described not for its own sake but as a human register of shifts in academic life.

There will be those, I am afraid, who will find this approach too anecdotal and too limited to be convincing. To those who may particularly object to the narrowness of my experience in a few elite colleges and universities—Columbia, Williams, Oxford, Yale, and Princeton—I reply that while the new community colleges might seem to offer better vantage points from which to see the broad trends of democratization and vocationalization of American education in the latter twentieth century, this prospect would not show the full meaning of what has been taking place. The view from those sunny places—why do they always seem to be in the sunbelt?—is so clear as to be blinding. Only in the old elitist colleges and universities did the battles between the traditional academic order and the new educational ways get fought out, inch by grudging inch, and only in these institutions was something like a full sense of what has been at stake in the culture wars to be grasped.

It might further be objected that a story describing educational change largely in terms of what has happened in literary studies, a marginal field in our time, is likely to ignore resistance to change elsewhere. In other words, English departments may be thought to represent the extreme, not the normal, example of what has happened. To these critics I would repeat what a textbook editor, a good friend long dead named Ron Campbell, once said to me: "If you want to know what is actually disturbing a university, visit its English department." And whatever its status as an academic subject, literary studies has been an excellent point from which to observe the conflicting views at work in the universities in the latter half of the twentieth century. There on the intellectual marches you did not just hear in the distance the forces that were transforming the university, they blocked the entrance to your classroom, and they had tenure in your department. Furthermore, in literary studies the full implications of vigorous types of relativism and demands for social change in higher education were more apparent than in fields better protected by sturdy concepts of truth from the high winds of controversy. Here, in English departments, new ideologies such as those of deconstruction, feminism, African-American studies, anticolonialism, and gay and lesbian movements soon found an academic niche and in time revealed their full theoretical and educational effects. Literary studies is, I think it fair to say, the Northern Ireland and Bosnia of the great culture war that has been fought out in the universities since the end of World War II. And like those places, it offers a view not of things unrelated to the larger world but rather one that reveals more clearly than happier places the kinds of energies at work elsewhere in education, the ends they seek, and the likely consequence of their success.

But enough of generalization. Let me now offer you what I learned, and what I learned about learning, from a lifetime in colleges and universities.

1

Theater and Reality in Greenwich Village

columbia, 1946

Exultant not only to have survived the war but to be on my way at last to a college education, I returned after five long years in the navy to the December snows of Saratoga, Wyoming, population 650. Other young men were straggling back from across the world, and we met in Charley Gould's Rustic Bar, in front of the huge stuffed mountain lions with outstretched tails that covered the wall behind the bar. Here we traded tales of the war, as long as the lions' tails, and sooner or later came around to talk of the future.

"What are you going to do now? Will you use the G.I. Bill?"

"Well, I just might go down to Laramie to the university and take some courses."

"There are lots of jobs around here now.

1

Things have really opened up."

"Don't you want to get out? The government will pay for the tuition and give you sixty-five dollars a month, anywhere. It's a great chance."

"Why leave home? We've been away long enough already, and it's a good place to live, lots better than California, and it sure beats Germany."

"My folks are getting old and there's no one else to work the ranch."

In the end most of them stayed and became the state policeman, the town carpenter, the mayor who ran the trucking company, hired hands, sawmill workers, and ranchers. The pull of familiarity is a psychological force as powerful as gravity, and who is to say that this attraction to the known is wrong? For all its nostalgia, though, the American small town seemed to me Winesburg and Gopher Prairie, places where people in the end wear out, bored with a lifetime of doing the same thing, seeing the same people, thinking the same thoughts.

For me, it was time to go, and Candide departed Westphalia with no more confidence in himself nor higher expectations of the big world. I was one of those who feel that the most satisfactory end in life is knowledge; not money or power or prestige, but an understanding of people and the world they inhabit. I assented to Socrates' view that the unexamined life is not worth living. I had in my innocence developed a view of knowledge that will seem laughable in our skeptical days. Read the right books and listen to the right people, think in the most intense and logical fashion, I believed, totally and without question, and all the darkness of Plato's cave of illusions would burn away in the bright sun of understanding. I did not think that truth remained to be discovered; I believed that in the main it already had been found and that I just had not yet been informed of the results. The true nature of evil and of good, the structure of the cosmos and what existed beyond it, the workings of cause and effect, the laws of history, the nature of the mind, the rules that governed social life, what distinguished good art from bad, these were all, I believed, lying about like golden nuggets on the American campus, just waiting to be picked up.

I bought a decrepit blue 1936 Chrysler at a high price and went to California to see my wartime comrade Dick Boone. Acting was what he wanted, while I wanted knowledge, and New York seemed the place to find both. The huge car was a juggernaut once you got it going down the road, wearing out brake linings like Kleenex, but the valves and rings were shot, so it had no power. Loaded with our baggage it had to be pushed up the steep driveway of the Boones' house above Glendale, and by the time we had crossed the desert and reached Las Vegas, Dick was trying to persuade me to take it to a used car lot, get what I could for it, and go to a casino and put it all on red for one turn of the wheel. He reasoned that if I won I would have enough to buy a newer car, if I lost we would take the bus and be better off anyway. My reasoning was that it was all my money that was involved, not a penny of his, and that I had better hang on to what I had.

In Utah snow was falling and the road was covered with ice. The car gulped so much gas that it had to be driven in overdrive to get from one station to the next, but it had to be taken out of overdrive to get some control on the slippery road. The overdrive lever was sticky, and one of us had to crawl underneath the car with a hammer, while the other braced both feet on the dash. When the Übermensch shouted "Now!" and pulled with all his might, the Untermensch hit the connection sharply with the hammer. This continued all the way across the country in dreadful weather—"How far to Joliet?" "Never heard of it"—until seven days later we thundered down the Pulaski Skyway into New York, nearly a century after the first train had made it across the country in six. I began to get some sense of how much larger the world was than I had thought when I took a cashier's check for a thousand dollars into the Corn Exchange Bank (it looked very sound) to open a checking account and was told, very politely, that the minimum balance was ten thousand, and that they couldn't cash the check anyway because they didn't really know—ignorance of this kind seemed unbelievable to me—if the Saratoga, Wyoming, State Bank existed. It took two weeks to get the check validated, and in the meantime we were broke, dependent for food on an old writer, Jimmy Hopper, still writing stories about the Philippine Insurrection, and his young wife, Elaine, whom Dick had known in Carmel before the war.

In time we ended up in one room in Greenwich Village, on Fourth Street. A partition at the back separated a filthy bath from a filthier kitchen and supported a small sleeping loft above. Some cheap water paint made it look better, and two iron cots with pallet mattresses made up the furniture. It was very like the navy, but free of navy discipline! Dick went off to the Neighborhood Playhouse, which was happy to accept veterans with the G.I. Bill, and I made my way up to Morningside Heights, where Columbia had set up an extension school for returning veterans. No doubt they made a little money on it, but they ran it well, staffing it with regular faculty and giving fine courses. All this was possible only because of the G.I. Bill, and here is probably the place to say something about this first step in the postwar democratization of higher education.

The Servicemen's Readjustment Act of 1944, more generally known as the G.I. Bill, was passed by Congress not so much to reward the 15.5 million people in the services at that time as to ward off dangers that might appear when at the end of the war huge numbers of soldiers and sailors were dumped into the economy. Eleanor Roosevelt had gone overseas to talk to the troops and had been greeted with raucous shouts of "Take it off," which so unnerved her that she told the press that war had brutalized the men so much that they should be held for a time after the war in camps where they could be recivilized for entrance into society. Congress was more worried, however, about what millions of jobless veterans might mean economically, remembering uneasily the Great Depression of the 1930s, the bonus marches, and the revolutions led by disaffected veterans in Europe after World War I.

With these concerns in mind, they set up a postwar plan for veterans that would pay unemployment insurance—the famous 52/20 club, $20 a week for a year—help with job placement, provide loans to build homes, give everyone mustering-out pay of $300, and pay a monthly stipend of $65, later $75, plus up to $500 a year for tuition, books, and equipment for anyone attending an accredited college. The $65 a month would pay for food, and the maximum of $500 a year would cover tuition at even the most expensive college in the country, Harvard, if you could get admitted. Married students got slightly more. Any veteran could attend for at least one year any college that admitted him or her, and an additional year of eligibility was provided for each year of service, up to a maximum of four.

About 15 million veterans used one or another of the various programs run by the Veterans Administration, but only about two and one-quarter million attended college from 1944 to 1956 on the G.I. Bill. It was estimated that of this group only 20 percent, of whom I was certainly not one, would have gone to college without government assistance. The program was most attractive to those who had served during the actual war, and the peak enrollment years of veterans were 1946–1950, after which it tailed off fairly rapidly until the program ended in 1956. By then there was a Korean War bill in place, but it was not nearly so popular as the G.I. Bill.

Not everyone was enthusiastic about the G.I. Bill. The old elitist views died hard. Robert M. Hutchins, then president of the University of Chicago and one of the most prominent voices in American education, predicted in "The Threat to American Education" that as a result of the G.I. Bill "colleges and universities will find themselves converted into educational hobo jungles" (*Colliers*, December 30, 1944). The president of Harvard, the distinguished James Conant, in his annual report called the bill "distressing" because it did not "distinguish between those who can profit most by advanced education and those who cannot" (*Harvard Alumni Bulletin*, January 1944 and February 1945).

The veterans themselves had no doubts. Nearly half the students in college after the war were veterans. They were extremely discriminating, choosing only the best universities and liberal arts colleges, which were crammed to discomfort levels for lack of classrooms, dormitories, and married students' housing, while the poorer state and private colleges had empty places. The average veteran was twenty-five on entrance, with 56 percent below twenty-five and 17 percent over thirty. Half the veterans were married. Over the years the total cost was $5.5 billion for a college program that educated a generation of professionals—lawyers, doctors, professors, engineers—and began the full democratization of American higher education.

Selecting my courses at Columbia was a real pleasure. Modern philosophy, from René Descartes's rationalism to William James's pragmatism, seemed just the thing for someone keen to break into the realm of truth in a hurry. Political science, the history of political systems, would teach me the truths of government; creative writing would hone my literary skills; and math would reveal the bare bones of reality. What a delight the books were to buy, even with their cheap bindings and wartime austerity paper that seemed to be made of pressed oatmeal already yellowing and flaking. I have some of the books still: the slim ivory copy of *The Discourse on Method*; the blue cardboard of David Hume's *Enquiry*; the Modern Library short stories of Ernest Hemingway; a big, blue, and very expensive text describing all the forms of Western government, from Greek oligarchy to bicameral legislatures. Books have mana in Gutenberg society, and in many ways it is not necessary to read them but only to own the physical objects, to put them on your shelf where you can look at the titles, to absorb their sacred energies, which is really why scholars build personal libraries. But at that time I wanted to read them through and understand them as well, so at night I would sit in our room in the Village reading by the dim bulb hanging from the center of the ceiling about getting to the one solid thing that can be asserted without doubt and on which a world can be built — "Cogito ergo sum" — or, in a somewhat different vein, about Mrs. Macomber putting a bullet through the head of her husband instead of the charging buffalo. "Why ever would she want to do that?"

At least I read there for a time. Dick was soon recognized as a coming actor at the Neighborhood Playhouse, and he brought back to our room at night a number of other aspiring actors, many of whom, such as Kevin McCarthy, became well known in time. It turned out that actors learn their trade by an activity called improvising.

"Let's be a group of gangsters who have decided to kill Dick and Jane."

"Okay, but we get into a fight with you and escape. We try to stop cars to get a ride, and run up to people asking for help."

"Right, and we follow you, accusing people of helping you. After a while you get back to the room and we corner you here and have it out."

Then the roughhouse would begin, the prisoners would be lightly knocked about, clothing searched. Then the escape and hullabaloo in the streets where astounded citizens would be confronted by a wild-looking man and an attractive girl with her dress pulled off her shoulder. It was all a children's game, of course, good exercise, an exciting evening épatering the bourgeoisie, and it always ended back in the room and on the beds. As the springs creaked and new passion gasped, I retired to the gray-green toilet, strings of old paint hanging down the walls, pondering by the dim bulb Hume's argument that the mind is totally dependent on experience, that mental activity cannot discover the slightest thing about reality on its own. And so while I reflected on le bon Davy's billiard balls and whether one could know a priori what would happen if you hit one with another, pretense created pleasure in the grimy room just beyond the partition, until the exhausted lover-actors made their way off to some party and I could sleep in my rumpled bed. I had no sense at the time that we were enacting in that little apartment an epistemological drama between objectivity and subjectivity, trying to get at the truth and making it up, that would recur throughout my academic life.

In Greenwich Village things did not look so good for philosophy or for me, but I was slightly contemptuous, while at the same time envious, of people who had no interest in reality and had such a good time with make-believe. But there were attractive intellectual games as well, it turned out. My creative writing teacher, a very attractive young woman, always wore a red cloche hat while teaching—something she associated with Dorothy Parker and the Algonquin literary round table. She put us to various exercises, sketches of action, scenes of indolence, nature descriptions, and so on. All veterans, we drew on the war for material, and she was surprised to discover that when a patrol whispered "Vehicles!" it was not a learned word unlikely to be used by soldiers but the standard warning when you didn't know what the hell was coming down the road, wheelbarrows, trucks, motorcycles, or tanks.

One afternoon after class she asked me if I could stop by her office to discuss a problem. One of the older and surer members of the class was making suggestive remarks to her and cornering her in ways that made her nervous. She wanted my advice, she said, about whether he was dangerous and how she should handle him. Would it be safe to walk home alone in the dark evenings? Flattered to be asked about intimate matters by so sophisticated a creature as this girl in her bright lipstick, dark hair, and red hat, I told her that I thought it was just a standard G.I. attempt to try to make any good-looking woman, and that there was no danger in it. Perhaps I was right, but would I mind walk-ing home with her just the same—I might even come in for a bit to talk about writing. Her nipples, it turned out, were the same shade of red as her hat, which she removed, despite my pleas, for thrashings and turn-ings on the bed of pleasure. Her marriage had failed from too much Hamletian brooding and a consequent impotence, but my own appe-tites were at this time almost entirely without complication, as were hers, and without thinking too much about it we managed to have a very good time on those dark winter afternoons after the writing class.

Back in the Village below Washington Square, Dick Boone and I, who had been such good friends in the navy, increasingly irritated each other. We still quoted our favorite poet, e. e. cummings, and laughed at the way he skewered "the brass" of an earlier war—"straightway the sil-ver bird looked grave, departed hurriedly to shave"—but peace was too much for us. Theater and philosophy acted out their antagonism, Pre-tense bold and loud claiming the space for his own, while Reason, quiet but stubborn, insisted on certain rights. In the end Pretense was the stronger, and Reason moved out, finding an even grimier and smaller room in which to finish out the term. New York was not for me: I hated the crowds, the noise of the subways, dirty slush in the streets, and the constant edge of unfriendliness, if not downright hostility, that was the native manner. It was time for a country boy to move.

On an early spring day in 1946 I got the old blue juggernaut out of the corner of a lot where it had been stored, brushed off the dirty snow, charged the battery that I had kept in the corner of my room, and roared off without a map to drive around New England looking for the college. Not just a college, but the college. I was completely ignorant of the entire New England college ethos, the social status, the rank-ing order, the elitism, the admissions difficulty, but I had drunk deep of the myth of ivy-covered buildings, spartan living, transcendentalism and bold thinking, Concord and Walden Pond, and I knew that if I drove long and far enough I would find a place where deep study and wise mentors would resolve the troubling conflict between theater and reality, between Descartes's rationalism and Hume's skepticism, that my months in New York had revealed.

I came in time to Williamstown, Massachusetts, and there in that bowl in the Berkshires, The College suddenly spread out before me. The white Congregational church with its tall spire stood out against the purple mountains surrounding the town and the campus. Bells ringing in the evening, the Civil War monument to the graduates who died at Antietam and Cold Harbor, Georgian brick buildings and nineteenth-century Gothic stone, the long row of elm-shaded fraternity houses. I bought it all instantly, Colonel Ephraim Williams and Lord Jeffrey Amherst, Mark Hopkins on one end of a log and a student on the other, Stetson Library with its niches for the busts of the great—Shakespeare, Goethe, Montaigne—the tiny old stone observatory. Even the beer bottles cooling on the sills outside the dorm windows spoke of evenings of easygoing, deep talk among students, as well as sophisticated laissez-faire on the part of college authorities.

Ignorance is not without its benefits, and when I presented myself at the admissions office without an appointment, without the faintest idea of the elitist reputation of Williams College, the admissions director was amused enough to sit down and have a long talk with me, mostly about the recent war and our experiences. He too had been in the navy, and we had been in many of the same places and battles. I enjoyed the talk immensely and would have carried on all day, but after a while it clearly was time to go. I thought it would help if I told the director frankly that I would like to go to Williams but that I needed to know whether they would admit me—at least I knew there was a chance they might not—and when, so that I could make my plans. He remained grave, puffed the pipe that was required in those days, and said he would if my Columbia grades and SATs were all right. They were, and I was duly admitted.

2

The Other End of the Log

williams college, 1946–1949

I
n the bright fall sunshine, with the bells ringing for class, dressed in my fur-collared navy flight jacket, blue work shirt, and bell-bottomed dungarees, I stopped to look at the statue of the Civil War soldier with his cape, kepi, percussion rifle, and long bayonet. Other veterans came by, wearing army boots and fatigue jackets still bright with the flashes of the First Cavalry, Eighth Air Force, Big Red One, Eighty-second Airborne, Third Marines. These were men who had recently at an icy twenty thousand feet looked out of B-17s at the bomber stream a hundred miles long over Germany, who had watched the ramp of the landing craft drop to reveal the black sands of Iwo Jima, who had roared in a tank over the Remagen bridge across the Rhine, who had looked up at Monte Cassino, far above, as their regiments were shredded trying to get their rubber boats across the river at the foot of the mountain.

About half of the new class were eighteen year olds, alumni children from the usual feeder prep schools, Deerfield and Exeter, and from the fashionable country day schools of West Hartford, Lake Forest, and Shaker Heights. Normally, they dominated the college, but in 1946 they were lost among the veterans. A former infantryman, decorated with the Silver Star for his skill at street fighting in German towns, got drunk while waiting on tables at a solemn fraternity dinner of alumni and new pledges, and thinking to add to the fun leaped on the table, roared up and down, kicking the china and crystal aside to demonstrate the fine art of breaking down doors to get at snipers.

While appearances may have changed, the institutional infrastructures, both social and educational, remained much the same. Fraternities were still very much a part of life at Williams, so much so that getting a room and meals after the freshman year was difficult unless you were a member of a fraternity. The only alternative was the Garfield Club, a dormitory with a small commons bearing the name of a recent president of the college, son of the one president of the United States that Williams had produced—only to be assassinated in his first term. It was known with the usual anti-Semitic bias as the "Garfinkel Club" because of the large number of Jews, excluded from most of the fraternities, who, along with some of the odder varieties of Christians, ended up there, studying, playing bridge eternally, and longing to share in imagined bacchanals in the great fraternity houses whose long windows, behind deep green lawns and large maples, lighted the main highway through town.

Veterans of Midway and Normandy should have scorned such childish nonsense as initiation rites, solemn mumbo-jumbo rituals, and blood pledges of eternal brotherhood, but our adolescence apparently had not been skipped, merely put in cold storage for a time. We hastened to the House of Walsh, the local haberdasher who extended long lines of credit, to buy our unofficial uniform of gray flannel suits, white and blue oxford-cloth shirts with button-down collars, and heavy brown (never black) scotch-grain brogues. Thus attired as true New England college boys, we sat in our rooms and waited nervously for the rush committee members to visit and pass judgment on us.

When Smithers was elected to Chi Psi, one of the more fashionable fraternities, his parents hurried to Williamstown, where he gave them a tour of the house, including the marbled communal toilets. Wresting open the door of a stall to show his admiring parents the fraternal plumbing, he found one of his new brothers sitting on the john, face hidden in his hands. With the savoir faire of the true fraternity man, Smithers introduced his parents to the seated brother, who continued to hide his face while extending a single groping hand. Not to be flurried, Smithers stood chatting for a few moments about fraternity affairs, leaning nonchalantly against the open stall door.

The real counters in the game were, of course, what Scott Fitzgerald said they always were, as they still are: family, money, looks, athletic ability, personality. Only very rarely intellect or good nature. Never virtue. I was innocent of such matters, and having not the slightest comprehension of this ancient snobbery I babbled away happily about the war years and the books we were reading in class to the self-assured fraternity members who came around to interview me. Fatal. Fortunately, or perhaps unfortunately, some of the houses were less finicky than others. The Dekes, St. Anthony, and Chi Psi could pick and choose. But there were, down at the lower end of the pecking order, off the main street, some fraternities that badly needed help in paying the mortgages and keeping their ramshackle houses heated enough to be habitable in the long winters. In time, as all the big men on campus went to the more prestigious houses, almost everyone could expect to hear from one of these fraternities of last resort. There was argument about just which fraternity was lowest in this group, the Betas—"Let's all go down and piss on the Beta House," roared the voices of the night "flown with insolence and wine"—or Delta Upsilon. DU usually won, and there I ended up in an old Tudor half-timber monstrosity, with a furnace that gulped tons of expensive coal every day, and where the wolf always could be heard howling just outside the door.

The president of the house was a much older, very funny Irishman from Boston who sat in his presidential tower room drinking beer and telling stories all day long. Then there was Pennyworth, who could think of nothing but cunt—not sex, but cunt—and wore the tires on his new car bald in pursuit of it. Hamilton was already in training for his later work in Bebe Rebozo's bank and Nixon's Watergate finances.

Webley the prep school boy was infatuated with Nazis and filled his room with swastikas and ritual SS daggers. This in a house filled with veterans and even some Jews, the wonderful Heineman boys. There were also a couple of socialists who established their proletarian credentials by becoming the permanent waiters in the dining room. They shared the cheapest and smallest room at the back of the house, where they plotted ways to reveal our false consciousness to the rest of us.

They had their work cut out for them, for while we may have had doubts about the honesty and fairness of the American political and economic system, we were nonetheless dedicated to becoming a successful part of it as soon as possible. We told ourselves, of course, that when our time came we would improve the world, but we were hardly revolutionaries. Veterans in our early and mid twenties, the children of a devastating depression, our youth spent in the service, a new cold war already under way, the threat of atomic weapons hanging over us, we suspected that the establishment that ruled the country had, as Philip Wylie told us in his great wartime satire *Generation of Vipers* (1942), "balls of brass and the guts of a bear," but we made no waves.

We were mainly determined to enjoy ourselves in whatever time we had, and we certainly, unlike earlier and later generations of students, had no thought that American capitalism was irredeemably corrupt or that communism and Soviet Russia offered any hope whatsoever for the future. Our attitudes toward communism were pretty much formed by two great literary attacks of our time on that system, Arthur Koestler's *Darkness at Noon* (1941) and George Orwell's *Animal Farm* (1946). These two books, along with Orwell's later *Nineteen Eighty-Four* (1949), may well have been as effective in the Cold War as were containment and nuclear deterrence. Certainly they convinced my generation that whatever was wrong, communism was not going to make it better—in fact it would make it worse, much worse. About as far as I went in the way of protest was writing to Wyoming for an absentee ballot in 1948 and, worried about what I considered Harry Truman's dangerous pugnacity—"Give 'em hell, Harry"—foolishly voting for Henry Wallace, one of only a handful of voters in all of America to do so.

Money was a more constant problem than politics. I had come out of the war with a few thousand dollars, largely the winnings of a big poker game on board ship in Japan just before coming back to the States, but that was soon exhausted, so I sold the old blue Chrysler for a few hundred dollars. I wasn't going anywhere anyway. The $65 a month the government gave veterans would just about pay for room and board, and for the rest I did a variety of odd jobs like collecting cleaning and laundry on commission for the local cleaners, working in the rare book library putting lanolin on the cracking leather covers of the old books, and working as a bartender in a good restaurant, the 1896 House, just outside town.

On the instructional level at least, Williams College was still pretty much the kind of educational institution idealized by Lionel Trilling in his essay "On the Teaching of Modern Literature":

> That quiet place at which a young man might stand
> for a few years, at least a little beyond the competing
> attitudes and generalizations of the present, at least a
> little beyond the contemporary problems which he is
> told he can master only by means of attitudes and gen-
> eralizations, that quiet place in which he can be silent,
> in which he can know something—in what year the
> Parthenon was begun, the order of battle at Trafalgar,
> how Linear B was deciphered: almost anything at all
> that has nothing to do with the talkative and attitudi-
> nizing present, anything at all but variations on the ac-
> cepted formulation about anxiety, and urban society,
> and alienation, and *Gemeinschaft* and *Gesellschaft*, all the
> matter of the academic disciplines which are founded
> upon the modern self-consciousness and the modern
> self-pity.

This pretty much accorded with my own ideas of an education at that time, and to Williams College and its faculty, the stars and the plod-ders, I owe an enormous debt. I had seen the ruins of Nagasaki and Hiroshima without the faintest idea of where the destructive energy came from, and now I learned something of atomic physics, along with Adam Smith's marketplace and Keynesian economics. I heard at Williams for the first time about Charles Darwin and his theory of evolution, Sigmund Freud and the unconscious, the periodic table of the elements, William Shakespeare's plays, Gregor Mendel's genetics, the history of antiquity and of modern Europe, something of the French language, and other pieces of the furniture of the educated mind in our time. I also learned those things that last best in a liberal education, those habits of mind such as how to examine and sort out the evidence, how to analyze the facts, how to lay them out in speech and in writing, and how to argue them effectively.

All of this, however, was taught pretty much in a rote fashion that reached almost the level of parody in a course given by the president of the college, James Phinney Baxter, a naval historian and specialist in the development of guns and armor plate in the nineteenth century. Tougher and thicker armor would be developed, and then a bigger gun to penetrate it, and then thicker armor, and then a different shape of projectile. The course taught something, I suppose, about the kind of arms races that Russia and the United States were then starting on, but this was never mentioned, only the relentless thicker, bigger, thicker, bigger, with loving detail of plunging fire, dreadnought, torpedo, and ironclad.

About this time I heard the old saw that the only lesson that history teaches is that history teaches no lessons, but at the same time I also read George Santayana's often-repeated remark that "those who cannot remember the past are condemned to repeat it." I asked, but no one could resolve the paradox, and most of my courses in ancient and modern history seemed to offer just the facts with little concern for what could be made of them. Never was there the slightest hint that they might be interpreted as the repetitive follies of mankind that, like the brave old Duke of York, marched ten thousand soldiers up the hill, only to march them down again.

The Williams faculty was a well-intentioned and intelligent group of men — there were no women — but most of them were not, with rare exceptions, critical or adventurous thinkers. They were led by one of the last of the old autocratic college presidents, "called" from the Harvard history department to preside over the fortunes of Williams College in the thirties. "Phinney" looked and sounded like Teddy Roosevelt, and even with only one lung left from a bout with TB he still roared in a voice heard with fear through Hopkins Hall. He interviewed and hired and fired, with almost no consultation, every single faculty member.

A rather fine looking Georgian brick faculty club had been built by a rich benefactor who in return insisted that a certain number of faculty members visit him at his South Carolina plantation every year. A portrait on the heroic scale of this betweeded and shotgun-outfitted alumnus, with a spotted hunting dog licking his hand, hung over the fireplace in the club. A professor of art history identified the dog as the icon of a grateful faculty. Near the picture was a debarked and varnished tree branch, fantastically intertwined and complicated. Beneath it was inscribed the Alexander Pope couplet:

> 'Tis Education forms the vulgar mind,
> Just as the Twig is bent, the tree's inclin'd.

Discontent, as these images suggest, but not daring to be rebellious, the faculty suffered through long, hard winters in a landscape covered with ice and snow from November through March, with dark clouds on seven days out of ten. The teaching schedule prescribed four or five one-year classes, each meeting three times a week for fourteen weeks a semester, with frequent papers and tests. There were about a hundred professors for the thousand students. Many of them had started teaching at one of the major Ivy League universities, and failing promotion at the end of six or seven years had come to Williamstown for an assistant professorship, or even in rare cases a tenured associate professorship. To me, with their tweed jackets, pipes, and learning, the Williams faculty seemed incredibly sophisticated and successful, but many of them had failed by standards that they themselves fully subscribed to, and so, long after everyone else had forgotten, they could never forgive themselves for not becoming a professor at Harvard or Yale. Buying a power saw and rebuilding an old house, or taking to drink and the neighbor's wife's bed were standard ways of handling the guilt of failure.

Lack of money intensified their problems. The average beginning faculty salary at this time was about three thousand dollars a year, the top about five or six thousand. I went to supper once at an admired teacher's house to find him and his wife sitting at a table covered with bills which they moved about as if in a game of Monopoly, trying to work out some strategy of what to pay now and what to put off. Many of the students were rich, and the ancient contrast between the wealthy student and the impoverished tutor put a subtle though strongly denied poison into the atmosphere.

Scholarship did not flourish in this atmosphere. Why bother? The science labs were usually locked up, and no test tubes bubbled away inside. And though Williams in the postwar period, in keeping with the general increase in academic standards that followed the war, was beginning to tie promotion and salary to publication, only a few faculty members worked very hard at their subjects. Teaching was the purpose of a liberal arts college, they said, and too much publication could make a less effective teacher who spent little time with his students.

I soon found that one encounters only a few really great teachers—with luck, maybe even a *really* great one—during the course of an education. There were several at Williams in the late forties. Fred Schuman was a student of international relations who was often accused of being a communist, which he was not, by the more conservative alumni, who regularly demanded that he be fired. He defended himself ably against the charges, and his class was a must for serious students. A man of rationality, he could not avoid the irrational when one of his children came apart mentally, and Schuman blindly turned to Dianetics. It seemed to help, and he, the philosopher-king of Williamstown, wrote about the wonders of Dianetics and tried to convert anyone who would listen to this latter-day superstition.

Clay Hunt, a scholar of Renaissance poetry, was the teacher who had the greatest influence on my early education. A Kentuckian with a Ph.D. from Johns Hopkins, he was a manic-depressive, and a closet homosexual, who taught with frantic enthusiasm and broad learning. Drinking, smoking, talking, and eating with gusto, he was outrageous in everything, trying to shock his classes and the faculty members, squirming about uncontrollably as he flushed, grimaced, and roared with laughter at his own cruel but witty sallies. He had, or came close to having, a photographic memory and would thrust his reddened face in yours and quote long swatches of poetry, usually, I learned in time, with a few small errors. Leaving a party one night after Clay had been particularly loud and learned, I found a faculty member on the porch in the dark, holding his head: "How can you compete with someone with a memory like that?"

A reviewer of a book Clay later wrote on his favorite poet, John Donne the metaphysical, described his criticism as belonging to "the lemon-squeezer school," and he was one of the most intense of the New Critics. A poetic text—Clay dealt not in prose—was an invitation to carve up the language in a thousand ways, locate endless ambiguities, display immense amounts of curious learning, and in the end bring it all together with some triumphant twist of logic. To many he will sound repulsive, and there were those who could not stand him, but I found in him a rare energy of thought, intense feelings, and a conviction that knowledge was both strenuous and almost a physical pleasure. He made literature and criticism seem active and meaningful, and I followed him from one class to another and spent my senior year in honors work with him reading modern poetry, which at that time meant plentiful doses of T. S. Eliot, William Butler Yeats, William Carlos Williams, John Crowe Ransom—on whom I wrote a thesis— D. H. Lawrence, Robert Frost, and Wallace Stevens.

The Williams faculty may have had doubts about the veterans when they first poured onto campus, but for years afterward they, like other faculties, looked on the late forties and early fifties as the golden age of college teaching. "Spontaneous overflow of powerful feelings," to quote a Romantic poet, in the middle of fairly commonplace discussions, could suddenly make the intellectual life very exciting. My economics professor, Paul Swazey, had been forced out of Harvard for his communist leanings, and his critical discussion of capitalism in Econ 1 regularly struck hot, bright sparks from young men champing to make a fortune on Wall Street. The instructor in the history of religion tried to teach the higher criticism of the Bible, distinguishing the parts of the Pentateuch written by the J (Jawhist), the E (Elohist), and the P (Priestly) writers, only to get entangled with people who had been religiously newborn in foxholes in fundamentalist discussions about every word in the Bible being written by God.

But on the whole, the veterans were as areligious as they were apolitical. Students were still required to attend church or chapel once a week, and cards were collected to certify attendance; but you could go to any church in town—the brief early Sunday Roman Catholic mass, no sermon, was the most popular. Failing all else you had to attend the college chapel on Sunday evening when the chaplain, fortified by strong waters, held forth about his navy experiences in which he had seen—most unlikely, thought the veterans—sailors hurl themselves overboard in blood-reddened water filled with sharks to save their dying shipmates, all in the spirit of Christian self-sacrifice and the brotherhood of man!

Even poetry could explode the classroom from time to time, as it did in a memorable introductory English class of mine that was learning how to read poetry and write papers out of the famous New Critical textbook Understanding Poetry, by Cleanth Brooks and Robert Penn Warren, first published in 1938 but getting its real classroom test in the years after the war. "Sentimentality" was the ritual word of poetic excommunication for Brooks and Warren, and it was pronounced nowhere more solemnly than in their discussion of Percy Bysshe Shelley's "Indian Serenade":

> Oh lift me from the grass!
> I die! I faint! I fail!
> Let thy love in kisses rain
> On my lips and eyelids pale.

This was too much for Brooks and Warren, and they fulminated: "The statement, 'I die,' comes with very different effect when wrung from the lips of a man of few words, cautious and well balanced [the type obviously admired by Brooks and Warren] than it does when shrieked out by a flighty, hysterical sentimentalist." On and on they went, unable to let well enough alone: "Sentimentality we may define as the display of more emotion than the situation warrants . . . obsession with one's own emotions . . . emotional one-sidedness." They may well have been right, but it is an unfortunate passage, one that starkly reveals the ethical narrowness of these stoic southern Americans.

On the day "The Indian Serenade" was discussed, someone who agreed with what Brooks and Warren had to say about sentimentality jumped on old Shelley with both feet—"I can't stand this stuff any longer"—only to be countered by another voice and another way of feeling:

> "What's wrong with the poem after all? The guy's in love. Love's like that, you lose control, you do foolish things, you feel sick, you exaggerate."
>
> "Well, sure, but it's still sentimental. It's just him rolling in his feelings. We don't even know what she looks like. Maybe she doesn't even like him and he's just wasting his time."
>
> "So what if she doesn't like him? [the voice rising] We don't need to see her, it's his feelings that we're interested in. Love doesn't have to have anything to do with a girl, it's just love."
>
> "I still say its sentimental!"
>
> "Okay, so it's sentimental. What's wrong with that? I like sentiment, I don't see anything wrong with it, and any poem that doesn't have lots of it is a bore."

By then they were both shouting, and when the instructor tried to intervene, he was ignored. Others were by this time chipping in from the sides. Both participants obviously had a personal stake in all this. Both seemed to have been in love in some kind of difficult circumstances, and probably the one had suffered openly and a lot, while the other had bottled up his feelings. Faces were red by now and fists were clenched, there were even a few shoves, but others calmed them down, and the bell rang to end the most passionate discussion of poetry I have ever participated in.

Doubts about the certainty of knowledge seemed to occur everywhere. A fraternity "brother" charmingly known as Bobo was engaged to a girl at Smith College, about fifty miles away by a twisting road, and spent much of his time in Northampton. He was a pre-med and worried about his grade in biology, but he was never in Williamstown long enough to go to the lab to look at the microscopic creatures we were supposed to draw and turn in as evidence of our lab work. A parody of Samuel Taylor Coleridge,

He prayeth best who loveth best
      All things both great and small.
The paramecium is the test,
      I love him least of all

was often quoted by the biology teacher, Mr. Hoare, but he stressed at the beginning of the course that we were to avoid artistically touching up the things we saw: "Draw it as it is." I took him at his word, sketching nature not in imagined symmetry but in all the irregularity—I even roughed it up a bit for effect—that I thought I saw under the lens.

Exhausted and pale after an illicit night in a Smith dormitory and a reckless early morning drive on snowy roads back to Williamstown, a haggard Bobo would ask to borrow my lab drawings. He drew quite well, much better than I did, and in copying my sketches he neatened them up considerably, a little dramatic shadow here, a highlight there, and smooth sinuous curves for amoeba and paramecium. A most unscientific approach, I thought, until I noticed that on the lab papers I was regularly getting Cs and he was getting Bs and As. Art was once again, as it had in Greenwich Village, triumphing over fact. But just what were the little buggers like in reality, rough or smooth? The instructor apparently held contradictory views. He told us they were rough but paid off for smooth. Did the observer and his microscope distort the object? Hume and George Berkeley and all their questions of idealism and empiricism suddenly came back to life. I eventually struggled through to a B, and while Bobo did get an A, he went on not to med school but to a life in the insurance business.

Disturbing evidence that knowledge was not quite so firm as might be desired began to arrive from many areas, such as a brief general course on cultural anthropology. What the subject had to say was simple but startling to me at that time and to most of the other students: people not only live in different ways, they think and feel in different ways, no one of which can be said to be true, or right, or essentially human. Short books like Ruth Benedict's *Patterns of Culture* (1934), probably the most popular work of anthropology ever printed, changed my entire way of understanding human culture during an evening's reading. Like most of my generation I had unconsciously absorbed the Enlightenment concept of a universal human type, logical, active, gregarious, which European culture had developed far more successfully than any other society. Here in Benedict were Apollonian Zunis alongside the Dionysiac Dobu and the paranoid Kwakiutl, each acting out a different reality. But all were human. The course introduced us to other books equally revelatory. Susanne Langer's *Philosophy in a New Key* (1942) replaced man the scientist with man the symbol maker. Benjamin Lee Whorf and Edward Sapir showed how different languages create different realities.

Mr. Newhall—academic titles were not used in those ancient days, any more than Phi Beta Kappa keys were worn—wounded in the Great War, was a fine historian of modern Europe with one dead hand encased in a black kid glove carried in a black silk sling. One day when we met on a walk and stopped to talk, he volunteered that it is one of the great ironies that in proposing to teach truth, education makes skeptics of its most observant scholars, those who refuse to go about like the sheep in Orwell's *Animal Farm* bleating, "Four legs good, two legs bad."

But the big lessons came not in the classroom but in those places where learning was tested against the most intense human experience. Nowhere did this encounter generate more heat, and even a little light, than in the relations between the sexes.

When the lemmings in their burrows under the northern snows increase in numbers to the point that they begin to make life impossible for one another, a young male turning a corner in one of the tunnels in the ice and coming suddenly on a female is likely to drop dead on the spot. The sudden spike in the sexual urge, Mr. Hoare told us, consumes all the blood sugar in an instant, and death follows immediately. As these incidents multiply, the famed migration of the lemmings understandably begins, and they pour out of their dens in the thousands to rush suicidally to the sea where they drown.

No Williams student, so far as I know, dropped dead at the sight of long, stockinged legs, jiggling breasts, or the swirl of silky hair, but, continuing to live as we did in an exclusively male society, none had difficulty understanding the lemmings' problem. Nor did the students rush in a herd over the cliffs and toward the sea, but they did pour down the icy roads from Williamstown to the women's colleges in the valleys below, to Smith, Mount Holyoke, Vassar, and Wellesley, where fortified with strong drink they wrestled with young women of good families in the back seats of cars barely heated by running motors. The women were four or five years younger than the men but wise enough to understand and protect themselves from the risks they were being importuned to take. The whole scene was beautifully portrayed years later in the encounter between Jack Nicholson and Candice Bergen in the movie *Carnal Knowledge*, in which an Amherst boy and a Smith girl grapple for dominance. When he wins she stares at him malevolently, backward over her marvelous white ass, while he kneels behind her and regards her with a satyr's triumphant but faintly disappointed leer.

Our psychology class and Freud threw some light on our situation. *The Psychopathology of Everyday Life* (1904), with its enumeration of slips of the tongue and of the pen, convinced me without difficulty that dark energies, largely sexual, were stirring about in the deep of the unconscious mind, the very existence of which was news to me. Getting to know those wonderful characters—Rat Man, Dr. Schreber, Anna O.—confirmed what young men more or less believe anyway, that Eros or the Pleasure Principle is life's basic energy, and since society cannot allow it full expression if anarchy is to be avoided, limitation, repression, sublimation, indirection, and censorship divert Eros at every turn. Because Eros can neither be entirely suppressed nor fully expressed, hysteria, neurosis, depression, and a feeling of life only half lived are the human lot. The inescapable tragedy built into a life of required repression was grandly summarized in *Civilization and Its Discontents* (1930), where Freud told us that because we could neither satisfy our instincts nor obliterate them, anxiety is the human fate.

Freud understood our problem precisely, but he was not comforting. The overall effect of Freud was not, as public opinion usually has it, to license free love, but to describe the tragic story of the hopelessness of ever finding complete fulfillment sexually. We understood—this is how it felt—but the permanent frustration of Freud's message was not welcome to us.

Then in 1948, Alfred Kinsey's lengthy study *Sexual Behavior in the Human Male* appeared, seemingly to liberate us. Ray Washburn's bookstore could not keep enough copies in stock. We stayed up all night poring over tables of masturbation frequencies, homosexual episodes among college students, nocturnal emissions, petting to climax, types of intercourse, and bestiality. This last was unappealing, and we were not surprised to learn that only something like three percent of young men ever practiced it. But the rest of Kinsey was the stuff of life, answering questions like Who did it? How often? With what effects? A nameless hero emerged from Kinsey's bar graphs and pie charts, the successful lawyer who ejaculated thirty times a week for thirty years; but most young men, Kinsey said, between adolescence and age thirty —just our bracket—managed it only 3.3 times a week. We knew that point-three event only too well! We learned too that the most sexually experimental men were exactly those of our social and age group: young, atheistical-Protestant, college educated, urban, and white collar. We were the ones who most likely had been involved in a relationship one or more times with a member of the same sex. Seventy percent of us had orally stimulated and been stimulated by a woman, we masturbated frequently, and were constantly excited by sexy pictures. We liked women dressed in an attractive manner, went to suggestive films, and discussed sex with members of our own and the other sex.

Kinsey was a statistical zoologist, and his sample of fifty-three hundred white males—since criticized as being too small and containing too many convicted felons (probably he found their sex lives more interesting)—made a point of the greatest importance to us. Public morality asserts one abstemious type of sexual behavior as normal and therefore uses one law to cover all sexual activity, while in truth the amount and variation in practice is enormous. One man has thirty emissions a week, another only one in seventy years. The "publicly pretended code of morals" in society, marriage, the law, education, and religion is also founded on false information and on false premises. These social institutions all assume right and wrong kinds of sexual activity, and they posit that people are sexually abstemious. In fact, according to Kinsey, life is suffused in sex, everywhere, at all times, and of all varieties. Whatever is pleasurable not only goes but gets done. The judge, the preacher, and the psychologist if they faced the truth would think the world suffering from nymphomania and satyriasis. As for guilt, says Kinsey, contradicting Freud directly, "few adult males . . .

are particularly disturbed over their sexual histories," and they therefore suffer almost no neuroses or psychoses for any kind of sexual activity. Even pedophilia, and perhaps incest, though not condoned, were said by Kinsey probably to be less harmful to the participants than were the hysterical treatments of them by the courts and a prurient public media. We all read Kinsey, the young women as well as the men—this was the "real stuff." In our secret selves we had thought we were depraved beyond help, but we now knew we were really only like all the rest, and need not worry about it.

But we were by no means at the top of our sexual learning curve. In our momentary enthusiasm we failed to see that Kinsey the zoologist had ignored the enormous complexity of actual sexual relationships, their intricate involvements with other elaborate value systems, with practical matters like pregnancy and disease, with the propensity for bonding with the sexual partner, with discrimination and fear, and with deeper currents of the psyche, the kind that run through what Tolstoy wisely called "that abyss of error in which we live regarding women and our relations with them." To all these matters, and much more, I was about to be introduced.

The women's college of Bennington, about ten miles from Williamstown over a dreadful Vermont road, was founded in the thirties for the daughters of the very rich, and it prided itself on its avant-garde views and unusual courses. It was exactly the kind of school described by Mary McCarthy in her novel The Groves of Academe (1952), though she actually had in mind a similar college, Sarah Lawrence, where she had taught. At Bennington, as at McCarthy's fictional "Jocelyn," epic poems were interpreted "in a mythic semblance, using the plot of the Epigones, that is, of the Seven who came after the Seven, and the structure of the whole was that of a series of Epicycloids arranged around a fixed circle." One-on-one tutorials were given by the faculty on this or any other subject the student could imagine—Freud's hydraulic imagery or the lost tribes of Israel—and small classes were taught by some of the most distinguished intellectuals in the country: Peter Drucker in economics, Francis Fergusson in theater, Stanley Edgar Hyman (he always of the three names) in mythology. These classes did not begin like our Williams courses with the rudiments of a subject—in economics, for example, the Federal Reserve System or Joan Robinson's multiplier—but were, in keeping with the august figures who taught them, and the future responsibilities in society of the women who took them, at the macro level from the outset: "The Principles of Capitalism," "The Idea of a Theater." A work period in the winter months took the students out of the Vermont snows to various kinds of life experiences—politics, union organizing, factory work—that expanded their understanding of the world, particularly its blue-collar, more politically liberal activities.

Bennington students were all from wealthy families, and they were recognized by themselves and others as intelligent but a bit unusual. "Flaky" is a later word that would retrofit them precisely. They exulted in their oddities, which made them interesting, and despised boys from Williams, a repulsively square college. Williams boys were in turn very nervous about Bennington girls, whom they considered difficult and intensely intellectual, and heavy on megatheory. To me, however, the Bennington students were fascinating in their strangeness, and I romanticized them to a dangerous degree.

The New England spring hills were green, the white houses shone in the sun, and the fresh springs ran in dark, swift water down through chalk pools, over falls to the rushing river. By this time I was taking a course on Renaissance lyric—"The grave's a fine and private place, / But none, I think, do there embrace"—and reading pastoral verse about nymphs and shepherds frolicking beside clear rushy streams. "Come live with me, and be my love, / And we will all our pleasures prove," sang the passionate shepherd. My nymph's hair was the color of the fortune in gold her family had torn out of the western mountains, and she drove a big Chrysler convertible with wooden framing, the metal sections repainted to match the exact shade of her hair. "At least I'm smarter than she is," exclaimed an impoverished Bennington instructor, watching her from his office window as she drove this flaming chariot at five miles an hour down the gravel drive of the college. He *was* smarter, too, a lot smarter, but her neck was a tower of ivory and her breasts were round as melons. Strangely, she would show them to me freely but did not like them touched. When we went to bed, as we soon did—or more accurately went to the back seat of cars and to sleeping bags on cool Vermont hillsides—she kept her brassiere on, and I kept my hands on her back or below her waist. Otherwise she treated sex in a more or less matter-of-fact way, part well-bred upper class, part Bennington quasi-intellectual. During long evenings spent at bars or wrestling in the darkness of her college room, my nymph, who was reading Richard Krafft-Ebing's *Psychopathia Sexualis* for a tutorial in abnormal sexuality, spoke frankly about such matters as her masturbation patterns, beginning at age four, and the relative advantages of vaginal, anal, oral, and manual intercourse.

She was leading me into an ocean beyond my depth. The raw facts of sex were not the problem—"tell me more"—but I was wild with jealousy when she casually told me that she would see me through the week but that on weekends she went off to visit a young man who was a ski instructor in winter, a sailor who crewed on Newport racing boats in Narragansett Bay in summer. We never met, he and I, but both of us were fully aware of the other, and Phoebe would tell us how much she enjoyed, or didn't enjoy, depending on whether she felt cruel or loving, the company of the other—"He really isn't much fun to talk to"—or even the precise sexual details—"It's funny how differently men smell when they come." My role, and my strong suit, I soon learned, was to talk as effectively as my rival skied and sailed, and no Renaissance courtier ever tried harder than I did to lay out his intellectual wares in a lively and interesting fashion. In this way the formal rhetorical education begun in the classroom found practical use as I described Darwin's natural selection, or explained—"Oh, callow youth!"—the interactions of the Freudian ego and id.

I assume that in order to compete, the athlete must have skied as recklessly as I talked, hurling himself down precipitous icy mountains, schussing with abandon on the edge of the deepest abyss. In a bizarre modern way she was playing us off against each other, not because she wanted either of us really—she married neither—but because the game of sexual power and mate selection is the most natural and delightful of all activities.

My rival had the weekends while I had to make do with week-nights cut short by class preparations and bartending. Still, for a time it looked as if I had prevailed. In the curious custom of the time, she wore my fraternity pin, was "pinned" to me, which was a minor form of engagement, and sometimes promised to give up my rival, but did not. I waited by the only telephone—that place of many sorrows—in the fraternity house trying by any ruse to keep my brothers off the line so that I could get calls from Phoebe that usually never came. I lay awake on weekend nights after coming back from work at the bar and imagined, half in agonized jealousy and half in voyeuristic pleasure, my rival's brutal penetrations, each groaning upthrust of her round buttocks, each spasm, as they tore their "pleasures with rough strife / Thorough the iron gates of life," until, exhausted, I fell asleep.

This was not the love that I had expected to find on the green meadows by the rushy streams of Arcadia. Williamstown during a post-war catch-up summer session was a heavenly place—"Annihilating all that's made / To a green thought in a green shade"—a few quiet classes in the sunny days, long reading sessions in the empty library, picnics at the nearby limestone pools where you slid down the natural slides from one deep green pool to another, hoping there were no broken beer bottles on the bottom. Old friends who had graduated came back from Boston and New York, and sometimes we drove into Vermont to an abandoned quarry that had filled with water. A tin garbage can filled with ice and beer was carefully floated across the quarry, its free-board barely visible above the water, to a high rock, where the day was spent drinking, telling jokes, swimming, laughing, and admiring Phoebe in her new-style bikini, which had just about the same explosive power as the atomic bombs on the South Pacific atoll after which it was named. Sometimes the overloaded beer container would sink, and then we dived deep down to bring up the brew, bottle by cool bottle. We sat through the afternoon into the evening around a fire singing the familiar songs from the war that now seemed lost forever in the past, never to return again:

> Fuck 'em all, Fuck 'em all,
> The long and the short and the tall.

Always there was the drinking. Ours was a hard-drinking time in America, and we in our mid-twenties, just out of the service, took enormous amounts of alcohol for granted. We laughed at the young girl who came for dinner at the fraternity and got her calibers wrong, asking for "a French 45"; but while we may have been more sophisticated than she about the names of cocktails, we were as indiscriminate in what we drank. Drinking to the point of drunkenness was expected, and we did so two or three nights a week. House-party weekends were the worst. Girls were imported from all over the East Coast for the fall Amherst-Williams football game. This was serious business for the pretty young girls, an exciting chance to dress up and have a good time, and also an opportunity to meet the kind of young men they were likely to marry and live their lives with. My nymph came down from Bennington and enjoyed it all, but most of the dates had a wretched time of it over these weekends, trying to deal with raucous drunks, pawed in cars and dark corners, left to fend for themselves while the men, like a bunch of young Indians in an Iroquois longhouse, went through their tribal rituals. Chaperones were hired by each fraternity, but they were expected to stay in their rooms unless screams were heard. Snooted by the Vassar girl in the powder room, their dates passed out or having abandoned them for someone else, trying to get a ride back to the private house where they were to spend the night—was this a preview of marriage for the women of the educated classes? Probably, given the later divorce rates.

For the Williams boys these occasions were opportunities for an orgy. We began drinking on Friday morning before the girls arrived, and kept it up until Sunday afternoon when they escaped. Sunday was the day to recover with milk punch, and, deciding to throw a memorable party, the Saints' fraternity house—Saint Anthony!—invited everyone to the bash and brought a bathtub out on the lawn and mixed milk, ice cream, and whiskey in it. Their house was located on the main highway into town, and on a bright fall day the road was filled with cars out for a drive to see the yellow leaves. By midafternoon some of the "Ephmen" —after the founder, that stern old colonial soldier Colonel Ephraim Williams, who would probably have shot all of us—had climbed like monkeys into the branches of the trees along the highway. A drunken date was persuaded to take off her clothes and get into the tub, where she sat filling our cups with punch. The traffic was backed up for miles, all the townies were gathered to see what the crazy college boys were doing now, the state police were there threatening mass arrests, the dean was trying to reason with the drunken officers of the fraternity to get them to restrain the mob that was threatening to march down the street and take over the town.

Dusk came at last, the dates were put on the train, Phoebe drove back to Bennington, the students disappeared into the fraternity houses, the traffic jam ended, and the college officials managed somehow to pacify the police. It snowed all night, and next morning as the bell rang to announce the beginning of classes, the young men of Williams College, bright and scrubbed and looking as if nothing had happened, walked briskly down to their classrooms to what the faculty and their parents imagined to be their primary business for being at this seat of higher learning.

When my nymph's family came east for Christmas, I, not my rival, was invited to meet them on Christmas Eve at a fashionable East Side hotel in New York. The evening began badly with my very modest presents for Phoebe, a remaindered copy of the poems of Baudelaire and a bottle of Sandeman's sherry, in a black pottery figure of a man with cloak over the eyes and Spanish hat. These contrasted poorly with the rich gifts the family exchanged, and the evening was one of icy politeness as I drank and talked too much. It was the evening of a great blizzard: nothing was running, cars were abandoned all over the streets, and I wandered out into two feet of snow, drunk, and zigzagged across Central Park to the Heinemans' apartment where I was staying.

Phoebe was still trying to make up her mind about me, and I was still fascinated with her, taking incredible risks to have her in odd places and at chancy times that Christmas. I think she actually liked the riskiness of the situations, and they stimulated me to the point of erotic madness. But in the end it didn't work. I went back to Williamstown, and she took her Bennington winter job in Brooklyn. One weekend when I came down to see her she told me that she definitely was not in love with me, that the engagement, which never quite was, was now definitely off, and gave me back my pin. I wandered down to the subway, feeling surprisingly well, and when I threw the pin up the dark tunnel, down which the light of the train was coming, there was an enormous flood of relief. I felt better than I had in years, no longer in love, no longer trying to please someone else, no longer being managed by some uncontrollable passion. A very narrow escape, I thought then and think now, from a poor-boy rich-girl marriage between two people who really didn't like each other very much.

But in the meantime, I was still puzzled about just what to make of it all. Could this have been love? Does passion permit all these extraordinary changes? Can pleasure cause so much pain, and can the sources of life be used for so many less worthy purposes? How can it be actually a delight no longer to be in love? Neither Freud nor Kinsey any longer seemed to have the answers, but about this time I read Somerset Maugham's *Of Human Bondage* (1915). It was not a great art novel, only one of those somber realist epics of middle-class life favored at the turn of the century, but it riveted my attention with its naturalistic treatment of sex. Philip Carey, a medical student, falls in love and nearly ruins himself pursuing a young waitress, Mildred Rogers, with a complexion so green that chlorophyll seems to run in her veins. Despite all the attention and love he lavishes on her she cares nothing for him, responding to each of his invitations with no more warmth than, "I don't mind." Maugham drove his point home with a hammer:

> He did not know what it was that passed from a man to a woman, from a woman to a man, and made one of them a slave: it was convenient to call it the sexual instinct; but if it was no more than that, he did not understand why it should occasion so vehement an attraction to one person rather than another. It was irresistible; the mind could not battle with it; friendship, gratitude, interest, had no power beside it. Because he had not attracted Mildred sexually, nothing that he did had any effect upon her. The idea revolted him; it made human nature beastly; and he felt suddenly that the hearts of men were full of dark places.

In matters of sex, Maugham told me, the law of the jungle rules, and there is "always one who loves and the one who lets himself be loved." It is different but no better for the woman. Mildred knew from childhood that "If you want men to behave well to you, you must be beastly to them, if you treat them decently they make you suffer for it."

The "shock of recognition" was overwhelming. It was not that Maugham had exactly portrayed my own affair in a minor key with Phoebe, but he at least provided a sense of the strangeness of the world of love into which I had entered so innocently. Years before, during the war, I had casually answered my stepfather's pointed question, "What do you plan to do with your life?" with "Go to law school, I guess." I really thought then that living through the war was a worthy enough goal for anyone, but he wanted something more solid, and law school seemed a reasonable thing to try. It still seemed so when I began college, but as time passed, my courses in political science and economics seemed uninteresting and my efforts in them not particularly successful. I somehow always got the facts right but never assembled or interpreted them with any flair. In literature courses, however, I did almost nothing except for reading the texts, and still I always seemed to get at once to the core. It will be hard for anyone today, when literature is said to be totally political and empty of any referential truth, to realize how attractive the study of literature was in those early postwar days and how informative it could seem. Maugham had, even in a popular novel, after all thrown far more light on my deepest feelings than had Freud or Kinsey. There were many, of course, who even at that time looked down on literature, considering it easy, modish, pretentious, and too pessimistic in its view of things. I was still far too naive, however, to have any real sense of how "soft" a subject literature was in comparison with the sciences, nor did I know yet how little the world valued and rewarded literary scholars in contrast to those who, like economists, psychologists, and historians, satisfy the world's primary sense of how you get to know the truth of important things.

There were, after all, still great writers in the land. The poets Eliot and Frost were still alive, the playwrights Arthur Miller and Tennessee Williams were writing *Death of a Salesman* and *Streetcar Named Desire*, novelists like William Faulkner and Ernest Hemingway published books that were read and discussed by educated people everywhere. Literary criticism attracted minds of the very first order, like William Empson and Kenneth Burke. F. R. Leavis told us that a literary education was the only one that fitted a person for a full and meaningful life, deeply tied to the roots of our culture. We laughed when Tallulah Bankhead dismantled Norman Mailer, who had just written *The Naked and the Dead*, in which the censor had forced him to use "fug" instead of "the word that won the war": "Oh, yes, you're the young man who doesn't know how to spell 'fuck.'" But literature was serious business, an important part of a civilized life and a substantial prop of culture. It seemed to have become, in fact, the substitute for religion that Matthew Arnold had predicted nearly a century earlier, telling deep truths about the most intense human experiences, love, war, death, hope. *Of Human Bondage* had made me understand Lionel Trilling's words, "art yields more truth than any other intellectual activity," and so it was that on these almost accidental grounds I decided to go in the direction of an academic life spent in research and teaching the great line of writers in English—Chaucer, Shakespeare, Milton, Pope, Johnson, Wordsworth, Dickens, Yeats, Joyce, Eliot, the literary canon. I fully understood that choosing an academic life was to give up the rewards of power and money that the law or business could bring, but it seemed worth it to live life against the background of the Himalayas of language, the great works that revealed essential human experience. Chaucer's knight defined duty and service, Othello jealousy, Pope's dunces stupidity, Wordsworth nature, Dickens the city and goodness of heart, Eliot alienation and modern angst. A literary education was as broad as it was deep, forcing familiarity with chivalry and revolution, with gods and devils. And always you learned about, or better still, internalized these matters not through the abstractions of sociology or the large-scale events of history but as they were experienced personally, under intense pressure, by human beings—fictional, of course, yet still human and much like yourself.

Reading the paper one day I discovered that Dick Boone was playing in a grown-up Freddy Bartholomew's touring company in nearby North Adams, a dying New England mill town, old redbrick buildings and empty storefronts, the scene of an old Williams song that reveals what the students of yesterday thought about lower-class factory girls:

Here's to the girls of North Adams, North Adams,
And here's to the streets that they roam,
And here's to those dirtyfaced urchins, those urchins,
Don't kick them, they may be your own.

Bartholomew's production was *The Hasty Heart*, John Patrick's 1945 play about soldiers—in the inevitable multicultural Grand Hotel formula of the time, a Scot, a Yank, a Tommy, a black African, an Australian, and a New Zealander—in a hospital in Burma. Freddy was Lachlan the Scot, dying bravely and bitterly in a hospital far away from home, and Dick had the part of Yank. I went over to his hotel on a drizzly spring day, called him, interrupting a nap, and he came down to have a cup of coffee. During the war our friendship in trying times had meant much to us, but now we had little to say. He offered me a free ticket to the show that evening; I begged off and invited him over to dinner at the fraternity house the next night, but he couldn't make it. We shook hands and parted, knowing we would probably never see each other again and regretting it. I followed him through the years as he became famous as a Hollywood and TV actor—portraying Paladin in *Have Gun, Will Travel*, successful mostly because of his hard looks playing the parts of tough guys or sometimes downright villains—but I never saw him again. It seemed to me that the old life had ended then and something new was about to begin.

A good friend on the faculty, Jack Roberts, went to the hospital to die that spring, and since my course work for the degree was finished at midyear, the English department hired me as a lecturer to take up the slack, mostly grading papers in a modern novel course and in a course on the Romantic poets. I was also, inevitably, put to work tutoring students who wrote badly. I enjoyed the novel course, even if it meant reading endless papers on *The Way of All Flesh* and *The Island of Dr. Moreau* (these, along with *Sons and Lovers* and *To the Lighthouse* were still considered modern novels in 1949), but I was not so pleased with the teacher's curse, remedial writing. I'm afraid that I mocked those who could not write, putting crude comments in the margins of their garbled papers: "Just what do you mean by this bullshit?" The genteel professor for whom I was grading, Nelson Bushnell, known for walking through the English Lake District and writing *A Walk After John Keats* (this was the kind of thing literary criticism often was before the New Criticism), was horrified by my comments and gently explained that you just couldn't talk to students in this way.

I toned down my remarks but was not convinced of the need to ease off until one day in a conference I was hammering away at a student about the awful pomposity of his paper and the importance of clarity and straightforwardness to a good working style. To avoid being too personal, I was looking out the window of an office in Stetson Library as I talked, but hearing a sobbing noise I looked at the student and saw great tears rolling down his face:

> "What's wrong, Grant? It's only a paper, not a matter of life or death. You can learn how to write and do better."
> "Sir, sir, my mother wrote that paper!"

The majority of my classmates were well rounded enough by the time they graduated to roll to Wall Street, to law, to medicine, to business, to government. Your ball had to be a bit biased to roll toward the life of a college professor, but this profession seemed to me not only to lead to a true form of knowledge but an improvement in my social status, and so, without a lot of thought or information, I decided to be a professor of literature, and applied to several graduate schools.

Thumbing through the Williams catalogue that spring, however, I discovered that the college had since before the Great War given a fellowship every two years to Exeter College, Oxford. The Moody family, of Moody's Investors fame, had lost a son to fever in Sicily in 1913; he had graduated from Williams and then gone to Exeter. In his memory the family set up a fellowship to be given every other year to some deserving Williams graduate for two years of study at Oxford. By now it was 1949 and I was twenty-five years old. I really couldn't afford to spend much more time in the academy before getting on with life. But two years at Oxford and a chance to travel on the continent were too attractive to pass up, for I might never get such a chance again, and so I wrote an application and went around asking my friends on the faculty to support me, which they did—so effectively that I was awarded the scholarship. The news came by telephone from the chairman of the selection committee in the growing dusk of a spring evening, the elms and the maples just opening on the long dark lawns and the quiet streets of the rural New England town, and it seemed suddenly that the world had opened out before me. London, Oxford, Paris, Rome,

Florence, Venice, Munich. "Bliss was it in that dawn to be alive," as the poet Wordsworth had said of being in France at the beginning of the revolution. I had already picked up the literary scholar's habit of validating my own experiences—as the reader will have noticed—by their correspondence to some literary scene, character, or phrase. For literary people, an experience is authentic only if you can find a literary antecedent. I went from house to house, thanking my friends and insisting that they, their wives, their children too, have a drink from a special bottle of malt Scotch I had been saving for a celebration.

Graduation came, the procession led by the High Sheriff of Berkshire County, and I went back to working at the 1896 House for a last summer. I shared an apartment with a former merchant marine captain turned college student, Fred Capstan, who was working temporarily as a Fuller Brush salesman. On commission entirely, he slogged from house to house, his thick rotundity bristling with a huge and awkward variety of brushes, hoping to sell enough to pay for his day's drink and food. He was a Falstaffian tun of a man, and as the sun blazed out of the sky day after day that summer, Fred would return from trying to get housewives to buy of his wares, exhausted, irate, and having sweated so profusely that the dyes in his striped ties had soaked through his white collar. Having spent the day at the swimming pool, I was about to depart for the evening to work at the cool bar when he returned from his daily rounds, but I usually spent a few minutes laughing at him as he drank deep and cursed his fate and the unfairness of a life that condemned him to this labor of the mine and the galley. He had, he confided to me, a number of gold bars in a safety deposit box in a Paris bank, where he had put them after his merchant ship had been bombed and sunk in Rotterdam at the end of the war. Among other things, the ship had been carrying a goodly amount of bullion, and he had had the foresight to take some of it along when he abandoned ship, then made his way to Paris, where he had cached the loot in what seemed a safe place, a safety deposit box in a bank. He was now working, he said, to get enough money to go to Paris and pick up the gold, if the police were not watching it, so that he could live in a humane way instead of having to sell those fucking brushes to those fucking housewives.

He was always in debt to the Fuller people for the brushes they advanced him, and they were impatient people, skilled in dealing with just this problem from many years of experience. He was always hitting me up for a few dollars to keep, he said, the dreaded Fuller goons from coming after him, and he offered to share some of his gold with me if I would out of my first fellowship payment advance the funds needed to buy a passage to France. I was at least smart enough not to go for this one, but he was amusing, and I liked him, and I lent him more than I should have. Late August came and Fred, after a trip down to Hartford to curse the House of Fuller and return a carload of their unsold brushes, suddenly departed, on a vacation he said, before the rigors of the beginning of term.

It was time to pack my trunk and go down to New York, but when I went to get my passport from the shelf where it had been lying for the past month or so since it came from Washington, it was not to be found. I searched wildly, everywhere, for that bright green official document. I called my girlfriend, Sue—the sister of my first college roommate, the ill-fated Harry Scoble—in New York to ask her if she had picked it up by chance, and when she said no, I began to hint that she might have stolen it in order to keep me from going abroad and leaving her. At first she was amused, then incredulous, then outraged, and told me that she didn't care much for me anyway, so forget it! One of the Williams faculty had worked in the State Department, and through his kind intercession a new passport was issued, just in time. While I was waiting for it, nearly frantic that I would miss my ship, I picked up a copy of Life magazine and read an article about the demand for American passports in Europe. You could, said the article, sell them on the streets of Paris, no questions asked, for a thousand dollars or more. Hmmm! But then I was on my way, reconciled with Sue again, who came down to the ship with friends and champagne to see me off.

3

Chatter About Shelley

"Sterling Devalued" read the headline of the newspaper on the boat train to London, and I realized that my Moody fellowship of $2,000 a year, paid in dollars, could now buy pounds sterling at $2.80 rather than $4.00, the old rate. And since prices were still controlled and the cost of everything was depressed in the shabby postwar years, I was if not rich at least a lot more comfortable than I had been a day earlier.

But in Oxford there seemed nothing to buy, and life was very drab for someone who didn't know his way around. Food was still rationed, and the restaurants were dreadful. Beans on toast, sardines on toast, and duck eggs had become staples. My only suit sent to be cleaned was washed, shrunk, tied up with string in two neat bundles of brown paper and returned to me unwearable.

Like other Americans before me, I fled to Paris, where there was plenty to eat, a drink could be ordered at any hour of the day or night, and the brilliance of the city of light was almost overwhelming. I gawked at the Eiffel Tower, Napoleon's tomb, the Winged Victory of Samothrace, the Mona Lisa. Walking toward the Arc de Triomphe up the Champs-Elysées one hot afternoon, I stopped at an outdoor cafe at Ronde Pointe to order a beer. As I sat there admiring the beautiful girls, a familiar rotund figure, a dwarfish Sidney Greenstreet, waddled down the sidewalk, his collar soaked with the colors of his tie. His gray herringbone suit had been worn out between the legs, and some ingenious tailor had inserted a patch of very light gray flannel, which formed a half circle on his bottom, making him look like a hippopotamus going away.

"Fred, my God, what are you doing here!"
"Buy me a cold beer, Alvin, and I will a tale unfold that will make your hair stand on end like the fretful porpentine."

He plumped down at the table with a great sigh. He had been badly beaten up and had a black eye, some very painful looking cuts requiring stitches, and big blue and yellow bruises. He drank the beer down in a gulp, had another, and then another, before he told me that he had been mugged, his money and his passport taken, and, when he protested, beaten up by the thugs. Now he had no money except the few francs the embassy had allowed him while he waited for his new passport to come through so he could go back to Williamstown and finish his degree. "The gold bars in the bank vault?" Bank officials told him that the safety deposit box had been emptied by someone who signed his name and said it would no longer be needed: "Is there a problem?" they asked politely. "Would you perhaps like to file a complaint with the police and list the contents of the box? No? Too bad." How good it was to see me again, and could I possibly, he hated to ask, let him have a hundred dollars to keep him going until he could leave this dreadful place?

By now my mental circuits had closed, as I remembered the article in Life about how easy it was to sell an American passport in Paris. Probably he had tried to sell my missing passport in some bar or on some dark street in Pigalle and lost not only my passport but his own and his money as well. In the bargain he had gotten badly beaten, his trousers ripped in some unseemly way. This was the justice that only the gods ordinarily enjoy. I nearly smirked as I told him that I was broke myself, had to catch the boat train, and went off leaving him to pay for the drinks, which he had not the money to cover. Years later he wrote to tell me that he was starting a new venture to recover stolen treasure from sunken ships and asked if I did not want to buy in. Ignoring the request for funds, I wrote him a long letter, using the style of Hallmark greeting cards, wishing him all the best as he launched his ship once again upon the sea of life.

When I returned, the spires of Oxford had their ancient charm, and I enjoyed looking at the chained books in the Merton College library, gaping at the quad of Christ Church, finding my way to the busts of the Roman emperors outside the Sheldonian, which Max Beerbohm's character Zuleika Dobson had mistaken for the Twelve Apostles. Ranking things is the social skill at which the British excel above all others. Americans on a desert island would immediately begin making and selling things; Englishmen would start establishing who was superior to whom and by what symbols status would be made known. I soon discovered that for hundreds of years the Oxford colleges had been ranked with great precision. Somewhere near the bottom came, though I had no hint of it yet, the Turl colleges, located on the short street of that name, Lincoln, Exeter, and Jesus, all with provincial backgrounds; Christ Church, Magdalen, and Trinity were the posh colleges. A Magdalen student in Compton Mackenzie's Sinister Street, a fashionable novel in the early years of the century, remarks to his roommate that he had met a chap last night who said he was from Lincoln College. "I've never heard of it. Do you know where it is?" he asks his friend. "No, but perhaps we can find it on the map."

If the curse of American society is racism, Britain's curse is class. It is everywhere, as fiercely resented by those it puts down as it is stoutly defended by those it favors. The English upper and middle classes, I found out, really believe that the social classes differ from one another, not just by the accidents of culture but by some mysterious yet indelible nature of being. On a rainy day I toured a noble house, Packwood, where Jane Austen had worked for a time, and greatly admired the people and the civilization that had sponsored such remarkable architecture, well-designed gardens, elaborate furniture, and a gracious way of life. On the walls going up the great stairway were the family portraits, men and women, long-nosed, bewigged, craggy, wary, and haughty. Walking behind me were a poorly dressed young man, thin and white-faced, in a mackintosh, and a girl, pimply, almost featureless really, who had just arrived in the driving rain on a motorcycle. "Just look," he hissed at her, dripping water on the stair carpet, "at those degenerate faces, no life or energy left in them at all."

Exeter, with its Broad Church and west-country background and its large number of Americans, accepted for their fees, remained unremarkable, despite efforts to stress its few artistic graduates, the Caroline dramatist John Ford, the Victorian aesthetes Sir Edward Burne-Jones and William Morris, who had designed the stained-glass chapel windows. Eric—another romantic chaplain!—played Wagner all night in his rooms over the gate to the Cornmarket. But when the students burned a little incense in chapel before Sunday services, the suspicious rector sniffed the air most unhappily, and Eric cringed for his living.

The coal ration for my room was a hundred pounds a week, which sounds a lot, but it was soft coal and could easily be burned in the grate in a single long night of trying to keep the damp out. Wood could be bought from the scout, Bill, the servant in my entry, for an exorbitant price, but it too burned quickly. The food in the college dining hall was inedible, at least to me, and I found myself eating out a lot at the Taj Mahal, the Indian restaurant that shared the Turl with the three colleges. There you could get plenty to eat, everything well flavored with curry. Where they got their meat in the days of tight rationing was always a mystery, until they were later fined for buying cats. There was a night jar in the room, emptied by the scout, but "the bogs," the huge bathtubs and one rickety, mold-covered, dripping shower for Americans, was a long walk across the quad in a bathrobe and slippers. The British were obviously used to roughing it much more than Americans, who resented the amount of energy and time required to deal with the basics of daily life. Walking gloomily through the mist and rain one day on the way to the shower, I met the head tutor, a military man who had spent years bracing up the troops, who looked at me and said, "Kernan, why do you always seem so depressed? Cheer up." The bursar had been a civil servant, a tax collector in the Sudan, for most of his life, and when you were called before him for late payment of your college bills, known as the "battels," he clearly considered you some difficult fuzzy-wuzzy, and the only way to get on his good side was to stamp your boots, almost British army style, and stand at stiff attention. "Sar!"

In the buttery at night, the college wags sharpened their fine wits on one another and gave us Americans lessons in just how vicious social life and humor could be. To one boy with a head of hair so awful that it somehow looked fake: "Smithers, everything about you is bogus, even your sodding wig is bogus!" Roars of laughter, "Good old Robinson, always something clever." Smithers is probably by now the head of some government agency, with the best wig in London, but still thinking of bright things he might have said to good old Bob Robinson, who became famous in later life for attacking, said the reviewer of his memoir, Skip All That (1996), "politics, religion, war, peace, even the grass growing in the fields if he gets the chance." The beginnings of Robinson's career were mean enough, "faking readers' letters and rigging the crossword competition" in one of the Sunday papers, but he went on to live by his wits in print and on the telly by using the satiric razor he had honed in the Exeter buttery to cut up the great ones of his world. He described Richard Crossman, for example, as "a goggle-eyed leveller, remembered for nothing save losing his departmental papers while eating oysters at Pruniers."

Nothing seemed more odd than the quaint custom of sconcing. Every college had a different size sconce, and Exeter's seemed to be about two gallons, give or take a gill, or some other ancient Saxon measure. We had come here because we were students, but in the English way it was forbidden to talk shop in the hall, and if you slipped and said to the man across the table, "I was reading an interesting article today," some gleeful barbarian, face no longer blue but flaming red, would shout, "I sconce you, you bloody Yank, for talking shop. Bill, bring a sconce and give Mr. Kernan the chit to sign." A grinning waiter, my scout Bill at another of his jobs, would emerge from the pantry with a huge tankard of beer and present it to me. The trick was to drink as much as possible in one draught and then pass it to your right, where the man sitting next to you did the same, and so on around the table until the sconce was empty. The real champions, however, drained the damned thing in one long draft, even if it meant, as it often did, being sick on the spot or just outside the door on the steps of the noble hall. It was all done in the best of humor, and the only unforgivable sin was to take it too seriously; so we Americans stumbled along and got introduced to the bullying and ragging that begin with English schoolboy life and do not end with the university.

My tutor was notable but burned out and haggard from drink after pretending to listen year after year to his tutees' weekly papers on English literature from Chaucer and Langland in the fourteenth century to Arnold and Dickens in 1850, the death of Wordsworth being the terminal date of the English lit exams. An Anglo-Irishman, Neville Coghill had been a soldier in the trenches in the Great War, and war stories were what he and I found in common. He told with delight how when the troop trains passed through the French stations the soldiers would shout at the stationmaster standing at attention in full uniform, "Monsieur le chef de gare, il est un cocu," to see him rage at this insult to his manhood. I told him about sailing out of San Francisco harbor under the Golden Gate Bridge on a carrier headed for the far Pacific. But in talking of literature we seemed to have little in common. With my training in the New Criticism, I was most impressed when I found that Cleanth Brooks had been Coghill's student years before, but when I asked Coghill about it he put on his best Paterian high-aesthetic manner and replied, "Ah, yes, whatever became of that young man?" Later, when I knew him well enough to tell him the story, Cleanth was no clearer about what had happened to Neville.

Each week in the time-honored manner I was expected to appear in my short black scholar's gown to read to my tutor a five- or six-page essay on some aspect of English literature: Hamlet's melancholy, for instance, or Pope and the heroic couplet. I never got the hang of the Oxford essay. Having been trained as a formalist New Critic, my conception of a literary essay was to disembowel a poem or a play, laying all its parts out on the table and speculating on how they had once related to one another. I realized soon enough that this was not the way it was done in Oxford, and I tried for an easier, more occasional style, with elegant quotes from great writers. Some curmudgeonly remark from Dr. Johnson always went well—"the truth of the matter is, sir"—if you couldn't think of anything else. A graceful turn of phrase, an air of *sprezzatura*, a light touch rather than our American solemnity was what was admired. Criticism was an art rather than a science in Oxford, but I was unable to master an indirect and graceful approach to describing things.

When F. R. Leavis, the Cambridge don who took literature very seriously indeed, came to Oxford, the local wags dressed in velvet à la Reginald Bunthorne and Oscar Wilde, carried canes and lilies, and baited him until he roared with rage and stomped out.

Neville slouched deeper and deeper into his chair week by week, staring out the window at the endless rain. He was at his best with Chaucer, whom he later rendered in modern English for a Penguin Classic volume, and with Shakespeare, especially the staging. He loved to direct plays and mounted a splendid *Midsummer Night's Dream* in the garden, beginning in the early evening, of New College. Some years later he directed Richard Burton, who had been his student (as had W. H. Auden), in a famous Oxford University Dramatic Society production of Christopher Marlowe's *Doctor Faustus*. Elizabeth Taylor, then Burton's wife, acted Helen of Troy and provided the face that launched a thousand ships, but a voice that could not be heard in the first row.

Coghill's interpretation of Chaucer was minimal—all the tales praise different types of love—but he read the verse beautifully with his Irish accent and conveyed the wonderful fun of it all. He also made the Shakespearean plays, which had been for me only poems on the printed page, live on the stage. Going to the London theater and seeing great performances—John Gielgud as Leontes in *The Winter's Tale*, Laurence Olivier and Vivien Leigh in an unforgettable *Antony and Cleopatra*, Alec Guinness with a pillow stuffed in his doublet playing the Hamlet whose mother told him that he had "grown fat and scant of breath," Roger Livesey and Ursula Jeans in *Twelfth Night*—began to convince me, as Dick Boone and his improvisations in the room in Greenwich Village had not, that the theater was the greatest of all art forms: compact, structured, direct, life immediately experienced, tense with the effort to manifest some meaning or move some course of action. Lyric poetry, for all its delight, began to seem too cryptic, too removed from the actual experience of life, while the novel, at least in the Victorian form that Henry James styled "loose, baggy monsters," was too blowsily expansive and too confident about what could be known.

It was not only a time when the London theater was at one of its peaks, it also seemed, at least briefly, that poetic drama was being reborn. T. S. Eliot's *Cocktail Party* was the success of the season in 1950, and he wrote a powerful defense in *Poetry and Drama* of the use of poetry in the theater. Christopher Fry was filling the theaters with comedies, *The Lady's Not For Burning* and *Venus Observed*, in which the dialogue was in a verse stuffed with exaggerated metaphors. It is all completely gone now, but with the audiences laughing at Fry and listening carefully to Eliot it seemed that the Elizabethan poetic theater was about to return to grace the reign of the second queen of that name.

As I write this, it is a pleasure to realize that I owe Coghill more than I had thought, a sense of the direct, emotional power of language and theater, and surely this is where the real life of literature will always reside. But, unfortunately, these were not the subjects that the Oxford English honors school examined on. The Eng Lit honors degree was still fairly new in Oxford, having been established only in 1894, and then only after a great fight. It came even later at Cambridge, only in 1917. English literature had been a part of higher education through most of the nineteenth century at the University of London, where it had been lectured on by a series of professors—Christopher Morley and Mark Pattison, for example—as a branch of British history, as texts in the development of the English language, as the "poor man's classics," and as an encouragement of patriotism. By the 1890s, however, a grander Romantic conception of English literature as the sacred product of the creative imagination was widespread; and, led by John Churton Collins, a group of literary people was determined that the line of great poetry and prose that led from *Beowulf* and Chaucer and Shakespeare through Pope and Jonathan Swift to John Keats and Wordsworth was of sufficient importance to deserve, alongside history, political economy, and classical "greats," a place in the university curriculum.

In spite of their enthusiasm, the literati were unable to say when it came to the crunch just what literature would teach. When asked by James Boswell to define "poetry," Samuel Johnson had replied that it was much easier to say what it is not than to tell what it is. And so it was with "literature." The proponents of a degree in literature were clear about what it was not. It was not a branch of history, nor was it the handmaiden of philology, or a compendium of illustrations of the development of the language. But under sharp questioning by suspicious Oxford dons about just what literature was, they could only repeat vague words like "taste," "feeling," "beauty," and "imagination."

The characteristically Romantic indefiniteness about the nature of literature exposed the proposal to the broadsides of the Regius Professor of History, the medieval historian Edward Augustus Freeman, who thundered away that if you did not know what a subject was, how could you possibly examine in it, and if you couldn't examine you had no subject. "There are," he pronounced, "many things fit for a man's personal study, which are not fit for University examinations. One of these is 'literature.' . . . [We are told] that it 'cultivates the taste, educates the sympathies, enlarges the mind.' Excellent results against which no one has a word to say. Only we cannot examine in tastes and sympathies. The examiner, in any branch of knowledge must stick to the duller range of 'technical and positive' information." Freeman believed that literature could be a respectable university subject only as a branch of the study of language, and he said so in terms that have haunted literary study ever since: "What is meant by distinguishing literature from language if by literature [is] meant study of great books, and not mere chatter about Shelley?"

In the end Freeman had his way. English literature was voted down as a subject the first time around, and when it returned a few years later the Honours School in English Literature was primarily a philological course of study, which is what it remained at Oxford in my time. Although a candidate was expected to read his way through all the major English authors, Sir Thomas Wyatt and Henry Howard, Earl of Surrey, John Donne and Abraham Cowley, John Dryden and William Cowper, Samuel Richardson and Samuel Johnson, he or she—there had been a few women doing Eng Lit from the start, which in the opinion of many definitely marked it as a "weak" subject—was also expected to pass a Latin exam on entrance and to study Anglo-Saxon for one year. In addition, of the nine examination papers making up "Schools," five directly involved linguistic theory and history of the language, while the other four never strayed very far from philology.

Attending lectures was often the only way to prepare for certain subjects in the Schools, since the information on which the exams would be based often could be gotten only there. The dons who would set the exams usually didn't bother to write books about their views. C. L. Wrenn, the great Old English scholar, was crucial for *Beowulf*, and everyone flocked to a large university lecture hall where Wrenn, who was nearsighted, held a book in front of his face and mumbled into it the material that we desperately needed to pass the exam he would set. J. R. R. Tolkien, who would become famous for his hobbits in a few years, lectured on *Sir Gawain and the Green Knight* in University College (a marble Shelley with a large flaccid penis writhed on his nearby monument) in a high-pitched voice that was lost in the hammer beams of the great hall, and in an accent that would defeat an American even if it had been spoken directly into his ear. Only the irascible C. S. Lewis, famous for having tutored the Prince of Wales and having written *The Allegory of Love*, a book proving that love was not natural but an aristocratic cultural invention that had not appeared before the eleventh or twelfth century in the courts of Provence, gave lectures on Renaissance poetry—the Drab Age and the Golden—that were informative, well organized, and quite amusing. In time he would become a cult figure, best known for his ability to teach High Church principles in science fiction and, improbably, as the hero of a Hollywood love story, *Shadowlands*, in which he is taught to love, late in life, by the American poet Joy Davidman. But Lewis's lectures, interesting though they were, would not help much with Schools. You could use his material for answering only one or two questions, but *Beowulf* would fill half a day!

But exams seemed far in the future, and I worried more about other parts of life. Devaluation had made it possible for me to get married. Along with Wesley Posvar, a lieutenant in the U.S. Air Force, a Rhodes scholar, and later president of the University of Pittsburgh, I rented a converted house called the Old Manor in Sunningwell, a small Berkshire village a few miles out of Oxford, just below Boar's Hill. Sue arrived in early December on the *Mauretania*. She moved into the Randolph Hotel, where she engaged in long and laughing conversations

with admiring Indian students, while I stayed in Sunningwell to fulfill the residency requirements for marriage in Berkshire. On the day of
the wedding, December 13, the Sunningwell woman who drove us to
the registry in Abingdon addressed Sue as "Miss" when she got into the
car and as "Madam" when she emerged from the registry, no longer a
"spinster." The Channel crossing to the continent for our honeymoon
was very rough, and when I tried to escape a large number of French
children crawling over my luggage, my bride of a few days followed
me up on deck, where in the darkness and the teeth of a howling gale
she voiced the suspicion of all wives, that I was a heartless beast who
really didn't love children. I bought a bottle of cognac in France and we
passed it around the smoke-filled train compartment, drinking toasts to
ma femme. In Austria, the cheapest country in Europe, we detrained in
the Vorarlberg and took a sleigh up the high bare mountains, stopping
for wine before a roaring fire at an inn on the way, until at night—
Excelsior!—we came to the ski resort of Zurs, no trees, lots of snow,
rocky pinnacles all about, and Bauhaus-style buildings of glass brick
and stark white plaster.

My bride could not ski, but I had assumed that the opportunity to
do so in the high Alps would fill her with joy. It did not, it turned out—
she longed for sun and beach—but if she had to go to the mountains
she wanted cuckoo clocks and lederhosen, not avant-garde architecture.
I enrolled her in the beginners' class and then took the lift to the high
slopes with great vistas of distant mountains, long swishing runs, bright
sunlight everywhere. By noon, when I got back to the hotel, Sue, tor-
pid from the anesthetic, was in the local doctor's office having her ankle
put in a cast. I was filled with remorse and ready to leave at once. But,
no, supported by the boot, she had gamely promenaded on the broken
ankle. There was swelling and the cast would have to be left open for a
week or ten days until it subsided and a closed cast could be put on, and
only then could we travel. I had not budgeted for a broken limb. Every
day brawny young Tyroleans picked Sue up and carried her higher in
the hotel to a smaller and cheaper room. At dinner we no longer looked
at the names of the wines but merely at the prices, and on New Year's
Eve we could afford only the cheapest bottle, so acid that it set the teeth
on edge. But it worked, and we happily clumped about the dance floor

on the new closed cast with a bright red ribbon tied around it, welcoming the 1950s in song. It is customary now to sneer at the fifties as a mean era of McCarthyism and Ike, of *The Ed Sullivan Show* and tail fins on automobiles, but if you had grown up in the depressed thirties as we had, and gone to war in the forties, the fifties were welcome.

Stumping about Paddington Station on our return to England, with her white cast, Sue was accosted by a stammering young man, "You, you, you're the princess from the Pantomime!" This made her day, even after she learned that the actress playing the princess in the local pantomime had fallen off the stage the previous evening from too much drink and broken her leg in the pit. I remember the young man as rather simple, but she remembers him as a charming young Englishman with a modish stammer.

Marriage was nearly as new to Oxford as it was to us. Only at the end of the nineteenth century had the dons been allowed to marry at all, and even now marriage was, if not slightly shameful, at least not very fashionable. The women and children remained out in the suburbs during the week while the men stayed snugly in their rooms in college, read, lectured, tutored, ate at high table, and found society in the senior commons room. This situation led to some bizarre events. When the famous but not very popular historian A. J. P. Taylor returned home to find his wife in *flagrante* on the kitchen table with the drunken poet Dylan Thomas, his landlord, Magdalen College, to whom he complained, museumed the table. Lord David Cecil, a notable aesthete of the time and the English literature tutor at New College, sat in his car intently reading Keats while his pregnant wife, in blue workman's coveralls, was under the Austin Seven fixing it so that she could drive his lordship to college.

I was by no means so blasé as Cecil, nor Sue so acquiescent as his wife. We kept house, and I worked at home rather than in the library, reading the primary texts rather than the secondary criticism, ignoring the philology altogether.

All the water from thousands of acres on Boar's Hill drained directly into our old brick sump, but when we asked Madame Duval—she was vastly flattered when I asked if her name should be spelled as two words on the check—our absentee landlord living on our rent and trying to marry a gangly daughter in London, to have it pumped, she replied airily, "Ah, you Americans, you take so many baths," and did nothing. It was difficult living five miles out of town, with a mile walk to the nearest bus route, usually with rain coming down in buckets. Too many evenings we left the theater at the beginning of the second intermission to catch the last bus home. As a result of these truncated theatrical experiences, I was much better grounded in the first two-thirds of numerous plays than their endings, which made for an interesting view of theater. On moonlit nights it could be splendid as we walked down the long lane into the village, past Bishop Jewel's fine church, reciting the famous lines about Dr. Fell, who had once been rector there:

> I do not love thee, Doctor Fell,
> The reason why I cannot tell;
> But this alone I know full well,
> I do not love thee, Doctor Fell.

As we neared the barn at the end of the lane, instead of "the Emperor's drunken soldiery" we heard the inbred village children—thumbs and palates were the obvious problems—giggling at their sexual play in the hayloft.

Ace Posvar, with whom we shared Old Manor, was rich, by student standards, getting a first lieutenant's pay, flight pay, and a Rhodes scholarship. He also had PX privileges at the London embassy, and through him we could get groceries, whiskey, and cigarettes cheaply. We borrowed from him regularly, and he kept strict accounts—"2 bots. Canadian Club, 1 cart. Lucky Strikes, 7 quids"—in a little black notebook. Since we never entirely got out of his debt, our relationship to him soon grew into something like that of a tenant farmer to the company store, fawning and insolent at once.

He also had a big American Chevrolet. In this machine, Ace, his flaming red hair shining, his freckled face glowing with good humor, his horn blowing, would race through the countryside, scattering the villagers as he went. We hid beneath the dash, thinking they would stone us if he stopped, but instead the admiring maidens would wave, primp, and exclaim to one another, "Coo, ain't 'e smashin'." As soon as the "vac" came, Wesley would head for Germany, where he had an American girlfriend, Mildred Miller, a fine mezzo soon to become famous for her Cherubino in Mozart's *Marriage of Figaro*, who was singing in the Stuttgart Opera. Anyone who wanted to could ride along, getting across the Rhine and into *Mitteleuropa* in a short time at small expense. The ride cost something in patience, however, for Ace, first in his class at West Point, was already a Pentagon bureaucrat through and through, with a huge briefcase filled with official papers, and whenever we came to a border post in the middle of the night, even if the sleepy guards waved us through he would stop, wake up the commander, and insist on going through the full drill of showing his papers and getting them stamped.

At dawn we would come to the medieval city of Bruges with the sun rising behind it, where we would have coffee and cheese in the public square before moving on to Brussels for lunch. At Aachen in the late afternoon the war ruins began to come close to the road, and by night we were in Cologne, where all the bridges over the Rhine were out except one, and the spires of the great cathedral stood above a flattened city. One night, looking for something to eat, we descended into the underground Bahnhof Keller, where the Germans stared blankly at us and drank beer after beer. By the first light the great round tables were each ringed by twenty to thirty of the men, all sound asleep with their heads on the table. Up the Rhine to Frankfurt, then Stuttgart, where we stopped to hear Millie sing, and then on to undamaged Munich, where the black and white American soldiers got into vicious fights with one another in the platz.

For Americans abroad for the first time, the lure of the continent was irresistible, and the frequent Oxford vacations, two of six weeks' length between terms, plus one long summer vac, made it possible to travel frequently. The English students socialized while up at the university during the three terms—Michaelmas, Hilary, and Trinity—and then went to dull homes to settle down and get some serious reading done during the vacs. But for the Americans it was a chance to see Europe. Once in Europe we split up for the summer to look for high culture and low rents. Austria was best because of its favorable rate of exchange, and Sue and I went to Vienna for the summer of 1950, where we took a room in a pension, hired a Scottish woman long resident in Europe to teach me for pennies the German I would need to know for graduate school, and to see the remarkable sights of the great city. But now it was a city in ruins. Carol Reed's famous film *The Third Man*, with Joseph Cotten, Trevor Howard, and Orson Welles as the sinister Harry Lime—"Switzerland has had peace for four hundred years, and what has it produced? The cuckoo clock!"—mythologized the postwar city with its dark empty streets, its cellar restaurants where cigarettes were cut in half to be sold, the Riesenrad, the great Ferris wheel with its wooden cars in the Prater, and the Danube that was browner than blue. It was all just as the film showed it, and we scurried quickly along the empty arcades at night, walked carefully around the trash-filled Weinerwald, stared curiously at the Russian soldiers on guard at various points, ate *gulasch suppe* and drank pilsener beer in ratskellers filled with evil-looking plotters, one with a live chicken in his briefcase, another with an assortment of twigs.

Vienna was still deep in the Russian zone of Austria, and when North Korea attacked South Korea and Truman sent the troops in, we packed and made for the ruined West Bahnhof to take what we feared might be the last train to Salzburg. Salzburg was lovely but expensive, and we soon made our way to Innsbruck and a summer school in German in the nearby Zillertal. Here, high up in an Alpine valley, we drank beer, competed in throwing paper beer mats at flies, went on long hikes and climbed mountains, and practiced basic German. To improve our pronunciation we sang lustily about millers who liked to wander the countryside.

Thinking that I might eventually write a dissertation on D. H. Lawrence, I had brought along as summer reading all ten volumes of a recent Penguin paperback edition of Lawrence, and now set myself to reading books I had never heard of before, like *Kangaroo* and *Fantasia of the Unconscious*. A few days of immersion in *Kangaroo* convinced me that Lawrence was right, we needed more sex, or at least the English did, but Lawrentian prose was probably not what literature needed:

> The moment—and the power of the moment.
> Again he felt his limbs full of desire, like a power.
> And his days of anger seemed to culminate now in
> this moment, like bitter smouldering that at last leaps
> into flame. Not love—just weaponlike desire. He knew
> it, The god Bacchus. Iacchos! Iacchos! Bacchanals with

weapon hands. She had the sacred glow in her eyes. Bacchus, the true Bacchus. Jack would not begrudge the god. And the fire was very clean and steely, after the smoke. And he felt the velvety fire from her face in his finger-tips.

Sex spoke to us at this time in another tone. We were rolling huge logs, playing like children in a large swimming pool fed by an icy mountain stream, when Sue felt pains so sharp that they caused us to consult the doctor and find that she was pregnant. This sobering news sent us off to Italy by way of the Dolomites and Bolzano, where in the station hotel a maid stole Sue's filmiest nightdress and my copy of Henry Fielding's least-read novel, *Amelia*, which I had turned to after giving up on Lawrence. We imagined her sitting in bed in the revealing gown reading the dullest of novels in a language of which she knew not a word. Having tried to read it for a month myself, I sympathized with her, and secretly thanked her for freeing me from ever reading it.

In general that summer books seemed not to mesh with life as well as they had earlier, appearing disadvantageously against the fullness of the European summer. Still, I had to go on preparing for Schools, and in Menaggio, on Lake Como, near where the Partisans caught Mussolini, I took out of my book bag the Old English epic *Beowulf*, which had to be mastered, line by line, word by word, for the exams. Without a dictionary or a translation, the story had me baffled until one day while buying lunch in the neighboring grocery I spied a lurid Italian comic book, *Beowulfo*. I bought it at once and read it from end to end instantly, impatient to learn at long last just what it was that the hero tore off the monster Grendel—I had toyed with a possibility worse than the fact— what his dear mother did when she appeared in the mead hall after the death of her beloved bambino, and what kinds of wild parties Hrothgar the *theod cyninga* gave in Heorot for his *aethelingas* including the swinish Unferth, whose machinations at last became clear to me. I now had the story, but I have never been able to get the pictures from that comic book out of my head. I see Beowulf to this day as a blond and rather fashionable Milanese, and the Grendels as a peculiarly beastly Sicilian Mafia family, *malocchio*, pursuing a heavy blood-revenge feud.

There was one small light hanging from a fly-covered cord in the middle of our room, by which we tried to read, always reading, old novels—South Wind and Mr. Polly—left by generations of English tourists in the hotel library. The motor scooters roared around the piazza until early in the morning, and the girls on the postillions shrieked with wild laughter. The Italians who ran the *pensione* were delighted when they found that Sue was pregnant, inquired warmly about possible names, and provided baked potatoes to settle the stomach. The guests were kind as well, taking us to the lido for parties, teaching Sue to play gin rummy, while I read doggedly on in *Beowulfo*. At last I finished it—a hell of a story!—and it was time to go back to Oxford. On the last afternoon we sat on the lido talking when some English girls ran past us. One stopped:

"Oh, how good it is to hear someone speaking English."
"Yes. When did you leave England?"
"Oh, this morning."

I had to take Schools the following June, and the baby was expected in March, so it was time to become serious. I sat day after day on a small chair inside a huge old fireplace beside a coal stove. One day I decided I was having a heart attack and got up and pedaled furiously into Abingdon to see the doctor. He asked me only how I had gotten there, and when I told him, recommended getting more exercise. I pored over the old papers given in Schools in earlier years, trying to get some sense of what kind of questions would be asked about English literature from "Caedmon's Hymn" to The Pickwick Papers. But it was not the literary papers that were the real concern, it was the philology. I had been farmed out to study the history of the language with one of those poor young graduates who lived in miserable digs on the outskirts of Oxford, hoping against hope for an eventual appointment to some college, keeping alive by teaching subjects the college tutors didn't want to be bored with. I went out once a week to Cowley to discuss the vowel shifts that had taken place in the primitive Germanic forests with this poor young man, who obviously had no chance whatsoever to ever make it into one of the colleges. He knew my future as well as I knew his, and when he realized that I was not going to master the history of the English language offered some helpful hints of how to get by without knowing much. "When you hit a word in a text that you cannot identify, simply correlate it with some modern word that it sounds like and then invent a bridge between them. Most of the examiners will be suspicious but may consider, so imprecise is linguistic science, your little word history an interesting possibility."

The day of reckoning was coming, but not right now, and we felt that a few days in Paris at Christmas might be good for everyone. Sue, by then seven months pregnant, consulted the doctor, and he advised that while the Channel crossing by ferry would be too rough, a nice smooth plane ride would be fine. We flew in a small plane from Croydon on what must have been the worst night of the year. Lightning flashed about us, thunder cracked, and the plane bucketed about, rising and falling several hundred feet at a time. Sue was so ill that we feared she might lose the baby, and our sightseeing in Paris was punctuated by frequent trips to the nearest loo whenever the smell of rich food floated through the air. And where does it not in Paris? Venus de Milo, down a long corridor at the Louvre, far from any toilet, was left with a puddle on the floor nearby.

In the manner of first babies, ours was late, and on the doctor's advice we bumped about the countryside on trips in the ancient little square Austin Seven some New Zealand friends had loaned us, seeing lots of sights, like Richard III's tower, but seemingly getting nowhere in persuading the baby to come into the world. But finally Geoffrey, named after the most delightful of poets, was born in early March, in the nursing home at Abingdon, where he was known as "the admiral" because at the time the Americans had forced the British to accept an American admiral as the commander of the combined allied fleet in their sea, the Mediterranean. Taking care of a new baby was a novelty to both of us, and far away from family we learned it on our own: night feedings, burping, nappies, swaddling English style, baby sitters, the "carry cot" that went everywhere with us, and the pram. Most of it fell to Sue, as I, now in the last term before taking Schools, was reading frantically trying to cover ground that had been missed. "How would you distinguish Crashaw from Herbert as a metaphysical poet?" "Is the four-foot or the five-foot line the natural form of English verse? Give examples." "What did Beowulf do to Grendel?" "Distinguish the basic metrical patterns of Old English verse." "Trace the development of the verb 'towze' before and after its appearance in Shakespeare's *Measure for Measure.*"

The Clutterbucks, English friends—he was a retired naval commander—offered us the use of their unimproved cottage in Cornwall, and Sue made her way there by train with Geoffrey while I put on my gown and white bow tie and began taking Schools: three hours in the morning and three in the afternoon for four and a half days. The dreaded papers in Old English, Middle English, and history of the language, all exclusively philological, were first, and even the Shakespeare paper consisted mostly of untangling linguistic snarls.

After it was over I waited a few days to be summoned for an oral exam, viva voce, but was never called. Not knowing whether this was ominous or reassuring, I closed our Sunningwell house, sent our belongings in wooden crates off to the Southampton docks to be held for our departure, and went down to Perranuthnoe, where we walked the Cornish cliffs, went on picnics on the shingly beach, and bathed in the cold waters, while waiting for the results of Schools. Water was taken from a cistern, and cooking was primitive, but the air was restorative. Following their success with the ten Lawrence novels, Penguin had just published ten paperback novels by Evelyn Waugh, of whom we had never heard, and we devoured the adventures of Paul Pennyfeather after he was sent down from Oxford, of little Lord Tangent, Margo Maltravers, Agatha Runcible, Basil Seal, and Tony Last, who ended his days in the jungle reading Dickens on the goodness of the human heart to the illiterate Mr. Todd who held him a permanent captive.

Captain Grimes I admired particularly, who having disgraced himself in the trenches in the Great War was put in a room with a pistol and a bottle of whiskey to "do the right thing." An hour later when his superiors returned the bottle was empty and the pistol full. Disgraced again after a period of school teaching, Grimes's tracks disappeared in Egdon Mire, and he was presumed dead,

> But Grimes was not dead. . . . He was a life
> force. Sentenced to death in Flanders, he popped up
> in Wales; drowned in Wales, he emerged in South

America; engulfed in the dark mystery of Egdon Mire, he would rise again somewhere at some time, shaking from his limbs the musty integuments of the tomb. Surely he had followed in the Bacchic train of distant Arcady, and played on the reeds of myth by forgotten streams, and taught the childish satyrs the art of love? Had he not suffered unscathed the fearful dooms of all the offended gods of all the histories, fire, brimstone, and yawning earthquakes, plague and pestilence? Had he not stood, like the Pompeian sentry, while the Citadels of the Plain fell to ruin about his ears? Had he not, like some grease-caked Channel-swimmer, breasted the waves of the Deluge? Had he not moved unseen when darkness covered the waters?

The mixture of wild mockery and of self-righting vitality was perfect, and a few days later I thought I saw Grimes, at least his spirit, when out of a huge wave dashing on a dreadful sharp rock, the head of a seal popped up, stared at me bright eyed, winked, vibrated his whiskers in sympathy, and then slid away under the water, unharmed by, enjoying really, the destructive forces he moved among so easily. How much more real power of life there is in the satirical Waugh than in the pretentious Lawrence. I thought then and think now that Waugh is the prime English novelist of this century.

Grimes was the patron I needed. I returned to Oxford to find that I had gotten not a First, or a Second, but a Third. Neville Coghill was embarrassed, for it reflected on him too, and he mumbled that he thought that it had been a hard year for Americans. If Edward Augustus Freeman's theory of education was correct—knowledge consists of examinations, to ask and answer questions—then I did not know much. A First was probably beyond my reach, but a respectable Second would have been fine for an American. But a Third! Better by far a Fourth, or even a failure, for these showed that you hadn't cared much or hadn't tried at all. Really quite toney. But a Third stamped you with dullness of a specially unpleasant sort. You had tried, but you just had not been very smart. It was said that Helen Gardner, the grimmest and smartest of the Oxford female dons, out to prove she was tougher than the men—and she was—had had it in for American men that year. Years later when I knew her well enough to ask, though, she denied it. I could only thank my stars that the class of my degree would not mark me for life in America and determine my career, as it would have in England. If I had been English, my Third would have condemned me to being something like the clerk of the waterworks in some provincial town far to the north. In America, except among the savants, a degree from Oxford was just that, a degree, without qualifications.

Considerably depressed, Sue, Geoffrey, and I took the boat train down to Southampton and went by lighter aboard an old Dutch ship, the *Veendam*. I stood on the deck and watched my skis as they were winched up from the lighter drop into the ocean out of the rolled rugs in which I had placed them. Too bad; but I would not need them in graduate school. Yale had kept my application and had kindly admitted me again, and soon we were in New Haven.

4

See My George Gascoigne

"**W**ha, hello theah, Red," said the soft voice from the top of the stairs at one end of Yale Station, the university post office. From the other end came the response in a somewhat harder southern voice, "Wha, hello theaah, Cleanth." This was Cleanth Brooks and Robert Penn Warren, the Castor and Pollux of the New Criticism, deep calling unto deep at the beginning of the fall term. I had encountered the New Criticism at Williams, where I had come to admire the kind of power that its close analysis of literature almost magically conferred, and to be getting my mail in the same place these giants got theirs was almost too much.

On the whole, graduate schools are not sunny places. At Yale in my time there were mad students who wouldn't go back to Australia, master thieves of books from the Yale Co-op, a mathematical genius who would talk only to a

Romanian-speaking psychiatrist, and a wonderful student who said he had so much respect for the Russian language that he refused to be examined in it to fulfill his language requirements. One graduate student decided that he was Batman. He bought himself a complete costume, harmless enough, but then he took to stalking the streets and jumping out of dark alleyways at night to frighten passers-by, usually attractive women. Batman eluded all attempts at capture until one day he was sighted in the graduate school grounds and chased into a bush in the quad. The dean arrived and poked at him with an umbrella picked up on the way out of his office, shouting "Come out, you scoundrel!" until the poor wretch emerged and was taken into custody by the campus police, then duly dropped from the graduate school.

The move to Yale in the fall of 1951 was to a professional training in literature, and there was no debate at that time about what constituted knowledge of literature. From a professional perspective literature was first of all a canon of great books, primarily fiction. The emphasis was on English and American writing, but some knowledge of the classics was still expected, if only in translation: Homer, Sophocles, Virgil, Horace. Familiarity with all the major historical periods of English literature, medieval, Renaissance, Enlightenment, Romantic, and modern, was also on the books. In addition, we were expected to master the supporting background studies and criticism in our primary field of study. We were required to know the biographies of the major writers and to be familiar with the features of their cultural settings: the great chain of being, the divine right of kings, Reformation, rationalism, industrialism, post–Great War alienation. Reading knowledge—with a dictionary on the second try—was also expected in three languages, one classical, usually Latin, and two modern, usually French, German, Italian, or Russian. Finally, a year's study of Old English—*Beowulf* again— was required, plus an additional year of some other philological subject, such as Old Norse, Icelandic, or history of the English language. At least this was the ideal of a professional literary education in the 1950s, and while there were not enough hours in the day to manage it all, this was the standard to which we aspired and by which we were measured.

Though we might agree on what constituted the facts of literature, the best way to understand them—how to read literature, that is—was very much in doubt at the time. In 1951, New Criticism was still an exciting new approach, just coming into its own, based on the work of such critics as I. A. Richards, F. R. Leavis, John Crowe Ransom, Allen Tate, and chiefly the great Anglo-American poet T. S. Eliot, who convinced two generations that poetry is so important that it has to be taken totally seriously and entirely on its own terms. Literary study had for too long been content, these critics argued, with simply paraphrasing literature, studying the authors who wrote it and the historical situation in which it was written, expressing vague and inflated emotional responses, often applying some kind of conventional moral lesson to the text.

In the place of these older methods that looked at everything but the literary work, the New Criticism concentrated on the idealized and isolated verbal artifact itself, looking at certain key linguistic devices: form, structure, imagery, symbol, point of view, irony, and ambiguity. These were identified as the primary rhetorical patterns in which the creative imagination expressed the full range of things open to sensibility, in language so perfect that not only every word but every sound and every mark of punctuation was at least potentially functional in interaction with all other parts. Imagery and metaphor bound the dispersed pieces of the world together, and symbols like "rain" or "voyage" came close to the heart of actual things. Despite its own emphasis on precise observation, the New Criticism did not tie literary works to scientific exactitude. The tropes of irony and ambiguity allowed opposites ("this both is and is not Cressida") to coexist, and extensive possibilities ("shall I compare thee to a summer's day?") to present themselves simultaneously. Paradox—"I could not love thee Dear so much, Lov'd I not honour more"—expressed the ultimate unity of a world of endless apparitional oppositions. It was charged by some that the New Criticism was a late form of aestheticism, an art-for-art's-sake type of interpretation, concerned only with the beauty of the poetic structure, which Brooks called "the well-wrought urn," and W. K. Wimsatt "the verbal icon," cold, abstract, removed from life, interested only in words. But while it did center its gaze on the poetic artifact, drawing boundaries around it in order to analyze it more effectively, the poetic object itself was normally understood to draw its worth from the human and natural world it arranged, what Ransom called "the World's Body." Aesthetics were of the greatest interest, but only because they were the means by which the deepest truths of things were manifested.

The most popular and powerful teachers of literature at Yale by the 1950s were leading New Critics all: Maynard Mack, the Pope and Shakespeare scholar; Louis Martz, who wrote about and taught metaphysical poetry and published a detailed analysis of this type of writing in *The Poetry of Meditation;* Wimsatt, the leading theorist of the New Criticism who spelled out his ideas in "The Intentional Fallacy"; Cleanth Brooks, who taught modern poetry; and René Wellek, the Czech exile who with Austin Warren came as close as anyone ever did to giving the New Criticism an authoritative formal definition. Their *Theory of Literature,* which was something like the handbook of the New Criticism, was erected on the Platonic premise that there was only "one poetry, one literature, comparable in all ages, developing, changing, full of possibilities." Literature for the New Critic was "not an archaic survival but a permanence whose nature and function . . . have not basically changed."

The proponents of these formalist views were still engaged in a bitter struggle with those who read literature in terms of the society in which it was written. There was not at Yale an absolute hostility over the two approaches, but the lines were drawn sharply between New Critics and historians like the great Boswell editor Fred Pottle, who, along with his dedicated wife, Marion, spent his life editing the long-forgotten cache of Boswell papers from Malahide Castle and elsewhere that were bought by Colonel Ralph Isham and given to Yale in the twenties and thirties. His description of the papers, *Pride and Negligence: The History of the Boswell Papers* (1982), depicts scholarship and the literary scene at Yale from the twenties to the fifties.

No detail was too fine, no individual too obscure for the Pottles to identify as they worked in "the Boswell Factory," editing a handsome series of Boswell journals that began to appear in 1950 with the hugely successful *London Journal.* In this volume the young James Boswell describes how he came to London and "rogered" all the whores he could find while meeting and charming with his bright conversation and sprightly personality the great ones of the world, including

Samuel Johnson. It was sex that, somewhat embarrassingly for the dry, Maine-bred Pottles, made *Boswell's London Journal* a best-seller and a book-club selection. The book was an enchanting combination of the dustiest scholarship with the busy town life of the mid–eighteenth century, written by a diarist fresh from Scotland with a genius for the English language. But without the scholarship the vitality of the past was dead, locked up in Boswell's ancestral home of Auchinleck, or in the croquet boxes in the stable of an Irish castle.

Pottle was also a sophisticated theorist of the historical view of literature, and in *The Idiom of Poetry* (1941) he made a powerful argument for the literary historian's position that it is the responsibility of the interpreter of literature not to proclaim some eternal truth about poetry, as the New Critics said, but to attend to the major poetic "shifts of sensibility" that occurred at different historical times. In his view, the history of poetry was one of "total discontinuity," not of some unchanging ideal form, from which only the historian can recover the sensibility of the earlier time in which a work was written, thereby enlarging our sense of the wide range of literary culture and our knowledge of people very different from ourselves.

But the New Critics mostly had it their way, and for the theorist Wellek a historical view like Pottle's was merely "reconstructionism"—an ominously proleptic term, considering that in time, and not such a long time either, the New Criticism itself would be "deconstructed" and all its works mainly forgotten. The most dramatic Yale confrontation between the New Criticism and the historical view came some years later when Pottle remarked that it was impossible for the New Critics, according to their principles, to say that any reading of a literary work was wrong. Maynard Mack, determined to prove that this was not the case, wrote a brilliantly destructive report on a dissertation that was filled with extravagant readings of a set of poems, which led to the failure of the dissertation. If you could examine on a subject, as Professor Freeman knew, and fail something, what better demonstration that your methodology was scientific?

On the occasion of Pottle's retirement party years later, when I was myself a tenured professor at Yale, I went up to him after the dinner to congratulate him, forcing myself to call "Fred" a man whom even his elders addressed as "Mr. Pottle." He fixed me with a steely but not unfriendly eye and said, "You were never my student, I believe." To which I had to respond, "No," and as he turned away he said, "A pity." Talk about New Critical ambiguity! (though he would have called it irony). You could read it either way, and I have never been sure whether he thought, as I hope, that I would have done him credit as a student or whether he felt that he might have saved me from later folly.

The New Criticism was too attractive to resist, offering so many new, sprightly things to do. Even as I chose it, however, it displayed its darker side, not in the classroom, but in the larger world of politics. In 1949 the Bollingen Prize, the country's most prestigious literary award, administered by the Library of Congress, was given to Ezra Pound for his *Pisan Cantos* by a jury of New Critics, including Tate, Auden, Eliot, and Robert Lowell. Pound was by then a cult figure in the literary world, the father of literary modernism and thereby one of the founders of the New Criticism, who had revised Eliot's *Waste Land* and found support for James Joyce while he was writing *Ulysses*.

But in 1949 Pound was under a very black cloud. He had ranted against Jews and democracy before the war; during it, while living in Rapallo, he had propangandized for the Axis in weekly radio broadcasts from Rome. Captured at the end of the war, he had been imprisoned in an open-air wire cage near Pisa, where he wrote the *Pisan Cantos* as the latest sections of his long and rambling poem *The Cantos*, written over thirty years. "Exquisite lyric and stupid rant," said Irving Howe, in a judgment that time has echoed. But the literary establishment rallied to defend Pound, and in the hope of avoiding a treason trial a great deal of influence was brought to bear, chiefly by Archibald MacLeish, then librarian of Congress, by Robert Frost, our major living poet, and by Ernest Hemingway, America's leading novelist and a specialist on war, who had been a drinking buddy and sparring partner of Pound's in Paris in the early 1920s. After a sufficient number of strings had been pulled, Pound was judged insane and committed without trial to St. Elizabeth's Hospital in Washington, where he remained, a romantic prisoner, roaming the grounds at will for ten years, visited by his mistresses and mobs of literati.

Undeterred by the smell of treason, the Bollingen judges, determined to demonstrate the aesthetic view that art is above politics, awarded Pound the Bollingen Prize on the formalist New Critical principle that "To permit other considerations than that of poetic achievement to sway the decision would destroy the significance of the award." When reading these words it is important to remember, as the judges did not and as most of the literary world has been willing to forget, some of the things Pound actually said in his broadcasts from Rome. For example, on April 30, 1942:

> Don't start a pogrom—an old style killing of small Jews. That system is no good whatever. Of course if some man had a stroke of genius, and could start a pogrom up at the top [it is not certain that Pound knew about Hitler's Holocaust at this time], there might be something to say for it. But on the whole legal measures are preferable. The 60 kikes who started the war might be sent to St. Helena as a measure of world prophylaxis, and some hyper-kikes or non-Jewish kikes along with them.

The Bollingen Prize dramatized the dangers of divorcing literature from morality and from the historical circumstances in which it was written. But for the moment the New Criticism in its most reckless form prevailed, though many of its disciples, myself included, were never so easy with it again. In later years when the wheel came full circle and it became dogma that all writing is political, Pound's anti-Semitism was dug up and used to help prove that the modernist literary establishment in the first half of the century was, along with its New Critical theories, fascist at its core. Eliot's own anti-Semitic remarks were used to try to destroy his reputation as the most powerful poet writing in English in the twentieth century, but his poetic greatness made him not so easy a target as the blathering Pound had been. After his release from the mental hospital, Pound spent the rest of his life in Venice, in his apartment on the Dorsoduro with his mistress, Olga Rudge, and he spoke not a public word, and very few private ones, in his last dozen years.

The Pound case reminded us that there were real-life consequences to believing this or that, and that people could be held responsible for what they wrote and taught. There were other demonstrations of the same problem. Joseph R. McCarthy in Washington was accusing left-leaning professors of being communist traitors, and in 1951 with the publication of *God and Man at Yale: The Superstitions of Academic Freedom*, William F. Buckley, a Catholic conservative who had recently graduated from Yale College, extended the attack to a close look at the sacred doctrine of "academic freedom." The book was a sensation on campus, for it had much to say about Yale, and a best-seller in the bigger world where in the age of the bombshell of Whittaker Chambers's *Witness*, people in increasing numbers were beginning to believe that universities were protected enclaves of "godless communism." Buckley argued provocatively and brilliantly that the administration and faculty of Yale, despite Yale's having been founded on religion and being still supported by free enterprise, were systematically teaching atheism and socialism in the classrooms.

The evidence of the attack on religion was more amusing than telling. The anthropologist Raymond ("Jungle Jim") Kennedy, killed in Borneo in 1950, had made frequent crude remarks about religion—"chaplains accompanying modern armies are comparable to witch doctors accompanying tribes"—in his popular lecture course, the largest in Yale College. The defenders of religion were little more its friends in Buckley's view. In the course on the Bible as literature—known to the students as Cokes and Smokes because of the informal nature of the class—taught by still another university chaplain, "Uncle Sid" Lovett, religion was treated from a historical perspective and was so trivialized that students took the course only because it was the biggest "gut" in the catalogue.

But it was in economics that Buckley found his real target. Here, attacking the new Paul Samuelson textbook based on Keynesian theory, he charged that the introductory econ course taught that income in the United States was "unfairly" distributed and that this inequality caused the business cycle of depression and inflation. The professors of economics, according to Buckley, taught that the cure was to be found in the intervention of the state into all aspects of economic life and the redistribution of income by such means as a progressive income tax, a confiscatory inheritance tax, deficit financing, discouragement of thrift, and welfarism. All of this sounded outrageous at the time, for we academics, students and faculty alike, were mostly all, just as Buckley charged, confirmed liberals.

Buckley got to us most shrewdly when he argued that what Yale and other universities defended as "academic freedom," leaving the teacher to teach what seemed to him to be the truth, was in fact a device for propagating liberal views. Academic freedom, he argued, was not extended to communists on the left or to radical conservatives on the other wing, and while he didn't worry much about the communists, he instanced on the right the case of his mentor, the conservative professor of political science Willmoore Kendall, who made himself unacceptable to his colleagues by insisting on the guilt of Alger Hiss and supporting Senator McCarthy. So incensed were his liberal colleagues at Kendall's views that when he offered provocatively, and perhaps not entirely seriously, to resign for a payment of forty thousand dollars, they actually persuaded the administration to buy out this gadfly. Q.E.D., Buckley went on, academic freedom is only the cover name for a militant liberalism that has dominated the universities from the 1930s. But we children of the Depression, raised in the Age of Roosevelt, were so indoctrinated with liberal views that we took them as simply given and obvious truth. They *were* the truths that academic freedom made it possible to teach. It never occurred to us to doubt that Hiss was innocent, that McCarthy was a total liar, that the state was the best means for remedying all evils; and so we joined with everyone else in reviling and laughing at Buckley.

These political and ideological attitudes were widespread, but graduate students are for the most part a very odd self-selected breed of cat with their own agendas. The melancholics are withdrawn to the point of silence, and the neurotics are always ready to snap. The undergraduates took it for granted that graduate students were "weenies" and "nerds," and in the fifties we pretty much accepted this judgment. One friend, Bob Brown, with whom I played an amusing game in which we spoke to each other only in lines from Shakespeare, found himself telling his director, a very stern taskmaster, that he could not finish his dissertation and was planning to give up on his Ph.D. To describe what the fatal interview was like he turned to a recent film drawn from a Joseph Conrad story, *The Outcast of the Islands,* in which a man who has gone native (Trevor Howard) crawls in the mud of the river bank, shouting at the perfectly upright, unmoving back of his former patron, an old sea captain (Ralph Richardson), sitting in a canoe disappearing into the mist downstream.

Social class had a lot to do with it. Graduate students in the arts and sciences, unlike the undergraduates or the professional students in law, medicine, and business, were drawn in the postwar period mostly from liberal arts colleges and the middle class. The financial rewards were too small to attract the more affluent and socially savvy people to what Bernard Shaw described as a life of "being half mad from reading undergraduate papers." But each of us thought he was very smart, at least until we encountered in graduate seminars people who were not only our intellectual peers but in many cases our superiors. Imagine suddenly finding yourself in a class on the Romantic poets taught by some giant intellect like W. K. Wimsatt and numbering among its students people who would in time dominate the field: Harold Bloom, Frank Brady, Geoffrey Hartman, Tom McFarland, Harry Berger, Donald Hirsch, and Charles Ryskamp. Harold beat his head on the table and groaned when Smithers read his long, dull paper, while Frank, six-feet-something tall, slid under the table until only his chin rested on it, and Harry walked to the window and stared out. Perhaps few classes were quite so dramatic as this, but they were all testing. Every meeting was a struggle to say something intelligent enough to establish your credentials without revealing the depths of your ignorance. We competed for grades and for the approbation of our teachers, not only because we wanted some guarantee that we were intelligent and learned enough to be in this business, but also because they would have a great deal to say about where we would get jobs. We gasped when one of the few women students, Leonora Leet (who was later to write *The Cup of Love*) replied to Louis Martz's suggestion that the paper she was reading was running well over the allotted time—"Don't you think you'd better finish now?"—with a starchy, "I will be finished in a moment."

For all our oddness, the Yale graduate students were a most remarkable group of talents, and the careers of many of its members have been sensational. Harold Bloom was, I suppose, the master competitor, our "covering cherub," to use his own later coinage, in whose shadow all his confreres would work for the rest of their lives. He came to the Yale graduate school in 1951 a marked man, described by his Cornell teacher, Meyer Abrams, himself no slouch, as "a prodigy, beyond anything I'd ever seen," and his gnomic sayings were the gossip of the graduate students. He flaunted his Jewishness as well as his learning at a time when anti-Semitism was still very much alive at Yale, and his quarrels from the first with the reigning New Critics of the day, Cleanth Brooks and Maynard Mack, had something to do with this. His first books, *Shelley's Mythmaking* (1958) and a big book on all the Romantic poets, *The Visionary Company* (1961), defied the New Criticism by praising the Romanticism it had discounted and insisting, like the poets he admired and quoted, that the imaginative faculty, not tight verbal structure, is the mark of great poetry.

Harold's energy was prodigious, his style vatic, his knowledge of humanistic letters extraordinary, his memory photographic. Students told of an occasion in the English study in Sterling Library when a question arose about how many stanzas there were in Edmund Spenser's *Epithalamion*; he offered to recite them all, and did, while they counted. Above all, he had a kind of literary perfect pitch. Every work he picked up came to a kind of full literary life in his hands. He displayed the work always *sub specie aeternitatis*, and at the same time his control of detail and tone was exemplary.

His appetites were as vast as his ambition. He ate hugely and would boast in time that he had had numerous women—*mille e tre?*—some of them his students. Insomniac, he wrote and wrote, book after book, and later entered into a publishing venture with Chelsea Books for nearly four hundred volumes of criticism on various authors and individual works. And always, from beginning to end, the keynote of his criticism was the same: "The canonical quality comes out of strangeness, comes out of the idiosyncratic, comes out of originality."

Because of his exaggerated mannerisms and his literary precocity, we all predicted that the philistine Yale students would murder Bloom when he was hired as an instructor in 1955. Nothing could have been further from the mark. They loved him, ate up his posing and his outrageous statements, his habit of kissing everyone on the head and addressing them, like Fagan, "oh my dear." He was a great teacher from the moment he stepped into the classroom through all his teaching life. He understood, as the rest of us emotionally buttoned-up graduate students did not, the uses of showmanship.

Sprezzatura, the prized Renaissance rhetorical art of making the difficult seem easy, he knew not. He made the easy seem difficult and important, throwing his head back, closing his eyes, intoning from some faraway place. He was a great unkempt bear of a man, one who suffered publicly and was able to bear the pain only long enough to bring his students and readers news from the far reaches of the self as expressed in poetry. His was a titanic ego, yet he always knew his students and contemporaries as people and inquired about their most private concerns in an understanding way. And everyone, even his bitterest critic, was flattered that he was that interested in them.

He and I were friends, but never close friends; our spirits were too contrary to stall together in the same department, and we both knew it well enough to be wary with each other most of the time. But one could not avoid the terrifying standard of achievement he set, and by which the rest of us were inevitably judged. Straight romanticism needed to be tumulted to attract the attention Harold wanted, so he mixed it with Jewish mysticism and the Freudian family romance. Older literary studies assumed, for the most part, that writers stood on the shoulders of their predecessors, and influence studies, one large aspect of earlier literary criticism, took it for granted that the effect of older writers, Virgil on Milton, for example, was always beneficent. But Harold applied Freud's Oedipal model to the relationship of writers and argued that the younger poet, the "ephebe," lived in the shadow of his great predecessors, was overwhelmed by their achievements, and could only write pale imitations of the patriarch. "Weak poets" were castrated by their elders and wrote only second- or third-rate imitations of them. "Strong poets," on the other hand, rebelled against their "belatedness" and misread the ancients in creative ways that freed their own voices. It is a likely enough story, and, indeed, we other graduate students certainly did labor in his shadow, but he was telling us something that we were too conventional to learn. For us the past was idolized as always beneficent, never constituting a threat to our own achievement that had to be challenged if we were to find our own voices. But anxiety suited our uneasy age, and living poets for a time beat a pathway to Harold's door, anxious to be publicly named by him a strong rather than a weak poet. He made quite a good thing out of issuing periodical certifications of A. R. Ammons as a strong poet, John Ashbery as this, Lowell as that.

For all his romanticism, Harold was a careerist of unusual abilities. His book *The Western Canon* earned him a $600,000 advance in the 1990s, an unheard-of sum for literary criticism. In the matter of appointments he also pulled off the unthinkable, managing to hold simultaneously two of the most distinguished chairs in the academic world, Sterling Professor of Humanities at Yale and Berg Professor of English at New York University. Whether he has been paid full salary in both places is not certain, but a *New York Times* interview spoke of him as "moonlighting at New York University since 1988." Not long before, it had been an unforgivable faculty sin to hold two teaching appointments at the same time: professors were supposed to divide neither their loyalties nor their time. When the black philosopher Kenneth Mills was discovered in 1972 to have taken another job at SUNY Stony Brook while still holding an appointment at Yale, a Yale administrator visited him at night and told him summarily to choose one or the other. But by the end of the eighties Harold was admired, at least by the young, for having engrossed two major academic positions, and by 1994 he would be given what had become the ultimate popular accolade, an article — "Colossus Among Critics, Harold Bloom" — devoted to him in the Sunday magazine of the *New York Times* (September 25): "Everything about him is outsized, an encyclopedic intellect, exuberant eccentricity, a massive love of literature."

But these triumphs were all far in the future, and in the early fifties he labored like the rest of us at getting through graduate courses that ran for a full year, during which you were expected to write six to eight short papers plus a longer term paper at the end. Most classes began with the reading of one or more of these short papers each week, and since they were usually very dull, these occasions were dreaded. We wanted to hear the professors talk about what they knew so well. We had come here to learn from them, but it was the practice in most classes for the teacher to say little or nothing, insisting that the students develop and maintain the discussion. This method furthered self-reliance, and once in a rare while it even taught us something, but mostly it produced tedium and confusion.

The reading lists were enormous, with many of the required articles and books in foreign languages, for it was still believed that it was necessary and possible to command all the literature of your field. In a way, the size of the bibliography was a help, for mastering it had become so obviously impossible that it forced us to consider what part of it was the most useful, and doing so made it clear that some of it was worth nothing and much of it was repetitive, even contradictory. The very mass of scholarship, ironically, was calling into question its own value. But as with so much else, we absorbed this knowledge silently, finding it inconceivable as yet to question the progress of knowledge.

For the single students life was lived almost entirely in the Hall of Graduate Studies and the library, but those who, like myself, were married, scurried about looking for a cheap place to live and some kind of work that would keep things going. I had saved enough of my four calendar years of eligibility for the G.I. Bill—not using it at Oxford where tuition was low—to be able to pay graduate tuition for two years and get a small stipend, but Sue and I both had to work, she at typing manuscripts for professors and I at whatever came to hand. At the end of the first year in graduate school we had another child, our daughter Kate (who later graduated from Yale, in the class of 1974), and with two small children we barely scraped by. I worked one year selling Good Humor ice cream, driving my open white truck with its clanging Pied Piper bell and keeping my German grammar—my study in Austria had not been sufficient, and I had failed the first test—in the refrigerated box among the Popsicles. Later I got a job teaching at Quinnipiac, a local proprietary college that operated out of the old Elks Club on Whitney Avenue.

Timing was always the tricky thing with this job. I had to coordinate my attendance at my Yale classes with the various courses in remedial writing and in the American novel I was teaching at Quinnipiac. We had a 1935 Dodge coupe that was a very sluggish starter. I would rush out of the Quonset hut in which we were living with barely time to make class, only to find that the engine would not start. Take out two spark plugs, scrape their points, coat them with graphite from a pencil, try the engine again. Doesn't start, clean two more plugs, damn, then two more, and then the final two, the deadline for class drawing nearer all the time. If this doesn't work, remove the air filter, pour some ether compound in the carburetor, and hope the engine doesn't catch fire when it starts with a red fireball and a great whoosh!

The school was run by two tightfisted Yankees, old Sam and Mrs. Tater. She would hold your paycheck in her right hand and only as you placed grades for your courses in her left hand would she release the check. Her crabbed approach worked, and by the 1990s Quinnipiac had a large rural campus, a law school, a famous political poll, and an Albert Schweitzer humanities center. By hiring a number of Yale graduate students Quinnipiac gave good educational value, but some of its teaching and most of its administration were done by those pale ghosts who wander from one unknown school to another, hoping desperately to get something published in some obscure journal, to finish their degrees, to land permanent jobs at a halfway decent university. I liked these academic ancient mariners and learned a lot from them about the folkways of teaching, addressing all of them as "Dr. Mudrick" or "Dr. Liebert," though they had never come within light-years of finishing a dissertation. They enjoyed the joke and were flattered by it at the same time, and we got along fine.

The Quinnipiac students came from blue-collar homes in the mill towns of the Housatonic Valley and were sent to college at great sacrifice to learn to be receptionists in medical and dental offices, accountants, and secretaries. In those days some liberal arts component was still considered necessary to any college degree, even the associate's. The level of study, though, was very low, and I filled in once without any difficulty for my brother-in-law, Harry Scoble, in a course on business math, though my math skills are not notable. In English it was spelling, case agreement, pronoun referents, and attempts to write simple declarative sentences. Forget the subjunctive. I learned a lot about grammar and found that I liked teaching as a skill in itself, quite aside from what was taught. Even parsing sentences can become fascinating in time, and it gives you something to do on the blackboard. Discipline was a problem, but the students were accustomed to accepting authority when it was asserted, and when one day I threw a huge anthology at the wall above a student who had fallen asleep leaning against the back wall of the classroom, and hit him by accident full in the face, there was only laughter, from him and others, not a walkout or charges of assault.

I taught a course in the modern American novel, *Sister Carrie, The Sun Also Rises, The Grapes of Wrath, The Great Gatsby, All the King's Men.* I tried to pick works that I thought would speak directly to the students. Theodore Dreiser, I thought, particularly would come home to their own lack of money, in passages like the one where Carrie realizes that she is going to die if she doesn't find the money for a warm coat with winter coming on, and just as she realizes that she can't save the necessary money meets the salesman who takes her into a restaurant, feeds her, and offers her a ten-dollar bill. But poverty—Sister Carrie's, in the Joad family, or among Willie Stark's Louisiana constituents—was not what interested my Quinnipiac students. They liked adventure in Hemingway and high life in *The Great Gatsby.* Literature for them was escape, not description of things they already knew well. But by concentrating on such questions as "What are the rich like in Fitzgerald?" I managed to combine their fantasies with my formal analysis and keep the classes going. I still thought that literature would throw light on their own lives, show them truths about themselves and their families that the priest, the politician, and the advertiser busily covered up. But they did not want to move out of the cave, and it began to seem folly to try to insist on their knowing things that they could not change and to undermine the illusions that made it possible to live life with some pleasure.

Back at Yale, however, you were still expected to know things, lots of things, and the qualifying exam had to be passed at the end of classes and before beginning the dissertation. This was an oral exam on the full range of English literature, from Old English to the present, lasting only an hour and coming usually after two years of taking courses. Its terrors were proverbial, and while it didn't last long, you were expected to answer accurately questions on any English book or author from the past fifteen hundred years. Horror stories were told of the student who sat at the end of the table answering questions and nervously chewing his lip until his white shirt was covered with blood; of a nun who fainted and slid under the table, where the male professors wondered if they should do something for her until Karl Young, an expert on medieval religion and the namesake of a chair I later held, rose, held up his hand, and informed his colleagues that canon law forbade a lay person to touch a religious one, even if she was in extremis. The hero of Yale English orals was the great Pottle, who had done so well in the 1920s that all his examiners filed out at the end to congratulate him. Everyone shook his hand and said what a fine job he had done, and then, in the manner of academics, stood around with nothing to say until Pottle spoke up: "Well, anybody going to the library?"

My own examination was not so heroic, but it was blessed with good luck. While stopped at traffic lights on the way to the exam I skimmed Samuel Johnson's "Preface to Shakespeare," which I hadn't read earlier. I entered the dark-paneled room in the Hall of Graduate Studies, sat down at the table, smiled nervously at the distinguished professors, and waited for the first question. It came with due solemnity: "What main points did Dr. Johnson make about Shakespeare's style in his 'Preface to Shakespeare'?" I could actually see the pages as I rolled relentlessly onward.

There is nothing like a good beginning to give you confidence, and this success powered me to one happy answer after another.

> "Name a Satanic character in American literature."
>
> "Captain Ahab."
>
> "Right. Do you have a definition of metaphysical poetry?"
>
> "How about Dr. Johnson's 'heterogeneous ideas yoked by violence together'?"
>
> "All right, Johnson is always interesting, but do you have any more modern definition?"

My questioner by this time was Louis Martz, the specialist on metaphysical poetry, and I risked quoting a version of Cleanth Brooks's definition, "forcing the many into the one." Martz didn't like that theory much either, for he had his own views, but with Brooks sitting across the table he could not object very strenuously. So we went on:

"Are there any metaphysical poets in the Victorian period?"

"Browning is sometimes said to be metaphysical, but he isn't really—he only sounds like it in some of his lines."

"Can you quote one of those lines?"

"Irks care the crop-full bird? / Frets doubt the maw-crammed beast?"

I stumbled a bit on the lines, and John Pope was pleased to help me out. But in the end I struck out on Henry James and his symbols. I had read only some of his short novels like *Daisy Miller* and *The Spoils of Poynton*, and I tried to get a discussion going of the antique furniture in *The Spoils of Poynton*, but the examiner hadn't read this book and wanted golden bowls and wings of the dove. Still, it was a good performance, as much a rite of passage as it was a test of knowledge, marking the successful initiate as a genuine member of the tribe of English teachers.

At thirty years old with two children and the G.I. Bill exhausted, two years was the most I could manage in residence in the Yale graduate school, and I began to look for a job. But first something had to be done about a dissertation. The English Renaissance theater was the subject I wanted to work on, and this meant working with Charles Prouty, mainly a textual scholar of Shakespeare. Prouty was engaged in producing an edition of the Shakespeare First Folio in conjunction with Helge Kökeritz, an expert in medieval and Renaissance English pronunciation, known as Koko to the students who took his course in the history of the English language to avoid some other even more difficult philological courses like Old High German. Kökeritz was a Swede by birth and a philologist by training who, because he had a distinct Swedish accent, prided himself on his ability to pronounce English in its ancient forms. He and one of my tutors at Oxford, Eric Dobson, were the world's foremost experts on early English pronunciation, and they disagreed totally. Knowing this, the graduate students were understandably skeptical, and Kökeritz's recording of some of Chaucer's stories from *The Canterbury Tales* was irreverently spoken of as the "By Yumpin' Yiminy Chaucer."

The Shakespeare folio edition was to be a reproduction of an especially fine original owned by the Yale literary society, the Elizabethan Club (which served tea and sandwiches to the literati in the afternoon). Since the pages of this near perfect copy were simply being photographed to produce the edition, the editors assumed there was no reason to do the massive work of checking the proofs page by page. But the designers and photographers working on the reproduction, knowing nothing of textual matters, had observed frequent "showthrough," a condition in which heavy inking on one page seeped through the paper and blotted lines on the obverse page. They meticulously cleaned up these spots in the master photo plates from which the book was printed, and in doing so corrupted the text in a number of places. They also, in their ignorance of early print fonts, sometimes knocked the ascenders off the old "long," or "staff," s, which looks like the modern f. At the same time they eliminated a lot of the "catchwords," the first word of the following page, which is printed at the bottom of the preceding page to help the printer assemble the pages in the right order. Absolute accuracy is the sine qua non in the textual editing business, and when the book appeared the critics pounced like blood-maddened sharks on the bewildered Prouty and Kökeritz, who couldn't understand how anything could have gone wrong. One critic spoke of Prouty's polemical introduction as a "dog returning to his vomit"; others charged that Prouty and Kökeritz were venal wretches trying to scoop a major edition of the folio that Charlton Hinman had been putting together for many patient years by comparing the eighty-seven copies of the volume gathered by Henry Folger in the rare book library in Washington that bears his name. Neither Prouty nor Kökeritz ever quite recovered from what maliciously came to be known as "the Bad Folio."

It was the custom in those days for graduate students, except a few geniuses, to work on topics that the professor, who was supposed to know the field, suggested as useful and rewarding subjects. Nowadays this practice would seem a sign of an unoriginal mind, but it worked well enough then in getting the student started—always the most difficult step—after which his or her own interests and abilities inevitably took over. When I went around to see Prouty, he was ready for me. "Marston is the right man to work on. Neither the poetry nor the plays have been *done* yet." This much was true. John Marston was a late-sixteenth-century English poet who wrote both satiric plays and poetry. He was a university graduate, one of the fashionable young men who came to London around Shakespeare's time to make their names and fortunes writing at first for the printers. Marston had a taste for satire, and he broke into the literary scene by writing a number of scurrilous and turgid poems of attack:

> I crave no syrens of our Halcion times,
> To grace the accents of my rough-hew'd rimes;
> But grim Reproofe, and stearne Hate of villany,
> Inspire and guide a Satyres poesie.

Marston soon translated his poetic satire to the theater, where in a series of plays, including *The Dutch Courtesan* and, most famously, *The Malcontent*, he turned his satire loose in the theater to whip the more sensational, particularly the sexual, sins of erring humanity.

Two earlier editions had established the texts and to some degree the chronology of his writings, so my mainly historical work was to locate the author and his works in a literary tradition of satire and in the setting of Elizabethan literature. This meant showing his relation to the Roman satire of Horace and Juvenal, which he had read in school, as well as the satire of his own times, describing how he adapted these traditions to the page and to the stage.

Gathering and sorting this information was as traditional in its procedures as the understanding of what constituted "an original contribution to knowledge," the old formula describing the purpose of the dissertation. An enormous amount of reading in the library and laborious note taking on three-by-five cards led to an accumulation of quotes and observations, all neatly indexed in the usual gray marbled paper box with its brass fittings, carried with you everywhere lest someone steal it. Strange kinds of organizing and understanding grew in the library. One elderly woman appeared every day for many years to work on her dissertation on Sir Philip Sidney. The task was endless, however, for each word of Sidney's writings sent her on a long excursion into the lore of the Renaissance. "Horse," for example, a word that occurs early in *The Defence of Poesie*, took years of searching through writings on the breeding of horses, dressage, training for war, cavalry tactics, and so on. There were other ghosts in the library stacks as well. One day while looking up an entry in Donald Wing's extension of the *Short-Title Catalogue*, a listing of all printed books in English up to the later seventeenth century, a faunlike man came up behind me and read over my shoulder. When I glanced around in some irritation, he drew back and said, "Great book, isn't it? I wrote it."

Another day, while digging away in the annotations of a seventeenth-century edition of Juvenal in the rare book library, I was interrupted by a man shouting at Marjorie Wynn, the expert librarian. "Do you know the three rarest nineteenth-century novels? I thought not. *Pride and Prejudice*, *Middlemarch*, and [I think] *Hard Times*." It was Chauncey Brewster Tinker, the patron saint of the Yale English department, and founder of the rare book library. When he finished he actually leaped into the air, shouting exultantly, "And I own all of them!" Fate was closing in on "Tink" at this time, for in the manner of so many of the eighteenth-century rationalists whom he had taught to a generation of distinguished and loyal students, he was about to lose his memory to what I suppose was Alzheimer's disease, though the name was unknown to us at that time. Despite his distinction, he had no funds to speak of, so his students arranged for a small house and a keeper for him in his last days. It was very like Jonathan Swift at the end gazing out his window at the Dublin rain, but, rather than the deanery, Tink was confined to a small tract house in East Hartford, a working-class suburb of Hartford.

Administrators at Rensselaer Polytechnic Institute, the science school in Troy, New York, wrote in August 1953 that they needed an instructor for extra English sections. I crammed my note cards into my files in preparation for leaving Yale and writing the dissertation in a place where no research library would be available. Troy was a decaying old Hudson River town, home of "Uncle Sam," a local worthy who became rich making shoddy cloth during the Civil War. High above the crumbling brownstone townhouses and cobbled streets of the old city, RPI sat like a fortress on the hill. The engineering students were sent in sections from class to class, and they were required to take two English courses, one in writing and the other a very imaginative locally designed course in practical linguistics intended to make them more sophisticated readers of all kinds of texts. S. I. Hayakawa, who became the combative president of San Francisco State College during the late sixties, and later a U.S. senator, provided the basic text, *Language in Thought and Action*. Although not a bad introduction to the subject, it was given to odd illustrations that suggested some troubles in Hayakawa's semantic infrastructure, such as a newspaper story he recounted that has for some reason stuck in my head. A man in a restaurant offers a dog part of his hamburger. The dog's owner refuses, saying that his dog never eats hamburgers, to which the offerer replies, "Fussy mutt, isn't he?" Furious at this insult, the owner of the dog goes home, gets his gun, comes back, and kills the hamburger offerer. Hayakawa used this bizarre little story to illustrate the maxim "Sticks and stones may break my bones, but words can never hurt me," with no sense of the intricate exchange of powerful feelings that lay behind the words. Apparently he really believed that if the dog owner had realized that words can harm neither him nor his dog, all would have been well. There were a few odd places like this, but on the whole it was a very good book to use as a basis for discussing how language works.

Four classes, in two different courses and each meeting three times a week, was the normal teaching load, and because the institute ran a night school for part-time older students you could sign up to teach a fifth class in the evening for extra pay. An aggressive former major in the Canadian army ran the night school efficiently, but he constantly complained that the students would not be there at all in a better-run society. "They ought," he would huff and wheeze, snapping his red suspenders, pacing up and down the room, "to be home getting a good night's sleep so that they could do an honest day's work for their employers tomorrow." He may have been right, but we were happy to get the extra wages for teaching them. At a salary of $3,800 a year, every dollar counted.

Because new instructors had to teach six eight o'clock classes (for the school week continued through Saturday in those days), the ones who taught night school found that some teaching days lasted more than twelve hours. But since I was writing my dissertation between classes in my office, the long day made it possible for me to do a lot of work with my accumulated notes during the day, when I was not trying to get the hang of Hayakawa. Sue typed the dissertation on the cracked glass top of an old patio table, and I corrected the pages during the day, making headway on getting the plays of John Marston in order.

We lived in paint-peeled World War II barracks that had been converted to faculty apartments. They were located high on the hill above Troy and the river, so they were wide open to the weather underneath. The winter winds are ferocious in Troy, and they swept under the buildings, up through the floors, and around the loose framing of the windows. One morning I woke to find a razor-thin drift of snow, about three feet high, running across the bedroom. I lay there for a long time staring at the ice wall and thinking that I had chosen the wrong line of work, that I would really have to quit and find something else if I wanted to support my family. But I did not know what else to do, and at this point I had too big an investment in academic life to turn back. Besides, being a teacher gave meaning to my life and was a worthy and honorable way to earn a living, if only you could earn a living! A Christmas bonus of fifty dollars seemed riches at the time.

Somehow the dissertation was completed, piling up chapter by chapter in a box that measured our hope for the future. As each chapter was finished it was mailed down to New Haven to my dissertation director for his comments. Prouty was not much of a reader of dissertations. In the entirety of my four-hundred-odd pages he made only two comments. On page 27 he wrote, "See my *George Gascoigne*," a book he had written about a minor Elizabethan author some years before. And on page 323: "See my *George Gascoigne*." In a way this made it easy since there was no time-consuming quibbling over the argument or the style, but it was hard for me to believe that he didn't want to learn all that I had said about Marston.

In March a letter arrived from the chairman of the Yale English department, F. W. Hilles, offering me a one-year, renewable appointment as instructor during 1954–1955, with the proviso that the dissertation had to be finished and the doctorate conferred in June 1954. The salary was $3,500, $300 less than RPI's, and there was no chance of haggling: take it or leave it, for there were others in a long line. I took it. I liked the people at RPI, but to be offered a position in the premier English department in the country was the kind of chance that not only improves your situation but determines your future. In order to take the degree, though, I not only had to finish the dissertation, I had to enroll and pay graduate school tuition in the term in which it was submitted and read, a matter of $500. I didn't have it, but I had to have the Ph.D. in order to make the move. I drove down the long road from Troy to New Haven to see the administrative graduate dean, Hartley Simpson, who worked away at his desk scarcely saying a word all day, sending out endless longhand letters, and then drank a bottle of whiskey every night to put himself to sleep. I expected no help but made my case for either a fellowship or a loan as eloquently as I could, and I was surprised to hear him say that it was at least possible that something could be arranged. "Go back to your teaching, and I will write you in a week." He did. "A scholarship has been granted you by the Yale graduate school in the amount of your spring tuition. Best wishes, Hartley Simpson."

The dissertation was bound in three blue copies and sent to the English department. Dissertations in the English department at Yale were read by three professors who had not been involved in the writing. Although the director of the dissertation was allowed to submit remarks—Prouty probably said, "He should read my *George Gascoigne*"— the vote by all the professors to pass or fail depended on what the presumably impartial three readers had to say. One reader complained that my explanation of everything went back to the Garden of Eden, and he was right, for the only way to be safe, I thought, was on introducing any idea like, say, satyrs, to lay out a full bibliography in the footnotes and to discuss fully Greek and Roman descriptions of these woodland creatures. I was right about the value of detail, the dissertation was passed, and the department recommended me for the doctorate.

Whitney Avenue has lost its shine by now, its elms gone, the big old houses decayed or turned into apartments and mortuaries, but coming down from Troy on a bright, sunny June day in 1954 it looked like the Champs-Elysées, and Yale in all its Gothic glory, just before urban blight surrounded it, still looked like Camelot. Conferring the graduate degrees was the high point of the commencement ceremony, conducted in Latin, and as I walked up to the platform in the Old Campus to get my diploma, looking at my wife and two lively children beaming, I felt that I had been admitted to the company of the learned.

The gods smile only briefly, though, and in a few weeks Sue's mother was diagnosed with inoperable cancer and sent home to die. In the way of that time (how long ago it seems), the daughter of the family was expected to care for dying parents—the two sons, being men, were exempted. Sue took our two small children down to New Rochelle to look after her father and to put larger and larger shots of morphine into a body that was wasting away to the point where there was scarcely a place to insert a needle. I stayed in Troy, teaching in summer school. In July I went down to New Haven to look for a place to live, and it soon became clear that there was nothing I could afford in the town. I tried to buy a four-room tract house in one of the more wretched suburbs, only to learn that my Yale salary as an instructor was too low to qualify for a mortgage on houses that were being bought by truck drivers and factory workers. My lack of credit was a piece of rare good luck, though, for in time I found on York Square, just down from the Yale gym, an old brick rowhouse that belonged to the university but had been empty for some years. One of the local high schools was just across the street in those days. The university, eager to have someone living there, struck a deal in which they would turn on the water in the old pre–Civil War lead pipes and check the coke-burning furnace to make sure its gases did not suffocate us, but nothing more, in return for a rent of sixty-five dollars a month. The gas water heater had to be lighted and turned off by hand, and every time I went out I worried the entire time I was away that I had left it on by accident. When I finally did and melted it down, the university, fearing fire, immediately installed a wonderful automatic water heater. The coke furnace was very tender and would go out in an instant if fed improperly, which usually happened just as it was time for me to leave for class on an icy day. When it did work it pumped enormous amounts of dust and sulfur gas up the ducts that ran through the old chimneys and fireplaces, clogging our breathing apparatuses every night and causing us to cough and hawk all day long.

Still, it was conveniently close to the university, cheap, and it could be fixed up. Sears and Roebuck became a regular run for linoleum and paint, and every weekend, and many an evening, was spent taking plaster off brick walls to make them look modern, painting the worn-out floors, building shelves, and in general trying to make the rooms look interesting. It was on five levels—cellar, first floor half belowground, main floor, bedroom floor, and attic—and we moved facilities, except for the one bathroom on the third floor, from level to level, kitchen here, living room there, looking restlessly for just the right arrangement. Truckloads of trash went out of the backyard, an old walk was uncovered under layers of cinders, and we mowed the weeds and planted flowers when grass would not grow in the stony soil. A maple tree and some ground cover in the tiny front yard created the atmosphere of a nineteenth-century townhouse.

In August I moved in alone—while Sue's mother still lingered in the long heat of summer—and began painting the rooms of the house and preparing for classes in the fall.

5

Keeping Them Quiet

The Yale English department hired the unheard-of number of ten new instructors in the fall of 1954. We were all glad to get the jobs but worried that we would end up like the children in Thomas Hardy's *Jude the Obscure* who hanged themselves, as the placard on the breast of one of them explained, "Done because we were too menny." The phantasmagoric quality about our lives, so mundane in many ways, so eerie in others, was caught perfectly by Kingsley Amis in *Lucky Jim* (1954), which was the runaway favorite novel of young faculty members at the time. Jim Dixon, his madly sane chairman, Professor Welch, and his neurotic colleague Margaret Peel, trying to trap him into marriage at their dismal provincial university, seemed our colleagues. Trying to meet standards we scarcely understood, judged by people who seemed to come from a world other than our own, fated to make dreadful mistakes, we only made them worse when we tried to make them better—as Jim did when he burned his chairman's wife's blanket with a cigarette, and then tried to hide the burn by hacking away its browned edges with a razor. "Lucky Jim is a novel about selfishness," said a stern critic forty years later, declaring Jim's escape from the university to a cushy job at the end of the book "entirely unmerited." But that was for us the point. No merit we could conceive of would possibly save us, only Jim's kind of luck. As the old song says: "Lucky Jim, Oh how I envy him."

"The Yale English department is now getting its instructors off the New York subway," said Benjamin Christie Nangle, the director of undergraduate studies and permanent associate professor, who drowned his disappointment in the changing times with bottles hidden away in his furnace. Ben was very sensitive to names, and as director of undergraduate studies with responsibility for putting together the numerous sections of mandatory freshman English, he whiled away many a dull hour until the sun was over the mast putting all the students with fish names—Bass, Pickrel, Trout—in one section, and all the animal names—Fox, Bull, Colt—into another. When roll was called at the beginning of each class, the results were thought to be hilarious. His masterwork was a section with all the unpronounceable names —Winchester Krysczewski, Manuel Dexterides, Gregor Ontopofurski, Apropos Dimitropopolous, Festus Adebonogo—which required about twenty minutes to call and usually ended in phonetic disaster. "Confusion now hath made his masterpieces," said the admiring, not knowing that multiculturalism and ethnicity were already slouching toward New Haven.

Ben had hold of something, though. Demography was changing things. It had all begun in the thirties, but it was the war that really ended the old faculty gentility, bringing G.I. students like myself to the campus from less privileged backgrounds. Faculty names were now a mixture—Bone, Warnke, Brady, Bloom, Young, Waingrow, Culler, Price, Feidelson. White males all, of course, no women, and no blacks, but the Jews were new, and they set the academic pace in the latter twentieth century. According to Robert Alter, "In the United States . . . though Jews are rather less than two percent of the population, if one looks to areas of activity such as journalism and criticism, or scientific research, or academic disciplines like mathematics, history, sociology, and English literature, a fourth or a third or sometimes more than half the leaders in the field can turn out to be Jews." In Yale English, Harold Bloom, Geoffrey Hartman, Charles Feidelson, Don Hirsch, and Harry Berger were my immediate contemporaries, and Stanley Fish and Stephen Greenblatt arrived a bit later. The range was great, from the courtly and shy southerner Feidelson to the demonic Bloom — "no teacher should look that anguished," someone said — but all were ambitious, and all of them seemed to me almost endlessly energetic, well read, and profoundly intelligent.

Alter denies that there are any specific Jewish traits that lead to academic success, but the Jews brought to the exegesis of literary texts the tradition of thousands of years of close reading of the most sacred of texts. They seemed wise beyond their years in their Talmudic understanding that there are many ways of getting at texts, none of them entirely sufficient, all of them requiring ingenuity and learning. Perhaps even more formidable, or so it seemed to me, was the Jewish admiration for learning. In America intellectualism and learning are not serious business — thought peculiar, in fact, outside the academy — so that those of us who were not Jewish remained always somewhat apologetic about what we did. But the Jews came from backgrounds that admired bookish achievements. And the refugees, like Hartman, were already familiar with the continental phenomenological philosophic tradition, from G. W. F. Hegel to Martin Heidegger, and from Friedrich Nietzsche to Walter Benjamin, that was to play such a large part in humanistic studies in our time. And they had the great advantage of seldom drinking alcohol, and then only in small quantities.

My mother-in-law was still dying, slowly and painfully, and my family was with her, but in the fall with the leaves turning and the nights chilly and bright, to be an instructor in the most notable English department in the country seemed to be a high calling, not dimmed even by six eight o'clock classes once more. We still taught on Saturday morning, called roll at the beginning of every class, started each fifty-minute session with a ten-minute quiz, kept attendance records and grades in an official blue book issued by the department, and gave frequent hour-long tests and a final. Tardiness was not allowed. I warned one student ("Buy an alarm clock!") that any further lateness would cause me to drop him from the course—we still had that arbitrary power—and he assured me that he would be there at eight sharp from then on. Next class he showed up half an hour late, and as he tried to sneak in I waved at the door—"Out, out." He was waiting outside at the end of the hour to plead his case, and when I remained adamant, he brought out his ultimate excuse: "But, sir, you don't understand—I have trouble waking up in the morning."

Evelyn Waugh caught exactly what new teachers feel when they first go into the classroom in his novel *Decline and Fall* (1929). Paul Pennyfeather takes a position at a school for boys, Llanabba Castle, run by Augustus Fagan, Ph.D.; Captain Grimes is also on the faculty. Knowing nothing himself, Paul asks one of the other masters as the bell rings for the first morning of class, "But what am I to teach them?" "Oh," says the older hand, "I shouldn't try to *teach* them anything, not just yet. Just keep them quiet."

By and large the wealthy Yale students thought of us as prep school masters. We were servants hired by their fathers at low wages to give them culture, to teach them how to write, and to expose them to the small amount of literary polish required by their station in life. We fought for status, desperately convinced of our intellectual superiority to those who looked down on us socially. We laughed protectively at their ignorance and laziness, and insisted that we were intellectuals, not mere teaching drudges, and proved it daily with dazzling displays of learning, quotes in the original Greek—carefully memorized but casually delivered—elaborate etymologies of English words, thumbnail descriptions of anything from the ontological proof for the existence of God to the Hindu doctrine of metempsychosis.

"Smithers, what do you think of original sin?" This early on a cold winter morning, as a way of getting into a discussion of *Paradise Lost*. Smithers thought it over for a long time before replying. "Well, sir, it's all right, I guess." The eyes of an older, more bored teacher would have dulled with disappointment at this unpromising answer, but among young instructors quickness of riposte was everything: (tolerantly bemused) "You don't sound entirely convinced, Smithers; what exactly are your reservations?" A merrier discussion was never heard than the following forty minutes as the students gradually picked up and played with the idea, novel to Americans, that there is something ineradicably corrupt about human beings, and that from them, even with the best intentions, as the founders of Yale College stoutly believed, nothing good can proceed.

But on other occasions the exchanges were more like what Chinese students during the Cultural Revolution would later call, with a much grimmer meaning, "struggle sessions." Sullen and unread students challenged to explain why Hamlet disliked his uncle, or just what Keats felt when he looked at the Grecian urn, were likely to reply in a churlish manner, "I don't know . . . sir." To which the appropriate answer, delivered with an ugly smirk, was thought to be, "What d'ya mean, you don't know? Are you stupid, or something?" Later generations regard this instructional method as sadistic, and by the time I retired it would have had me up before the dean on harassment charges; but in universities still for the most part male and with no illusions about how difficult it is to get the attention of a human being long enough to let a new idea slip into his head, it was the normal tone of instruction. It was also the traditional rough style of upscale universities, where a certain indifference to the students, mixed with a heavy manner of bored exasperation, was long thought to set the right tone in the classroom.

Teaching the young, like counseling the mad, is often more dangerous than it seems—can be the same thing, in fact, as I had occasion to learn one night when a huge and very menacing student arrived at my house to tell me about his imagined marriage to a movie star, who had now left him, perhaps at my advice. My suggestions that it was getting late only angered him the more, and it was dawn before I could convince him that I had nothing to do with his broken "marriage." But not all encounters with students ended so successfully. One of our football players, and one of my better students, young Samson, and some of his drunken friends were driving from bar to bar one night and rear-ended a car. Its driver, a junior biology professor, got out, walked back and bent over to look at the damage. Samson got out of his car, came up behind him, and smashed a fist, full force, into the instructor's face, breaking his cheek and nose. The professor's pregnant wife climbed out of their car and began screaming, and the campus police were soon there. As if Yale were still a medieval university and its students exempt from the law and the town authorities, the matter was handled entirely by the college discipline committee, and Samson and the others were rusticated for a year when their defense—"Jeez, we didn't know he was a professor"—was thought inadequate.

My wife, who after her mother died had brought the children to live in New Haven, often said that academics should have remained the unmarried clerics they once had been, and it was true enough. Life on the Yale faculty was the intellectual fast track. The competition was from the start almost unbearably intense. To survive, you not only had to teach well, you had to establish yourself as a scholar and, in short order, a writer on your subject with an international (read: English as well as American) reputation. This meant reading constantly, keeping up with the new as well as making up old deficiencies—who had ever had time to read all of Dante, or Robert Burton's *Anatomy of Melancholy?*— and publishing as soon as possible in the best journals and with the best university presses.

Family neglect was indigenous in the Yale faculty as fathers tried to "keep up with their fields" and publish, and difficulties were intensified by money problems. It was not really poverty in the sense that it was known in the black slums just above us up on Dixwell Avenue, but the genteel version in which auto repairs or dental work always brought a crisis, in which each unbudgeted expense had to be met by doing without or cutting back on something else. The senior faculty asked the obvious question, "Why don't they stop having so many children?" All I can say is that diaphragms seemed actually to encourage sex, and even the coming of the pill in the late 1950s did not stop academic procreation. Sociology, not biology, seemed to rule the reproductive process, for everyone we knew had several children, even those who were sterile or practicing abstinence. Partly it was the war, it was said. To make up for all the deaths, now we had to have lots of children, and since others had lots of children, we did too, and between us we produced the baby boom, the biggest population spike in the history of the country.

Before World War II it was assumed that anyone becoming a professor, particularly in the genteel humanities, would have some private income; but in the great explosion of democratic education after the war, people like myself, dependent on a salary, began to make academic poverty fashionable once again. The situation was something like the old tale of the holy man who tied his cat to a pillar with a pink ribbon to keep it from rubbing up against him while he prayed. After his death the piety of his followers was judged by the kind of ribbon they used to tie up their cats and how often they did it. In a similar way, scholarship was now measured by poverty, and some extraordinarily rich colleagues (there were still some) went to extraordinary lengths to establish that, although they might have a lot of money (it was impossible to deny), they were actually poor. One family bought an old battery that was too weak to start their car, which they then parked at the top of a hill so that it could, in the sight of all, be started with a push on cold mornings. Old orange crates—probably ordered from a decorator—were used for bookcases in another wealthy house, and still another wealthy family bought thousands of dollars worth of ladders and scaffolds in order to paint their house themselves. They were oddly appealing in their desperate need to be poor like the rest of us, but finally and inevitably they gave in to reality and bought big houses on posh streets, and luxury automobiles. "But did it have to be a Jaguar, Carruthers? Wouldn't a Chevrolet have done?" asked the chairman of the department, sensitive to the importance of, if not poverty, at least the appearance of only modest prosperity.

So much was being hard up considered the true mark of scholarship that it could transmute rags into a faculty appointment. On one cold morning with a foot of snow on the ground, I fell in with Polly Buck, the wife of the provost, trudging through the slush toward the university. Ahead of us, dragging a small child along by an arm, was a woman from the tenements higher up on Ashmun Street, dressed in tatters, an old rag around her head, broken galoshes on her feet, making heavy going through the snow. "Sensibly dressed woman," said Polly Buck. "Must be a faculty wife."

Clothes of somewhat better quality were bought by the faculty from Morris Witter on upper Chapel Street. Morris had a brother known as "Fi' buck" who went around to the students' rooms and offered to buy their suits, jackets, and coats from them for "five bucks." He never

paid more, and the students, many of whom had limited cash allow-
ances but unlimited charge accounts at J. Press and Rosenberg's, the
fashionable clothing stores, would sell clothing for five dollars that
they had just charged for hundreds at "J. Squeeze" in order to get the
cash they needed to buy a ticket to New York, where they could free-
load for the weekend at the various society parties. Morris would mark
up the clothes his brother bought, and when a faculty member walked
by: "Hey professor, I've got a Glen Plaid that will just fit you." Inside
Mrs. Witter sat on a high stool telling stories about the Hotel Duncan
next door, where according to her, "You are allowed to do anything
except scream." Morris had philosophical interests because of a missed
education, and a transaction with him was likely to involve quite a lot
of ethics and logic. One day without any warning he killed himself in
his basement apartment around the corner. From then on Yale lost a
good deal of its sartorial sharpness, and some of its humanity.

Young faculty members took all the extra jobs that came their way.
The Wellesley Club of Southern Connecticut called the English department and asked for a speaker on some literary subject, perhaps Shakespeare. The office called me, and it turned out that I had just the thing. A
colleague, Derek Colville, and I had put together a spoof on the "Who
was Shakespeare?" question that has always for some perverse reason
aroused great interest. We began by admitting that the poor boy born
in the country town of Stratford, his father fined for a dunghill in front
of the house, unable to sign his name the same way twice, an early
school-leaver, could not have been the author of those sophisticated
and learned plays. Who then was the author? Well, why not Edward de
Vere, the seventeenth earl of Oxford, who was often a candidate on the
grounds of his education and nobility? So, let it be Oxford; but as soon
as we certified Oxford as Shakespeare, we went on to the inevitable
next question, "But who was Oxford?" The earl had a vile temper, killed
people in his rage, drank extravagantly, and in general made a mess of
his life—a typical aristocratic ne'er-do-well. He couldn't possibly be the
author of those miraculous plays, so we then proceeded to show, using
mad codes and evidence torn piecemeal out of context from the plays
in the same zany manner used by the Baconians and other champions
of various claimants, that the crafty peasant Shakespeare had plotted

with other dissolute theater people like Robert Green to kill the noble earl, assumed his person, and proceeded to write the thirty-seven plays and the poems attributed to Shakespeare.

Learned wit, but the joke was so broad that I thought the ladies from Westport and Greenwich would roar with laughter. But as I got deeper into the hole I was digging for myself, the audience looked more and more serious. I sweated through it, and at the end there were a few polite remarks like, "I've always meant to study this matter more carefully, and now I will get down to it this summer and read some books about Francis Bacon and the earl of Oxford writing the Shakespeare plays." I hung around hoping to get my promised twenty-five dollars. "I have something for you," said the chairwoman to my delight, and relieved that I was going to get paid that night, I essayed another bad joke: "Well, so long as it's not some of the tuna fish casserole we had for dinner." "How did you know? There's oodles left over and you can take it home to your nice children and wife." The check did not arrive for several months.

This is all much more fun in remembrance than it was in fact, and looking back I think it was hardest on the wives. I don't suppose that there are many "faculty wives" left in a time when both members of an academic family are likely to teach, or both have jobs of some kind. In earlier times, however, the academic world followed the ways of the larger world, and wives for the most part stayed home and raised children, which didn't leave much time for reading Proust. And yet these women were expected not only to talk with husbands who were in the midst of an intense intellectual life, discussing arcane matters with their students and colleagues daily, but to mix socially with other academic families on occasions at which familiarity with the latest books and ideas was de rigueur, along with upscale social skills. It was tough going, and it was usual at a party to see the women gather at one side of the room to talk families, while the men gathered at the other to talk shop.

It took years of this to produce a real "faculty wife," but the type—like the pioneer mother or the New England sea-captain's wife—fully developed, was formidable. It could go either way. One poor woman with a tyrannical husband who was determined to make her act in a way that would further his career—it did not—regularly wet herself at parties, leaving a large stain whenever she got up from the sofa or chair on which she had sat unmoving all evening. Others, however, became hard as nails, sitting at the end of their dinner tables glaring at the guests and casting baleful looks at the hovering husband wondering what he had done wrong this time.

Socializing with the senior faculty in this setting was necessary but risky. We went one day to a large party given by Jim Osborne, a wealthy book collector who eventually gave a great collection of rare books to Yale. Jim was also a scholar, the kind of person who bought rare books for the love of them and to acquire unknown information, which he could then use in his publications. Like all such faculty parties, this one was stiff and formal. After some time Sue and I started to make our devoirs but on the way out fell into a discussion with friends and decided to stay a while longer. As we were standing in front of the table with the drinks and continuing to talk, I reached behind me to find the Scotch bottle to fill our glasses again. As my hand groped about for the bottle, it found another hand, firmly shaking it, and I heard the voice of my host saying, "So nice you could come. Do come again some time." I had no choice but to leave, and I paced the sidewalk for fifteen minutes waiting for Sue to appear.

In nearby Stratford, Connecticut, on the banks of the Housatonic, a very stylish replica of the Globe Theater had been built with timber donated from all over the world by a group led by Joseph Verner Reed and Eugene Black, the head of the World Bank, a Shakespeare buff who liked to argue with foreign dignitaries over such questions as whether the bed in "The Rape of Lucrece" was "berumpled." (It was not.) A good professional company was assembled each summer, with stars like Katharine Hepburn, Fritz Weaver, and Morris Carnovsky, to put on three or four Shakespeare plays. The most bizarre cast was surely that of The Tempest, in which Raymond Massey played Prospero, and Jack Palance, fresh from slowly drawing on his black gloves as the villainous gunman in the movie Shane, played Caliban. Roddy McDowell was Ariel. No expense was spared, and the papier-mâché island rock on which these stars cavorted was built in New York but was so large that it had to be sent to Stratford by way of Binghamton to avoid low bridges.

Black thought it would be a good idea to have a school attached to the theater, which the actors could attend and lecture in, mixing the theatrical approach with the academic. Someone was needed to do the administrative work, and presto, I had an interesting summer job. I read applications, arranged for rooms for the students, deposited checks, attended lectures, and taught anything that needed teaching. Buses carried us on performance nights to the Connecticut Stratford, where we picnicked, listened to strolling minstrels singing madrigals and airs, and in time went into the theater to see Katharine Hepburn play Cleopatra — "give me to drink mandragora" — in a Bryn Mawr accent, and Fritz Weaver as the Bastard Fauconbridge in *King John* carry a huge cowhide to lend weight to his threat to "hang a calfskin on those recreant limbs." On the Fourth of July he declared his independence by hurling the hated prop as far into the audience as he could. Cannons were drawn onstage to fire at the bepillared Civil War mansion that represented old Troy in *Troilus and Cressida*, the armies of York and Lancaster marched up and down in rubber fishing boots, and Carnovsky-Shylock sharpened his knife on the sole of his tennis shoe in anticipation of cutting out Antonio's heart. It was all great fun, and very good Shakespeare too.

The Yale Shakespeare Institute closed its doors after a time, and I turned to editing plays as a way of earning a few extra dollars and establishing my reputation as a scholar of the Elizabethan theater. Yale University Press gave me a contract to produce an edition of *Julius Caesar* for the Yale Shakespeare series, which was printed in 1959 in one of the famous little blue volumes. Signet Books, preparing to launch a collection of single-volume Shakespeare plays, each newly edited with glosses, textual notes, introduction, and four major critical essays, gave me a chance to edit *Othello*. As an advance on royalties Signet offered the princely sum of two thousand dollars, nearly half a year's salary at that time. I never thought the edition would pay off the advance, but by the 1990s it had sold well over a million copies.

The problem of constructing a single authentic text of *Othello* out of the two existing versions, a late quarto and the 1623 folio, with numerous small differences and a number of major ones, turned out to be an intellectual problem that focused on what can be known and how, in an unexpectedly precise and objective fashion. In older days editors simply corrected obvious errors and printed the version of the Shakespeare play they preferred. Or, more frequently, they assembled an eclectic text from the variants, using whichever reading seemed preferable, putting unique lines from several texts in the same play. To these early editors the different versions of the same play were stages in the historical development of a theatrical text over time, made to adjust it to changing playing conditions, different actors, or new fashions. In other words, there were many texts of a play, not a single "true" one, and the job of the editor was to assemble the most interesting text he could.

But the reigning theory of textual editing by the 1950s, a bibliographic version of the New Criticism, posited that in all cases where a play existed in variant forms there was a "true" or ideal version, the *exact* work that the author wrote, underlying the different texts, and that it was the business of an editor to restore this original text by working through the variants to the original urtext. This meant selecting a "copy text," the text that seemed on careful examination of all the evidence closest to Shakespeare's own manuscript—which no longer existed, of course. Corrections were made in that text only where it absolutely did not make sense, and all corrections were either taken from one of the other texts of the play or were supplied only on the basis of a convincing explanation of how the mistake had been made in setting and printing the book. These were the rules of the "scientific bibliography" associated in this country with Fredson Bowers, and if my edition of *Othello* was to be respectable, it had to be assembled under these terms.

Giving priority to the 1623 folio text of *Othello* was easy enough, since it was on the whole the better text of the two—fewer errors and better readings—but here and there it forced me into difficult positions, such as the folio reading of Othello's description of himself after he has killed Desdemona as a "base Judean, who threw away a pearl richer than all his tribe." The more familiar reading of the quarto text, "base Indian," had long been accepted as the correct reading. But "Judean," with a connotation of "Judas" or "Jew," made perfect sense as a reference to the Christian view of the Jewish betrayal of Christ, a matter that is very much in the poetry at that moment in *Othello*, and by my editorial principles I was therefore stuck with it, but it was not well received.

There is something very satisfying about editing. You may at the end of the day feel that the criticism you have written is worthless and throw it in the wastebasket; but if you sit for eight hours working on a text, choosing the right words, explaining the meaning of difficult phrases, you have by the end done a measurable amount of interesting and possibly even useful work. In this case, though, I was led slowly and carefully over the several months it took to edit the play to the conclusion that the text I had tried to produce, a supposedly perfect text, the arrangement of words that had once existed if not in a written manuscript then at least in the author's head, was only an illusion. The scrupulous editorial work was by no means wasted, since it fostered the closest attention to the words of the play; but that the posited object of reconstruction, the ideal text, had ever existed, let alone been reflected in my edition, seemed increasingly doubtful. What clearly did exist was a historical record, a succession of plays that changed over time, both in the theater and in the printing house, in response to endless currents of no longer visible actions and choices. I did not fully recognize at the time the shadow that this understanding cast over my New Critical views of literary work as "verbal icon" or "well-wrought urn," but it added to my growing questions about how rigorous a scientific approach to humanistic knowledge could usefully be.

Theory was really not what engaged our attention at the time, however, for we were far more likely to see our subject and our teaching in terms of their relationship to the social and personal problems of our time. Outside the academy, another world was taking shape in the fifties, prosperous, powerful, conformist, America the world power. Powerful but banal. Living in identical Levittown tract houses, manipulated by advertising, dominated increasingly by big business, exploited by cynical politicians, their thinking programmed by the media, more and more in debt on the installment plan to buy washing machines, cars and Frigidaires, the men in the gray flannel suits—Sloan Wilson's perfect image for his 1956 book about the trap—avoided emptiness by inhabiting without questions a culture that made illusion seem firm and sure. Sex was Marilyn Monroe, happiness was making money, government was General Eisenhower, fun was watching I Love Lucy on TV, and what was good for General Motors was good for the country. It was from this mindless conformity that we hoped to save our students.

We were in conscious opposition to that public world, seeing ourselves as an academic intelligentsia whose purpose was to seek the truth, not to pander to the great and powerful who ran our university as well as business and government. General Motors provided a car for every class of American—Chevrolet, Pontiac, Oldsmobile, Buick, and Cadillac—but we bought foreign cars. No tail fins for us. The first new car I owned was a Volkswagen Beetle, bought in the late fifties, a slick little black car with red upholstery, white plastic piping on the seats, and white side-wall tires—which someone slashed the first night we had the car.

Existentialism was the dominant philosophy in the postwar academic world, and it was ideally suited to exposing the emptiness and futility of life in the gray flannel suit. Jacques Guicharnaud in the French department had sat in a Left Bank cafe, Les Deux Magots, during the war writing away while Jean-Paul Sartre and Simone de Beauvoir worked at other tables in that holy place, and he brought us news of being and essence, alienation and absurdity, bad faith and nonbeing. But ours was not so much the existentialism of Paris as it was, like the French of Chaucer's Nun, that of Stratford-atte-Bowe. No one I knew had really worked through Karl Jaspers or Martin Heidegger, or had read all six hundred pages of Sartre's *Being and Nothingness* (*L'Etre et le néant*, 1943). Our sharpest images of what these thinkers were talking about were derived from Albert Camus's novels, such as *The Stranger* (*L'Etranger*, 1942) and *The Plague* (*La Peste*, 1948), and from his essay "The Myth of Sisyphus," in which the existential condition was equated with Sisyphus in Hades, condemned to roll his rock to the top of the hill, only to have it escape him and roll to the bottom, to be pushed up the slope again, forever.

With a sharp logical scalpel existentialism cut through the lies and pretenses, the bad faith with which the great majority of people and societies hide reality, especially of meaninglessness and death, from themselves. Beneath this surface it revealed the alienation, sense of absurdity, nausea, angst—Søren Kierkegaard's "fear and trembling" and "sickness unto death"—that attend a breakthrough into unblinking awareness that the world has no human meaning, no morality, no purpose, no plot. But despair was not existentialism's end. In terms that would in time come to seem melodramatic, it argued that true existence, full consciousness and humanity, came only from accepting the radical and painful freedom that recognition of our absurd condition forces upon us. To live meaningfully in the existential scheme of things is to act with the full knowledge that to act is meaningless except as a manifestation of freedom.

Some worldviews are good for a subject, and some are not. Deconstruction did not, I think, prove good for literature; but existentialism was good for literature. The majority of literary characters are, like Achilles and Hamlet, or Dido and Emma Bovary, existential heroes at odds with their societies who, usually accidentally, break through the surface of the social lie, develop an authentic self under the pressure of suffering, and finally act without any guarantee that what they do is right or even meaningful. Western literature has been existentialist from Job to *Waiting for Godot*, and existentialism therefore made literature appear not simply another art but the definitive image of the human condition.

It also made tragedy seem the most meaningful of literary forms. We no longer hear much of tragedy, but in the 1950s it was being discussed by everyone, and courses in various kinds of tragedy speckled the Yale curriculum: Aristotelian purging of pity and fear, as in *Oedipus*; Hegelian tragedy as a moment in the dialectic of the world spirit when two goods, the old and the new, for example, family and state in *Antigone*, are in direct conflict; Nietzsche's recurrent tragic destruction of man's Apollonian dreams of order by the Dionysiac frenzy that, as in *The Bacchae*, obliterates form and individuality.

Existentialism and tragedy are profoundly un-American ways of looking at the place of the self in the world, but in the 1950s they were in perfect time with the younger faculty's view that we were teaching students to have inquiring minds and not to accept without question established and obvious views. A remarkable revelation of the critical importance of this task appeared in the "obedience to authority" experiments, the very opposite of tragedy, staged in the Yale psychology labs by Stanley Milgram in the late fifties and early sixties. In this research, a character called the "experimenter," dressed in a white lab coat, directed a little scene between two people employed for a psychological experiment, one the "learner" and the other the "teacher." "The 'teacher' is a genuinely naive subject," wrote Milgram in his book *Obe-*

dience to Authority (1974), "who has come to the laboratory to participate in an experiment. The 'learner,' or victim, is an actor" hired to play his part in the scene. The learner is given a list of paired terms and told to memorize them, and then,

> after watching the learner being strapped into place,
> [the teacher] is taken into the main experimental room
> and seated before an impressive shock generator. Its
> main feature is a horizontal line of thirty switches,
> ranging from 15 volts to 450 volts, in 15 volt increments.
> There are also verbal designations which range from
> Slight Shock to Danger—Severe Shock. The teacher is
> told that he is to administer the learning test to the
> man in the other room.

The test consisted in the teacher giving the learner one of the paired words and telling him to name the second term. "When the learner responds correctly, the teacher moves on to the next item; when the other man gives an incorrect answer, the teacher is to give him an electric shock." Urged on by the experimenter—"the experiment must continue, no tissue damage will result"—the teacher administers heavier and heavier shocks, while the learner, failing to come up with the other word of the pair, writhes and grimaces in pain (feigned, of course, for no electrical current was actually hooked up to the person). "The point of the experiment," Milgram sums up, "is to see how far a person will proceed in a concrete and measurable situation in which he is ordered to inflict increasing pain on a protesting victim. At what point will the subject refuse to obey the experimenter?"

The answer to this question was extremely disturbing. All the teachers when urged to do so by the experimenter would go to the "intense shock" level, 300 volts, and two-thirds of them would administer the most powerful shock possible. No matter how Milgram varied the experiment—using adult men and women instead of students, requiring the teacher actually to hold the learner's hand onto the electrode, telling the teacher that the learner had a heart condition, moving the test site to a seedy office building in nearby Bridgeport to diminish the aura of scientific authority—the teachers still socked it to the learners.

The teachers had various ways of avoiding the reality of what they were doing, such as refusing to look at the learner, or blaming him for his stupidity; but in the end, eager to perform competently, they obeyed the authority figure of the experimenter as surely as Nazis like Adolf Eichmann ran the gas ovens. Hannah Arendt's startling book *Eichmann in Jerusalem: A Report on the Banality of Evil* (1963) made the same point as did Milgram's experiment, but in terms of the Nazi death camps: "A substantial proportion of people do what they are told to do, irrespective of the content of the act and without limitations of conscience, so long as they perceive that the command comes from a legitimate authority."

When Milgram's "teachers" were eventually debriefed, many of them were shattered by what they found out about themselves. The campus, when it learned of the experiments, was outraged at what was considered callous disregard for the rights of the subject and the inhumanity of science. But I think that we were even more disturbed by the possibility that all our efforts to teach our students to think for themselves, to be fully sensitive to the human situation, might only be grains of sand in the desert of the human mind and heart. Henry Reicken, in his review of Milgram's book in *Science* (May 1974), got right to the center of our fears: "The origins of obedience lie not in the personal characteristics of the participants, nor in the institutional auspices, nor even, indeed, in something so dramatic as a hardly repressed feral streak of aggressiveness. [Milgram's] analysis is correspondingly disturbing because it makes clear how banal the sociopsychological origins of obedience really are, and, therefore, how chillingly commonplace obedience is likely to be in any even minimally stable society." In other words, there is no mystery about it: we are programmed in the family, the schools, the churches, and the courts to obey authority, and we will obey authority no matter how morally dreadful its commands, or how well educated we may be.

But were we academics really any better? Was our ethic any better founded than absolute obedience to authority? The quiz show scandal about this time brought the question home, involving as it did knowledge of books and one of America's first literary academic families, the Van Dorens. It also raised a possibility that most of us had long ignored: that art can be the instrument not of truth but of falsehood.

The trouble with filming reality, the producers of the television quiz shows so popular at the time had discovered, was that reality isn't usually very exciting. Its characters are dull, its plot badly paced, its symbols blurred, its themes hard to find. So they began selecting the contestants in their quiz shows for their charisma, rather than any otherwise appropriate qualities, and rigging the plot. Charles Van Doren was the ideal White Hat: young and handsome, an instructor in the Columbia English department while still working on his doctorate, an American intellectual Brahmin, well read and mentally quick. But he was also corrupt, or at least corruptible. Week after week he was fed the questions ahead of time, and eventually, seemingly taking the big risk of losing the $32,000 he had already won for the chance of winning the grand prize of $64,000, he took the chance and became a hero. But the program was already under investigation, and Van Doren was forced to admit in public that he had participated in one of the big scams of our time. By now it seems scarcely remarkable, so accustomed have we become to the fraudulent, but at that time it hit people hard, academics especially. We wanted to believe in him, and in his intelligence, his education, his background, and perhaps even in the financial success and fame they brought him, and when these all crumbled, his failure brought us face to face with our own venality.

Television was to blame, we said, rightly, though we did not realize that we were watching the beginning of a communications revolution that would have radical consequences for higher education, and most particularly a literary education. The effects were not so obvious in the 1950s as they became after the appearance of Marshall McLuhan's *Gutenberg Galaxy: The Making of Typographic Man* (1962). The Great Books were still enthroned in the colleges and universities in courses like Yale's Directed Studies, an elitist course for a hundred of the best freshmen. Literature 1 was a pure masterworks of Western art course, beginning with Greek tragedy and the Bible and moving in the space of a year to Goethe's *Faust* and Eliot's *Waste Land*. It dealt with works from many languages in translation, treating literature as a universal and distinct category of writing, and mixing it freely with philosophy and art. The director of this program was the most formidable of English professors, Maynard Mack, who used it as a testing ground for young instructors from a variety of language departments: Victor Brombert from French, Tom Greene from English, Peter Demetz from German, and Adam Parry from classics.

Besides teaching a small discussion section, each of us had to take turns delivering the weekly lectures on the great works of Western literature. Maynard set the pace—he crafted his lectures as tightly as a poem while keeping his words direct and plain—but when we lectured he sat in the audience conspicuously and busily writing in a large notebook. So long as he wrote, you were OK, but when he looked up, paused, and then closed the notebook, you had ceased to interest him, and since he was the most powerful professor in the humanities, it meant your Yale career was probably over. Everything rode on those Tuesday lectures, and because we had almost no experience at lecturing and little familiarity with material like Second Samuel in the Bible, or *The Aeneid*, the learning curve was very steep.

One hapless instructor with no religious background was assigned to lecture on several Old Testament minor prophets like Amos and Habakkuk, but he had no handle whatsoever on these strange creatures. He plunged desperately into the library, where he chanced on anthropological writings that treated all prophets, including the biblical ones, as fakirs who entered trances by smoking hemp, induced hallucinations by eating dung, and practiced on the gullible by lying for months on their left sides at the city gates. This was exciting stuff, he thought, a real breakthrough into understanding the Old Testament, and so on Tuesday next he, proud of his newfound learning, drew elaborate parallels between the Hebrew prophets and various Indian and Arab mystics who took drugs, told fortunes, walked on hot coals, and lay on a bed of nails. The notebook slammed shut very loudly that day.

Perhaps an example of what we thought we were doing when we taught the Great Books will give an idea of a mode of literary interpretation that has now largely disappeared. It fell to my lot one year to lecture on Aeschylus's trilogy of plays *The Oresteia* (in Richmond Lattimore's great translation), performed in Athens in the mid–fifth century B.C. The plays portrayed the House of Atreus moving relentlessly down a bloody chain of crime-vengeance-crime-vengeance—Helen raped, Iphigenia sacrificed, the dead warriors at Troy, Agamemnon murdered,

Clytemnestra cut down by Orestes. "The Gods who live on high have decreed that wisdom comes to man alone through suffering," sings the Chorus of the play, and wisdom does not come easily when the smell of blood is in the air. Only after the revenge cycle—"beat on beat, driven by God"—has continued long enough to become unbearable is an attempt finally made to replace revenge with an impersonal system of justice administered by an Athenian court. But though the need is certain, it is still not clear what justice is. Apollo argues with pure male rationality, like some clever criminal lawyer defending O. J. Simpson, that Orestes should go free for killing Clytemnestra because killing a mother to avenge a father is no very serious crime, since the mother only carries the child, does not participate in him in any essential way. But this kind of sophistry is not found acceptable. If full justice is to be done, blood, the play says, must have blood, and the female Furies arrive to press this primal and irrevocable eye-for-an-eye claim. In the end Greek intelligence finds the answer in a system of justice, administered impartially by the state, in which no individual any longer has the responsibility for justice, and therefore each punishment does not constitute a new crime calling for new vengeance. But at the same time the need of the survivors to see the criminal suffer something of what he has inflicted on his victim is satisfied by the bloody punishments handed down by the law and executed by the state.

I analyzed the trilogy in a formalist manner, mainly following a scenic and imagery pattern in which again and again light and hope flare up, only to expire into darkness and despair, and then to be relit once more. A play that begins in darkness lit by the small, distant fire announcing the fall of Troy ends at last in the full blaze of noon of the Athenian theater and the Athenian court. I did not hesitate to point out to the students that the struggle for justice that is Aeschylus's subject is still played out every day in our courts, where rational laws free murderers because there is a shred of reasonable doubt, and the families of the murdered cry out and demand what we have come to call "victims' rights." This, I told them, or tried to extract from them in later seminar discussion, without apology for connecting literature with life, is where the real power of great literature lies, in its ability to portray feelingly and convincingly critical human concerns in terms that do not scant its full human reality and its desperate importance to our lives. All the aesthetic formalist aspects of the play—Aeschylus's extraordinarily tangled language, the profusion of imagery, the repetitive hope-failure pattern of the plot, the intense and brooding characters—were, in my opinion, ultimately in the service of the play's presentation of the human need for full justice and explanation of why it is so difficult to achieve. I was not arguing that the play has a "message," that it carries some social argument for a better court system; rather, it offers a universal description of where we humans live always in relation to justice. This is, I suppose, a view of the purpose of art that would most readily be called "moral," and I would not repudiate the term entirely, but I think that "existential" would be a far better term, for "moral" carries with it the suggestion of some rigid prescription, of a limited and coercive point of view, which is not the way great literature works.

6

The Two Cultures, Science and Literature

The college fellowships at the Yale residential colleges were small groups made up of faculty from the different departments of the university. Not every Yale faculty member was a fellow of one of the colleges, and there were always hurt feelings and charges of elitism until democracy won out in the seventies and all faculty members, and many staff, were made members of fellowships that immediately became so large that they also became impersonal. Fellows were given free lunches in the college on the theory that we would eat with the undergraduates and nourish faculty-student relationships. The master of Branford College when I joined the fellowship there, Steve Buck, exhorted us regularly to eat with the students, and from time to time he threatened to cut off our free lunches if we did not do so. The students didn't really want to eat with us, preferring to be left to talk with one another about fast cars, girls, and secret societies, though they were polite enough if you asked to sit down with them. It didn't matter. We fellows were more than happy to eat with and talk to one another.

The Branford dining hall was a splendid place, Gothic in design with long stained-glass windows, shining broad-planked floor, rich wooden paneling, and numerous small tables set with gleaming tableware and silver sugar and cream bowls. These were removed in subsequent years for fear of theft. The fellows' table stretched the width of the dining hall at the south end just below the great Burgundian fireplace that had been bought and transported from its original castle to New Haven when the Standard Oil money of Anna M. Harkness was building the colleges—no expense spared—in the 1930s. Day after day the fellows assembled around it and began conversations lasting from about noon to two o'clock, long after the dining room was empty of students. Many of the fellows were young and had been in the service, and most were polymaths by interest if not by training, eager not just to hear but to argue tenaciously with the physicist Allan Bromley about nuclear physics and the atomic bomb, or to add something to the book that Oystein Ore, the Norwegian mathematician who loved to play cards, had written about Geronimo Cardano, the Italian Renaissance gambler-scholar who had worked out some cubic algebraic solutions. John Blum, whose American history lecture course was the largest in the college, was editing the papers of Henry Morgenthau. The classicist Bernard Knox, who had fought with the British contingent of the International Brigades in Spain and as an American soldier with the partisans in France and Italy in World War II, loved to talk about war and about classical and Greek literature. The psychologist Irving Janis was investigating the dynamics of small groups and particularly how members of committees tend to move toward agreement with one another rather than toward the solution of the problem they were convened to deal with, often with catastrophic results. His papers were collected in 1972 as *Victims of Groupthink: A Psychological Study of Foreign-Policy Decisions and Fiascoes.*

Ed Lindblom in political economics was working on his studies of how social theory affected social policies and what the results of new theories were in actual practice. Sidney Ahlstrom was writing, slowly and painfully, his master work on American religions, and the table was graced sometimes by Eric Auerbach, the great German philologist who was famous for his book *Mimesis*, which he had written as a German Jewish refugee teaching in Istanbul during the war with only his small personal library available to him. Now that he was at Yale he felt that he had to make use of the vast resources of Sterling Library. Ironically, the result of riches was a dreary book on rhetoric, read and used by few; *Mimesis*, however, with its exquisite explorations of the way reality was perceived and rendered in texts from the Bible to the present, has become one of the literary classics of our time. It was at the Branford fellows' table that Auerbach one day had a stroke, from which he later died, and was carried down to the red leather couch in my office just off the stairway to the hall.

Literature was well represented in Branford College. In addition to Auerbach and Knox there were Ted Ziolkowski in German, the irascible Ken Douglas in French—killed by an icicle falling from a New York skyscraper, about what he expected of the world!—and Martin Price, Charles Feidelson, and Dwight Culler in English. These were all learned men and able talkers, and they needed to be, for among the illuminati assembled at the Branford lunch table there was real doubt about the respectability of literature as an academic subject. They were not hostile, but physicists and historians were not sure just what the object of literary study was, and if it was poems, plays, novels, fictions in general, what could really be learned from analyzing these make-believes? "Does literature progress?" one physicist asked, and when told that it changed but did not get better, that the older literature, Homer or Shakespeare, had in fact been in many ways more powerful than the modern, he threw up his hands in despair. "Why teach something that is less truthful all the time?"

In keeping with the spirit of the times, the pressure on literature was to be scientific, like other subjects. Great research universities like Yale were structured to institutionalize the scientific rationality that had dominated education during and since the nineteenth century. Yale was, to the chagrin of its science departments, more distinguished nationally for its great humanities departments than for its success in the natural sciences and the social sciences, but the intellectual paradigm to which the university was shaped was materialistic and positivistic. Knowledge was knowledge of some external objective reality, natural, historical, psychological, some universal truth, some essential quality of things, whether atoms or poems, which was to be analyzed by research and reported without subjective predisposition, as exactly as possible. We New Critics still believed that, though literature itself might be impressionistic, we worked very much in this scientific spirit. Article after article, book after book, we thought we were building up an accurate reading of literature, and that our formalist methodology concentrated unbiased attention on the objective literary text in the same way that the scientist looks closely and without bias at nature.

But in 1959 Sir Charles Snow, a scientist in the British civil service, published a book, The Two Cultures, depicting the isolation of the literary community from the scientific community, as if they were two remote tribes with totally different cultures. Snow—whose wife, Pamela Hansford Johnson, was inevitably known as "the abominable snow woman" —was the author of a series of rather wooden novels, the most famous of which was The Masters, and he offered himself as a model of participation in both the scientific and the literary worlds. But his book was not really so much an attempt to bring science and the humanities together as it was an attack on the "traditional" or "literary" culture, which he accused not only of being ignorant of the second law of thermodynamics, and unable to define a machine tool, but of being obscurantist, pessimistic, passive about the possibility of social improvement, and perhaps even fascistic. "Why," he disingenuously asked, "do most writers take on social opinions which would have been thought distinctly uncivilized and démodé at the time of the Plantagenets? Wasn't that true of most of the famous twentieth-century writers? Yeats, Pound, Wyndham Lewis, nine out of ten of those who have dominated literary sensibility in our times—weren't they not only politically silly, but politically wicked? Didn't the influence of all they represent bring Auschwitz that much nearer?" Literary intellectuals, Snow went on, are solitary, "natural Luddites," but scientists, he concluded, work well together, communicating easily with one another and contributing to the building of a better world.

The Two Cultures was a huge public success, and humanists began to bone up on thermodynamics. But not all humanists were impressed by

Snow's argument, and the "demon of Downing College," F. R. Leavis, in a public lecture gave Snow neither Touchstone's "quip modest," nor even the "reply churlish," but "the lie direct": "Snow is in fact portentously ignorant. . . . He is intellectually as undistinguished as it is possible to be. . . . *The Two Cultures* exhibits an utter lack of intellectual distinction and an embarrassing vulgarity of style." As for Snow's literary abilities: "As a novelist he doesn't exist; he doesn't begin to exist. He can't be said to know what a novel is." There is more, much more—vituperation so toxic that even so stout a defender of literary values as Lionel Trilling took pains to separate himself from it. But Leavis was a very tough guy, trained in the hard knocks of Oxbridge paranoia, a longtime champion in a war to claim priority for literature as the basic component of a humane education. In what Leavis considered a debased modern society, materialistic and cramped of mind, only the best kinds of literary work—"the great tradition," to use the title of his most famous book—offered some insight into what it means to be fully human, truly to participate in the fullness of the world, to share in the history of human effort to achieve the maximum of feeling and understanding. As he put it to Snow in regard to science: "There is a prior human achievement of collaborative creation, a more basic work of the mind of man (and more than the mind), one without which the triumphant erection of the scientific edifice would not have been possible: that is, the creation of the human world, including language. It is one we cannot rest on as something done in the past. It lives in the living creative response to change in the present."

Neither Snow nor Leavis was a stylist—both wrote very badly, in fact—and neither offered anything new to the long-standing and often-rehearsed argument between the poets and the philosophers. So far as argument went, as well as style, Thomas Love Peacock in *The Four Ages of Poetry* and Shelley in *A Defence of Poetry* had done a lot better a century earlier; but the Snow-Leavis quarrel brought, once again, the perennial science-humanities issue to center stage, and it made literary critics very sensitive about what they were doing.

The issue came closer to home when Robert Lane attacked Yale's failure to teach the scientific method. Lane was one of the more interesting people and aggressive talkers at the Branford fellows' table. A student of politics who thought his subject should be an empirical science, he brought Freudian theories to opinion surveys, developing questionnaires and in-depth sampling techniques that connected voting behavior to toilet training and Oedipal adjustment. Not surprisingly for the liberal Lane, anal retentives turned out to be Republicans who liked Ike, while Democrats were inevitably genital supporters of Adlai Stevenson. The universities were failing, Lane believed, in their primary responsibility to train students to be good citizens who think clearly and effectively, think scientifically, that is, about the order of the world and human society. Literary criticism seemed to him not the only but surely the worst culprit in this regard, confused in its own premises and encouraging in the students a muddleheaded subjectivity.

This all came out in a book, *The Liberties of Wit* (1961), in which Lane begins with very heavy irony, admitting that he may have "moved with booted feet into a garden of jasmine and lilies." His wife, Helen — dark, witty, sexy, and outspoken—was a novelist who did not leave unchallenged, in the home or abroad, the scientism of social science, and it was said that *The Liberties of Wit* let off the accumulated steam of many a domestic argument. Sounding like Plato once more banishing the poets from the republic, Lane argued that the nation wants and needs citizens with sound minds who come to terms with life, seek to build on solid foundations an understanding of reality, know how to test theories for truths, distinguish fantasy from fact, and above all have some consistent overview—what Thomas Kuhn would later call a "paradigm"—however provisional, of the order of things. Science, and to a lesser degree the social sciences, offer this kind of discipline, but the humanities, particularly literary criticism, fail signally, he said, in this regard. Literary studies had totally failed, Lane went on, to develop theories that are comprehensive, rational, public, and testable. To such basic questions as "what is literature?" "how does it function?" "what end does it seek?" "how does it relate to politics or social action?" literary criticism has no answers at all, or offers a bewildering variety of idiosyncratic and highly subjective views.

Lane was right, in his terms, for if being scientific was the sine qua non of a university subject, literature and the other humanities were, for all our pretenses to the contrary, in reality very lacking. On one occasion I distributed to a number of very distinguished colleagues a list of a hundred basic literary terms—comedy, novel, symbol, plot, meter, and so forth—and asked them to put them in some systematic order. The results were ludicrous, not only helter-skelter but inept, not because the professors were stupid—quite the contrary—but because they simply had never thought of their subject in this structured fashion. They were for the most part historical and "practical" critics who interpreted this or that text, or investigated one author or period, without ever really worrying about whether their interpretations followed from some larger theoretical structure. Terms like *symbol* and *image* were used interchangeably, and the novel could be treated as a myth like comedy or a formal mode like poetry. No one was bothered much when this theoretical chaos was revealed by my survey, and one of the members of the group, Robert Jay Lifton, the psychiatrist who was making a name for himself as a student of the effects on survivors of catastrophes like the Hiroshima bomb or the Holocaust, actually congratulated the literary people on lacking any system or theory, on the grounds that his own subject was, he felt, crippled by a surplus of fraudulent theory.

But the theoretical and methodological slackness of humanistic study continued to trouble us in universities that made science the model for thinking. Structuralism, which appeared about this time, was therefore embraced as a possible way to organize what were now increasingly, after the French practice, called "the human sciences," including literature. Structuralism made itself known to most of us in the writings of the French anthropologist Claude Lévi-Strauss, first in his travel book *Tristes Tropiques* (1955) and later in theoretical works such as *The Savage Mind* (1966). *Tristes Tropiques*, describing Lévi-Strauss's travels among the Indian tribes of Brazil and Paraguay in the 1930s, was a long and moving lament for the increasing disappearance of the vast living ethnographic museum of human cultures. Once the world had abounded with an enormous range of cultures, each composed of kinship systems, cuisines, body decorations, languages, and a host of other minisystems, that peoples had constructed in isolation from one another to make for themselves an ordered and meaningful world to inhabit. But now the old ways were dying in the Amazon forests and being replaced with the homogenized sludge of Western civilization in dull and dirty little interior towns with a few flickering electric lights, an empty church, and a dusty plaza. The *tristesse* was in the diminished lives of the Indians and the tattered remnants of their ways, a "long withdrawing sound" of old habits of tribal life that even the icy French rationalist Lévi-Strauss felt as a great loss.

But a Cartesian twentieth-century philosophe from the *hautes écoles* could not leave it at that. These dying cultures were not only to be sympathized with, their structures were to be analyzed and systematized: "The ensemble of a people's customs has always its particular style; they form into systems. I am convinced that the number of these systems is not unlimited and that human societies, like individual human beings (at play, in their dreams, or in moments of delirium), never create absolutely: all they can do is choose certain combinations from a repertory of ideas which it should be possible to reconstitute." The essential "combination" was said to be a binary division of all elements into a set of radical oppositions: the raw and the cooked, nature and culture, war and peace, good and evil, and so on, ad infinitum. To divide whatever the mind contemplates into opposing pairs is for the structuralist Lévi-Strauss the basic operation of human thought, and binary opposition is the fundamental pattern of culture building. The opposing elements are put into play by set rules of association, but they can never be collapsed into each other because to do so would cause both to cease to be, since it is only by contrast that they exist. For Lévi-Strauss, culture is an elaborate, ongoing piece of game playing, governed by a set of strict rules. Its purpose is the creation of an illusory "virtual" universe providing meaning and purpose.

Literature, in the form of myths and stories, is central to Lévi-Strauss's culture-making because it schematically reveals the organization of the raw materials into the required oppositional sets. And, like all the other cultural tools, it itself fits the rules of the larger game. Sophocles' *Oedipus*, for example, is for Lévi-Strauss not the traditional moral image of greatness brought low by pride, nor is it Athenian rationalism questioning its own validity, but a complex elaboration of a highly abstract binary opposition of the view that human beings are the chthonic products of nature and the contrary view that they are self-generated—autocephalous, as it were.

The possibilities of structuralism were intriguing to humanists looking to become more respectably scientific, but it was troublesome that structuralism substituted various more or less mechanical combinatory processes for the traditional imagination of the human spirit. But in *Anatomy of Criticism* (1957), the Canadian polymath Northrop Frye provided a structuralist theory of literature that preserved humanistic values. Where earlier criticism had been no more in his view than a mere chronology, or a series of random observations, unstructured by any overarching theory, Frye now proposed that we attempt a method of literary description as systematic as the notational system for recording music. "The first postulate of this inductive leap [of seeing all literature as a unit] is the same as that of any science: the assumption of total coherence."

In Frye's hands, literature became a kaleidoscope that when shaken always revealed a structured and coherent field. If he spoke in one sentence of Dante's fourfold mode of interpretation, he linked it in the next to Schiller's distinction between naive and sentimental poetry. Tom Sawyer's cave opened into the Cretan labyrinth of the Minotaur. Jonah's descent into the whale paralleled Christ's harrowing of hell and Orpheus going into the underworld to rescue Eurydice.

Basic to Frye's theory were four elaborated myths of comedy, romance, tragedy, and satire/irony. These myths relate to each other in a circular fashion, like the four seasons of the year to which they correspond, moving in the usual Fryean direction from the freest play of the imagination to its most limiting forms; from romance, the image of what the heart desires, to satire/irony, the world mankind fears. Then the cycle begins all over again. Each of the myths in turn has six phases, which move gradually away from the preceding myth and toward the following myth. The history of the four myths loosely fits the overall movement of Western literature from primitive stories, in which anything can happen, to realism, but for Frye the movement of literature is circular, not linear, and the pattern—spring, summer, fall, winter and romance, comedy, tragedy, satire—is constantly recurring, not only over the entire history of Western literature but in a particular period, and in the writings of a single author as well.

Though it tended quickly to get to be too much, Frye's touch made it seem as if it was at least possible that all the diverse pieces of a historically accumulated literature—oral epics, religious plays, prayers, novels, songs, and so much else—were the manifestation of a set of central symbols and a few basic myths. Frye was an ordained minister of the United Church, and he was, for all his scientific structuralism, a mystic, a systematic visionary like William Blake, about whom he had written his first book. Symbols were for Frye innate properties of the mind, like Blake's imagery or the Jungian archetypes, and as such "must derive some informing power from an ineffable mystery at the heart of being." Literature, in its parts and in its totality, was thus, for Frye, humanity's link to God, and its primary symbols reveal the things that the soul desires—the lamb and the garden—and those that it fears— the tiger and the city of dreadful night.

Anatomy of Criticism was written only to suggest what a structural paradigm of literature might entail, and it is not, Frye protests, "ever to be regarded as presenting my system, or even my theory." But he led us on with hints of the possibility of such a system, and in the vast labyrinth that he constructed we looked for Frye's system and blamed him bitterly when we could not find a literary tree of knowledge in a book that spills over with examples, ignores contradiction, delights in imprecise jargon, worries not about wrong facts, broadcasts pretentious theories, and sprinkles brilliant aperçus everywhere. I, like many other teachers of literature, spent an entire summer drawing endless provisional Fryean schemes; his publisher, Harcourt Brace, spent fortunes producing a textbook, Anatomy of Literature—in which Frye did not participate, and which never, I understand, sold very well—based on his "system."

I found the structuralist approach to literature fascinating and tempting, but I could never find any literary Great Code, nor did anyone else, and Frye's noble failure to construct an abstract theory of literature led me back again toward a historical approach. Paul Oskar Kristeller, the philosopher-historian of the Renaissance, provided a historical overview in a famous history-of-ideas article, "The Modern System of the Arts." Here he demonstrated that the conception of the fine arts—poetry, music, dance, architecture, sculpture, painting—as a unified group of similar activities, which we take to be natural and universal, had not appeared until 1749 (he was even able to identify the book in which the full system first appeared). If our conception of the arts could change over time, then our conception of their function and nature could also, and in the writings of Raymond Williams, a left-wing Cambridge don, I found a historical view that made some sense of what otherwise would be mere chronology. Williams, today an English Marxist saint, was one of the worst writers I have ever tried to read—not jargon, just plain poor grammar—but his masterwork, *Culture and Society, 1780–1950* (1958), was one of the seminal books in my education. Here he argued that the concept of high culture, of which literature and the arts were main constituents, began in the late eighteenth century to be defined as a counter to the increasing brutality, ugliness, and financial crudity of industrial liberal capitalism. He then traced the word and the concept of culture through its development in literature and art in the works of writers like Samuel Taylor Coleridge, Thomas Carlyle, John Ruskin, Matthew Arnold, William Morris, and T. S. Eliot. I had dinner once with Williams when he was lecturing in New Haven, and amused his socialist rigidity momentarily by saying that we would know that the political tide had turned when small children in Marxist states began to risk their lives to deposit their pennies in secret bank accounts that paid compound interest.

But all our efforts, structuralist or historical, failed to provide any kind of scientific structure for humanistic study. It began to appear that the things we were studying—literature, history, art, philosophy—did not lend themselves in some fundamental way to the scientific method. Our doubts found voice in several critical articles. In 1964 Susan Sontag published a short essay in *The Evergreen Review* titled simply "Against Interpretation." The argument of the piece was not very novel, but it was a cry from the heart of someone fed up with the New Criticism's "perennial, never consummated project of interpretation," the endless process of turning out new, ever more intricate readings of old works, demonstrating that under their surface lay other meanings that no one had as yet dreamed of. It was shocking but bracing to hear Sontag say openly that interpretation in our time "is largely reactionary, stifling. Like the fumes of the automobile and of heavy industry which befoul the urban atmosphere, the effusion of interpretations of art today poisons our sensibilities. In a culture whose already classical dilemma is the hyper-trophy of the intellect at the expense of energy and sensual capability, interpretation is the revenge of the intellect upon art." We dismissed her concluding remark that "in place of a hermeneutics we need an erotics of art" as stale romanticism, but it was increasingly difficult to suppress awareness that already there was too much criticism, that much of it was too clever by half, and that large parts of it contradicted other parts, and thus silently mocked any pretensions of progress and scientific inquiry.

Scholarship had its troubles as well. It had remained, despite rumors to the contrary, a respectable and powerful branch of literary study, and of this kind of work none was considered more objective and precisely scientific than bibliography, the establishment of the "true texts" of literary works, like the text of Othello that I had constructed. But now this too came under heavy direct fire.

In the sixties the federal government, through the new National Endowment for the Humanities, began to fund a project under the auspices of the Modern Language Association to prepare and publish precise and accurate texts of the works of the major American writers, Nathaniel Hawthorne, Herman Melville, Edgar Allan Poe, and the like. Money poured out of the Treasury, and large editorial factories were set up at the appropriate universities: Mark Twain at Berkeley, William Dean Howells at Indiana University, and so on. Large numbers of pro-fessors were recruited to work on these texts using the best scientific principles. No labor was spared. For example, a corps of scholars read through Tom Sawyer backward to be sure how many times in the various texts "'Aunt Polly' is printed as 'aunt Polly,' and how many times 'ssst' is printed as 'sssst.'"

The observation is Edmund Wilson's, the model of American pub-lic criticism, practical but conversant with theory as well. He had some years before proposed a plan for printing the American classics, which were often out of print, in substantial but unencumbered formats simi-lar to the Pléiade editions in France, a project realized only after his death in the Library of America. He thought that the NEH had promised the money for his project, only to find that the professors and the MLA had managed to get the funds transferred to their editorial project.

Not a man of easy temper—he fought the formidable Mary Mc-

Carthy to a standoff in marriage, and he refused to pay his income taxes for years—Wilson lashed out in two essays in the *New York Review of Books* in the fall of 1968 at the folly of the MLA project. He scorned the professors and their bookish pedantry, their long textual introductions, their hundreds of pages of notes, their collections of textual variants, their interminable delays (the project is still nowhere near an end even in the nineties), and their production of texts no human being would want to plow through. "What on earth is the interest of all this? What is important is the finished work by which the author wishes to stand. All this scholarship squandered on [Howells's] *Their Wedding Journey* is a waste of money and time. . . . Three pages are devoted to 'Word-Division.' "

The bibliographical professors were outraged at this attack on what they considered literary science, and they accused Wilson of making facetious remarks, name-dropping, and committing a number of minor errors like writing "University of Indiana" for the correct Indiana University. It was all a tempest in an academic teapot, but for those who listened closely it was also a telling public pronouncement by our most distinguished critic that there was something deeply wrong at the foundations of literary scholarship. It had labored to bring forth mountains and produced instead not mice but texts that, at vast expense, buried under tons of verbiage and pedantry what the best American authors had written. Everyone knew that much of historical and bibliographical scholarship had for years been producing trivial nonsense, but to hear Edmund Wilson saying that the emperor had no clothes was shocking and made us wonder how long it could go on. Not very long, it turned out, and the deconstructive theory of the seventies should be understood as, at least in part, an attempt not only to bring logical rigor to humanistic thinking but to expose the emptiness and meaninglessness of earlier pretensions of being scientific.

7

Publish or Perish

tenure at yale, 1960–1964

"U p or out" was the law of the Medes and the Persians for the faculty of a great research university, and "publish or perish" governed the lives of the junior faculty at Yale as elsewhere. We lived always with the knowledge that it was not enough simply to teach reasonably well, but that within ten years—four years as an instructor on yearly appointments, followed by two three-year terms as an assistant professor—we had to have produced at least one notable book and a number of articles published in refereed journals if we were to be considered for an associate professorship and tenure.

The rules were not new. One day William Lyon Phelps, who early in the century had lectured to big crowds all over the country on popular writers whose works were not yet considered classics, such as Willa Cather and Theodore Dreiser, met A. S. Cook, the crusty chairman of the English department and an Old English scholar, on the street:

> "What, Phelps, you still here?"
>
> "Yes, Mr. Cook, I've been an instructor for four years now, and I'm hoping to be made an assistant professor soon."
>
> [A pause]
>
> "Phelps, you're just the kind of young man we don't want here."

When Phelps told the story to the person who told me, he chortled and said, "And that was forty years ago." In his *Autobiography* of 1939 he wrote an interesting account of his career as a teacher at Yale during the early part of the century. So did another Yale instructor, Henry Seidel Canby, in *Alma Mater: The Gothic Age of the American College* (1936). The tradition of professorial memoirs in Yale English was extended to include a view of the 1930s and '40s with the publication in 1982 of Pottle's *Pride and Negligence: The History of the Boswell Papers*.

By the time I had been at Yale for six years or so, I had managed to scramble out of the introductory English courses and find opportunities to teach more exotic kinds of literature. You were expected to be an expert in some particular historical field of English literature—I was tagged a Renaissance drama man—and because of my general interest in theater, in time I had my own upper-level seminar in modern playwrights, in which I taught Scribe and Ibsen, Strindberg and Pirandello, Chekhov and Cocteau, as well as Shaw, O'Casey, and Tennessee Williams. You could cover a lot of ground in a course running through twenty-six weeks of classes.

One of my most memorable classes of undergraduates enrolled in this modern drama course. The Yale Dramat (the undergraduate theater group) was particularly strong in these years, taking on big productions like Williams's *Camino Real*. Double names being the thing in theater at the time, the leading man was Converse M. Converse, who played opposite a handsome young woman from the drama school named Evans Evans. Calvin Trillin, who later wrote about food and then became a syndicated columnist known for his pleasant humor, took the course but cut most of the time. Dick Cavett, later a well-known TV interviewer, and James Franciscus, known as Goey, incredibly handsome and headed for Hollywood, were the most perceptive and talkative. Years later Cavett interviewed Franciscus, who was then playing a blind teacher in a TV series, and took him to task: "How can you play a teacher with a straight face? Do you remember in Mr. Kernan's class when you got a 'minus 40' as a grade on a paper?" And he had. I was convinced, rightly I still think, that misspelling was a result only of carelessness and that if enough pressure was applied it could be eliminated. So I announced in the first class that every spelling error would result in a deduction of five points from the grade. When Franciscus's paper came in with twenty-eight abominable misspellings I, being a logical fellow in those days before spellchecking, followed through and gave him a minus 40. He argued passionately that there was no such grade, that it was illogical, as well as illegal, and unlikely to improve his spelling. His spelling didn't improve very much, but he tried, and ultimately he did quite well in the course and later in the theater, though he died young.

It was to this class that one day I brought Lillian Hellman. By then she was more famous for her defense of Stalinism and having lived with the detective story writer Dashiell Hammett than for anything to do with the theater, but she had written acclaimed plays in the 1930s. She was at Yale as a Chubb Fellow, and to earn her fee she had to, among other things, attend a class. I drew the short straw, and I had the students bone up on *The Little Foxes* and *The Children's Hour*, and we worked up some practical questions about how Broadway plays are put together. I was intrigued—after all, I knew little about the world of greasepaint and lighting boards—but when I began to talk with her over lunch about the contemporary theater, she professed no longer to know or care anything about it. Which was true. In fact all she wanted to talk about was a wicked case of indigestion—which I would have suspected without her saying a word about it—and the very painful problems she was having with her teeth. These are not interesting subjects, but she went on about them relentlessly, in great detail, turning aside my every attempt to change the subject as grimly as she had once refused to answer the House Un-American Activities Committee about her communist connections or those of her friends.

In time I got her to the classroom where Cavett, Trillin, Goey, and others were waiting with shining faces to ask questions about what kind of work had to be done in the second act of a play as opposed to the third act. She listened, belching now and then, farting only rarely, but in the end she airily swept all the questions aside as boring and meaningless. When we asked her about the musical *Candide*, in which she had had a hand, with its brilliant songs—"That old hag is no use in this gyp joint" is the line that came to mind—she professed only disdain. I suppose we were lucky that she didn't go into one of her notorious rages. Not knowing where else to turn, we asked her what she thought of Ibsen: "Haven't read him in years." About Strindberg: "A depressed and depressing Swede, not enough sunlight." About Chekhov: "Much like my own writing." Somehow the end of the seminar came, and with the excuse of another class I pointed her toward the English department office, where the chairman was waiting to take her to her lecture and introduce her. I never heard what she said, and never asked. Probably something about her teeth.

Fate was lurking in this meeting, though. In January 1980, Cavett— already well established as a TV interviewer of celebrities and other personalities—wickedly asked Mary McCarthy if she thought there were any American writers who were overrated. It was like throwing bloody meat in the water to a shark, and McCarthy began to reel off her list of the undeserving. Hellman's name inevitably came up, and Cavett—I'd bet he was remembering the class in the 1950s—expressed an innocent surprise:

> "What is wrong with her?"
> "A bad writer, overrated, a dishonest writer."
> "How, dishonest?"
> "Everything. I once said in an interview that every word she writes is a lie, including 'and' and 'the.'"

Hellman, about as tough an infighter in this kind of bare-knuckle cultural combat as could be found, sued McCarthy for defamation of character, naming Cavett and the Public Broadcasting Service as well, and seeking more than two million dollars. Only her death in 1984 brought the vicious battle between these two literary assassins to an end.

Support for tenure from the senior professor in your field was still considered crucial, and for me that meant Charles Prouty. Since his course in graduate school, he had become a kind of negative model for me, and throughout my academic life I frequently corrected my behavior in class or in meetings by thinking, "You sound like Prouty," or "That's something Prouty would do." I was particularly sensitive to a type of whining rhetoric in which he accused you of harboring some attitude you had never even thought of while featuring himself as the heroic last defender of some obvious value. "You will think it foolish of me, but I will never give up my lifelong defense of education."

But we rubbed along until a hurried call early one snowy morning when the streets were icy took me away from stoking my coke furnace to his bedside. There, groaning like Falstaff, he told me to go down to the campus and administer an exam to the son of Juan Trippe, the Pan Am magnate, so that the boy could leave early to go skiing in Switzerland. Swallowing my annoyance, I took the paper and was about to leave when I was told also to take several pairs of gray flannel slacks to the cleaners, and as I started out once more, Prouty made his final demand: "And take this radio down to the repair shop, and be sure to make them understand that they have to fix it right this time." "Fuck you, Charles" seemed the only thing to say, so I did, dumping trousers and radio on the floor, though I did take the exam and administer it. I felt better when young Trippe had to ask me his instructor's name in order to put it on his blue exam book. Years later after Prouty's death I called to express sympathy with his wife, adding that I was sorry that Charles and I had not gotten along better. She replied airily, "Oh yes, I've forgotten what you two quarreled about"; but apparently I have not.

The competition for the tenure appointments everywhere was Darwinian. Ann Young woke one dawn to the persistent ringing of the doorbell, and when she opened the door, there, standing in the snow, was the wife of a colleague of her husband waving in her face a bloody pair of men's underdrawers. "This is what your husband did to mine, and I want something done about it," she fairly screamed. At a party the night before, it seemed, the woman's husband had gotten into a ferocious argument with Dick Young, and Dick, with a very diabolic sense of humor and a sword cane he carried because of a leg lost to a land mine in the war, told him that if he didn't stop talking nonsense he would stab him in the ass. When the other fellow persisted in defining the Mexican GNP in a way Dick did not like, Dick whipped his sword out of the cane and stabbed him, not so deep as a well, but wide enough to draw blood. The mutilé du derrière bolted from the house and sat up all night with his wife brooding on this insult to the family honor. The wife was here now to demand apology. Fortunately Ann had a most soothing and sympathetic way about her, and they composed the matter with a cup of coffee, a few tears, and a new pair of undershorts.

Confrontations that drew actual blood were unusual, but paranoia always hangs like smog over the university campus. The trouble is partly that there is no quantifiable bottom line. In business, who makes the most money can often be established, but in the academy the fundamental issue, "Who is the smartest of us all?" cannot be definitively answered. Even the dullest drudge will always think that the Nobel winner got the prize through pull or luck, and "if only . . ." But an attempt was made to grade us. In the days before student grading of instructors and courses became an industry, Yale freshmen (not upperclassmen) were required to write comments about their instructors. Every year the chairman called all the instructors in and read them the judgments of their first-year students. We sat on the floor of the small English office in the Hall of Graduate Studies and chatted with the department secretary, famous for being a follower of Wilhelm Reich and having an "Orgone Accumulator" at home, wherein she sat for several hours every day to experience the rejuvenating powers of the astral rays focused by the box.

Ted Hilles, the chairman, was a remarkably kind man who was embarrassed by having to do so, but he read the student comments aloud to each of us: "This is the kind of teacher that I came to Yale to study with," the student you had given a B+ or an A would say. Then there would follow the report of students like Smithers, to whom you had given a C or a D: "This man is the worst teacher I have ever studied with, he is a disgrace to the Yale faculty and far infirior [sic] to my masters at Andover." A profound cynicism about student comments was born from the experience of hearing these absolutely opposite evaluations one after another and knowing how closely they correlated with the grades you had given.

But the judgment that counted was made not by students but by the senior faculty, and writing your first book and getting it published and favorably reviewed were what interested them most. I knew I had to write a book, and I thought about it a good deal, but I had no burning desire to do so nor any confidence that I knew anything out of which I could. The usual thing was to publish, with modifications, your dissertation. John Marston did not sound any better with the passage of years — "Quake guzzel dogs / Scud from the lashes of my yerking rime" — but I had a big investment in him, and without intending to I had become "a Marston man," even for a brief time "*the* Marston man," for there were no others at that moment. But soon my friend Anthony Caputi at Cornell toppled me from the summit of the Marston hill by proving that Marston's satirist — the persona who spoke his satire — was not a Calvinist, as I had argued, but a Neo-Stoic.

I had no more promising ideas, though, so if I was to write a book it had to be on Marston. Over the summers after teaching ended I dutifully read other Jacobean satirists (a very odd lot of shaggy, cloven-hoofed satyrs, I want to tell you); the Renaissance editions of Juvenal, Horace, Persius, and Martial, the Romans who were the English satirists' models; and all the contemporary criticism on satire and satiric stage tragedy and comedy I could find. By the time I was given a Morse fellowship of a year off with full pay for research and writing, I had sheaves of notes on Elizabethan satire. Day after desperate day I sat at my desk staring at the dissertation, trying to rework it and insert the new material, but at the end of long, long days I would read what I had written, drop it in the wastebasket, and go home to have a drink with my wife, determined to conquer satire the next day. (Leave for writing a book was not much of a year off for the instructor's family, who saw less of him than usual and what they saw was more depressed, and depressing.) Mine was no romantic writer's block, no Coleridge interrupted in his opium dreams of Kubla Khan, no Wordsworth tinkering for fifty years with *The Prelude*, but a tyro's confrontation with a mass of historical material and little sense of how to go about "understanding" it. I thought of myself as a literary archaeologist engaged in research, an investigator of a lost literary reality that it was my job to recover from the layers of forgetfulness with which time had willingly covered English Renaissance satire. I needed to know more in order to say more, I thought, but the deeper I dug in my material, the more tangled my prose and my ideas became.

Time was not unlimited, but inspiration struck me on Christmas Eve as I was leaving the office. There was something flawed not with my material but with my concept of a book. I had been thinking of myself as a literary scientist-historian looking deep into the object of study to discover the truth that was in it, but this was looking in the wrong direction. What I needed was not new, as yet undiscovered facts about John Marston and satire but some way of bringing to life the information I had by putting it in a larger and more illuminating context. I took the four hundred pages of the dissertation tracing satire back to the Garden of Eden and dropped them unceremoniously into the trash and went home to the family hearth.

When I came back after Christmas the writing went easily and quickly. A false etymology tracing the word *satire* back to satyrs, the shaggy woodland creatures of myth, half goat and half man, was believed by the Elizabethans to set the rules for satire—the word was even spelled "satyr" until the eighteenth century. Satire was therefore for the Elizabethans originally a kind of attack poetry used by satyrs, and their ancient mythic characteristics—sadism, prurience, harshness—dictated the appropriate satiric tone and style. While only a few of the worst English satirists put their satire in the mouths of actual satyrs, others like John Donne and John Marston justified the harshness of their satire, its strong subject matter, and its rough style by the original nature of satire and the character of fawning, lascivious satyrs. "Don't blame me for the crudity of my verse," the writers of satire were saying. "This is the way that true satire on the classical model has to be written."

I already had mounds of evidence on these matters, but now I understood that these Elizabethan satyrs and their twisted style were not to be taken as a literary anomaly, a curious, vulgar sixteenth-century literary error, but as the key to understanding something crucial about the history of all Western satire, one bizarre solution to a problem that had had to be managed one way or another whenever and wherever satire was written.

Other types of literature, like comedy and tragedy, may be uncertain of purpose, but satire exists to attack folly, and perhaps even to improve the knaves and fools it scourges, though this last seems more doubtful. Normal people find some way of ignoring society's massive hypocrisy—"the world was always like this," "you have to take the good with the bad," "we are all sinners," "if you get to know him he isn't really all that awful," "people who live in glass houses . . ."— but great satirists like Aristophanes, Horace, Ben Jonson, Swift, Pope, Byron, Orwell, Waugh, and our own Mark Twain and Nathanael West will have none of these evasions. They know knavery and folly when they see them, they understand how dangerous they are, they have the courage to call them their true names, and they have the verbal skills to strip the masks off hypocrites and fools and hold them up to laughter and contempt. Juvenal called the powerful moral outrage that drives the satirist to attack the hypocrisy and pretensions of the flagrantly wicked and the pompously virtuous *saeva indignatio*, fierce indignation. But the man who skins another alive gets a lot of blood on him, and great satirists have always had to find some way to relieve themselves of personal responsibility for the rough way they handle their fools and scoundrels. Some indirection, that is to say, is always required if the satire is to be both effective and safe. Pretending to be and acting like a satyr was only one of the more bizarre devices for handling this universal problem of satiric writing. Irony, pretending to praise what you are in fact blaming, and comic overstatement have been the standard rhetorical devices for achieving this required obliquity. Swift put his satire in the mouth of an idiot like Lemuel Gulliver, who is unaware of the idiocy and vice he describes, while a satiric novelist like Evelyn Waugh simply allows folly to reveal itself, scrupulously avoiding any comment on it.

By the time classes began in the fall of 1958, I was able to submit a manuscript on satire for the Yale Studies in English series published by Yale University Press. An argument erupted about the title, *The Can-*

kered Muse, which the editors at the Press thought too repellent to use. Ben Nangle, the editor of the series, defended it successfully, however. Cankered things he understood.

For many years authors who published with university presses had had to come up with subventions, either out of their own pockets or through sources such as university funds dedicated to that purpose, and to do without payment of royalties. *The Cankered Muse* was subsidized by the Yale Studies in English, but it was also one of the first products of an enlightened new policy by which the author received royalties after the sale of fifteen hundred copies. I was overjoyed to be published under any terms, and many years later when I received a royalty check for five copies, and in the next mail a notification that the stock of the book was exhausted and that it would not be reprinted, it still seemed a good deal.

It had once been an academic requirement, as it still was in Germany, that the dissertation be printed before the Ph.D. was awarded, and while those days were long past, publication of the first book, usually based on the dissertation, was a critical part of a scholar's career. The rite was not concluded, however, until the book had been reviewed. Favorable reviews in the right journals by the right people were critical to promotion, and the aspiring author waited impatiently, usually for a year or more, for the reviews to begin. Books by my contemporaries, Aubrey Williams's *Pope's Dunciad* and Harold Bloom's *Shelley's Mythmaking*, also published in the Yale Series, had recently been great successes, and I had little hope of doing so well. But then came one of those pieces of luck that determine careers.

After a long day of teaching I was walking home when a neighbor, Sunny Miskimmin, a woman of many sorrows, called out and, coming down her steps, handed me a copy of the *Times Literary Supplement*, or *TLS*. I sat down on the curb of Ashmun Street in the waning light and read, twice, through a piece of what seemed to me golden prose, realizing slowly that my academic fortunes had taken a sharp turn for the better. Then even more than now, when the *New York Review of Books* has to some extent taken its place in America, the *Times Literary Supplement* was the professional arbiter of success. To get a review in its pages at all was a plus; to get the full center-page review, as I had, was an honor usually reserved for the long established.

Apparently the regular reviewer of satire was on vacation when my book arrived, and it was given in his absence to Agnes Latham, known best for her fine edition of the poems of Sir Walter Raleigh. Writing anonymously, as was then the custom, Miss Latham praised the book forthrightly: "Mr. Alvin Kernan does not investigate all the problems which the subject poses, but in his examination of the satirical spirit as it manifested itself in the late sixteenth and early seventeenth centuries he propounds a general theory which holds good for that period and which necessarily, if it is accepted, is a contribution towards a wider interpretation of this uncomfortable, unlovely, universally functioning urge to rip up other people's garments and inspect the seamy side." Then, because she was interested in the argument, and because she was more a scholar than a careerist, rather than going on to state her own opinions about this and that, as many a reviewer does, she laid out the substance of the argument of The Cankered Muse on the rest of the page. Nothing could have been more rewarding than to see that laboriously-put-together, oh so painfully, bit by bit, view of satire praised publicly in clear and precise terms. She had understood, she was intrigued, she wanted to make the knowledge available to others. I wish every new author such a reviewer.

It was only a book review, a genre as common as the lice Miss Latham inevitably thought of in connection with satire, but from then on the professors knew who I was, and even the ones with whom I was not particularly sympathetic were approving. I had joined an academic club that I have railed against many times since but have never quite been able to leave. There were many clubs at Yale, but there were only two big ones. The first and far better known was the Yale Club: Boola-Boola, Bulldogs will never fail, old Blues, the Old Campus and the fence, Mory's and the Whiffenpoofs. This was the club that ran Yale, provided its senior administrators, sat on the Yale Corporation, invested its funds, and made a ritual of the annual football game with Harvard. To have been a graduate student at Yale did not carry admission to this club; its mysteries were made known only to Yale undergraduates, and most of all to members of one of the secret societies like Skull and Bones or Book and Snake. Fred Pottle was a fellow of Davenport College, as was Maynard Mack, a Yale graduate, but after a lifetime of achievement and world fame as the editor of the Boswell papers, even on the eve of his retirement a lunch with Fred was likely to bring out complaints about how Maynard had always had a much bigger and better office, on the second floor of Davenport College, and with wood paneling, while Pottle was given a cage in the basement with a cement floor and steel shelving. He attributed this slight to the fact that he had not gone to Yale College. Like Pottle and most of my peers, I was annoyed at never—even when I held a name chair and served as the acting provost of the university—being able to sign for a meal at Mory's, the club-restaurant where most of the business lunches on campus were held and where membership was automatic only for Yale undergraduates.

The second club was as powerful in academic affairs as the Bulldogs were in social and financial areas. This second club was, at least below the surface, even more snobbish than the first, and membership in it was one of life's few prizes that really satisfied something deep in people like myself. The members were people in all fields, senior and junior, who were thought to have real intelligence and at least the promise of intellectual achievement. Its home was the various college fellowships, and its meetings were at their lunch tables. Teaching really didn't count for much in this club; you were expected to do your honest best, and it was nice if it came off well, but no more than that. Eating at Mory's seemed not nearly so important as being able to join fully in the conversation at one of the fellows' tables or being listened to for a reasonable amount of time when you got up to speak at the meetings of the Yale College faculty in Connecticut Hall.

I never expected to make tenure in the Yale English department, but the golden fleece glittered so brightly that it was impossible to resist trying for it. Someone once remarked that tenure was the shortest-lived pleasure he had ever experienced, and after the fact that is true, but beforehand it beckons like the Grail. The quest is difficult for all but much more painful for some than for others. One very bright assistant professor was found drunk, with the skin burned off his feet, standing early one morning in front of Sterling Library. He had been trying to boil water for coffee when he spilled the kettle on his feet. Not knowing what else to do, he went and stood in front of the library, as if the all-powerful books could heal him.

Academics hate to make final decisions like awarding tenure, and strange things happen when they are forced to do so. The older professors in the art history department who were considering tenure for four brilliant young teacher-scholars—including Bill McDonald in classical architecture, Bill Crelly in European painting, and Spyro Kostoff in the history of architecture, great names all in later time—found the situation impossible, and besides, when it came down to it they really didn't think too much of any of them, so they fired them all.

Years later in the English department, when Howard Felperin had been voted tenure by the professors only to have the recommendation refused by the superior committee, the professors lost any enthusiasm they might have once had for him. Besides, they were annoyed at having to deal with the matter again. One of the professors had been sleeping through the meeting, as he usually did, but woke up when the vote was called on recommending Felperin for tenure once more, and asked what was going on.

> "We are just about to vote again on tenure for Howard Felperin."
>
> "Tenure! tenure! Felperin is not ready for tenure yet, if ever."
>
> "But you voted for him the last time we discussed the matter."
>
> "Well, if so I didn't think it was tenure we were voting."

Felperin, who had been celebrating and rather lording it over his peers during the brief time he thought he had tenure, was furious and ranted to his wife in the local Dunkin' Donuts, describing each of the professors in turn in some dismissive way. When he came to the kindly Gene Waith all he could think of was, "And that Gene Waith, that Gene Waith, he looks just like a cavalry colonel." His wife, a very cool beauty, bored with the whole thing, replied haughtily, "Howard, I couldn't care less." Howard, recounting the story years afterward in a bar in Australia, said, "And right then I knew that the marriage was over." It was, and so was his Yale contract; after a year on welfare he went off to Australia to carry the news of deconstruction Down Under, where he became the scourge of the Leavisites at Melbourne. Marjorie Garber, Howard's contemporary and his competitor for tenure, surveyed his fate coolly: "Nothing so much becomes Howard as adversity." In time she too failed to clear the bar, but she ended up on her feet at Harvard as the local Shakespearean, as well as an expert on cross-dressing and on the love of dogs.

Epic irrationality of the kind Felperin stumbled into was uncommon, though by no means unique, for the system of promotion was at best a very tricky affair in which things could go wrong at almost any point, and difficulties could appear suddenly from unexpected directions. The standard procedure was for the full professors in a department, after reading all the candidate's writings, to meet in solemn conclave, discuss the candidate, and vote. In those days the English professors sat in a horseshoe shape in a room at the top of the graduate school, and the chairman, sitting at the open end, called on each professor in turn to give an opinion on the candidate. After everyone had heard everyone else's views, the vote proceeded, aloud, in the same order. If it was negative, the chairman called the poor fellow that evening and tried to find soothing things to say. If positive, the recommendation was forwarded to the Humanities Committee, made up of professors from the various humanities departments and chaired by the director of the division. The committee members then read what they could of the candidate's works, interviewed the chairman of the recommending department, and voted whether to send the name on to the Board of Permanent Officers, chaired in alternate years by the graduate and the undergraduate deans, and composed of all the full professors in the faculty of arts and sciences. If no one in that august body decided to make some kind of an issue about academic matters having nothing to do with the candidate, or if no one had a long-smoldering personal grudge, or if the appointment did not involve some ongoing battle between "big-enders" and "little-enders," or if no one just felt like being difficult that day, the nomination would stagger forward to the provost. The provost would present it to the academic committee of the trustees, who would solemnly vote that so-and-so be given a permanent associate or full professorship, and the university secretary would duly notify the teacher of the decision on heavy vellum in an elaborate script. Tenure was, as was often said, "a carefully guarded privilege," but it is a wonder anyone made it through this lengthy, ramshackle process.

Politicking was sometimes practiced by those coming up for tenure, but it genuinely was frowned on, and your chances could be wrecked very easily by even saying something to one of the professors that he might interpret as an attempt to sway his vote or even to find out how he felt. The only sure way of avoiding saying something inadvertently out of nervousness was to stay far away from professors, and to engage them when you did meet only in the lightest of conversation. But even those defenses were sometimes not enough. It was the custom of a number of members of the English department in the fifties and early sixties to drink coffee, usually talking in a light way, coming and going between classes, at a table in George and Harry's, a hamburger joint on Wall Street. Mostly it was younger people like myself, but elders would sometimes join us, and Bill Wimsatt, who liked to talk with the boys, was a regular. On the occasion that the professors discussed the promotion to tenure of Frank Brady, the fine Boswell and Johnson scholar, Bill remarked that he had talked with Frank quite a lot at George and Harry's and that he never heard him say anything very impressive. The discussions were supposedly secret, but the next morning, and for a long time thereafter, there was not a soul other than Bill to be seen at the table. From time to time he would ask, plaintively, "Why don't any of you fellows come around to George and Harry's anymore?" "Too busy, Bill, got to get the book out." The restaurant is still there, though pizza has replaced hamburgers as the staple. But I wonder whether any junior members of the English department have ever again risked the curse of George and Harry's, though that most remarkable and human of men, nearly seven feet tall, whom Brady thereafter called Quinbus Flestrin (the name the Lilliputians gave Gulliver), has long been dead.

By 1964 I had been teaching at Yale for ten years as an instructor and assistant professor, and I was very concerned when the English department promoted me and a few others to an associate professorship without tenure. Traditionally the rank had carried tenure, but the new type of appointment was intended to hold us in place without a final decision. Louis Martz, then the chairman, called me into his office to tell me what the department had voted, and when my face fell at the news he tried to reassure me, saying, "It is absolutely the strongest vote of confidence the department could possibly give you. We will take up your tenure next year, but for the moment we want you to know how positively we feel about you and your work." He went on in this vein for some time—"it is everything but tenure"—and then suddenly stopped, realizing he was perhaps promising too much, that if they fired me later I might complain that I had been led on, and so he paused, and then said, "Of course it doesn't commit the department in *any* way."

I ran into him soon after on the street and greeted him with as much jollity as I could muster. He looked at me with a cool eye and said, "About time you gave me the latest copy of your vita." To which the only reply I could think of was, "*Vita brevis est.* Ha, ha." He smiled grudgingly and came back with "But *ars longa.*" He was right. By 1965 promotion to tenure was a two-book affair. Quality may have been more important than quantity, as was often said, but it was best to have two books ready for the tenure review, plus a number of articles in high-status journals. This left little time for dawdling. *The Cankered Muse* had done well enough, but to produce another book seemed hopeless, and for months I spent nights and weekends in my office pounding on the typewriter, trying to get something in place, spending hours staring out the window at the site of the famous "Humpty Dumpty riot" of 1952, which had erupted when police banned an ice cream vendor and his cart from the grounds. For two hours fifteen hundred students assailed the police, who turned on them with clubs and hoses until they were subdued. Eventually, the vendor was allowed to return to campus, and the students held a victory rally for him.

Riots were always near the surface in the spring, and in 1959 the snow was fatally right for snowballs. On St. Patrick's Day, when the drum and bugle corps of many Catholic schools and brigades of Irish lassies with bare white legs and short green skirts twirling their batons marched through the middle of the campus, the students began pelting them with snowballs. The marchers broke ranks and scattered scream-ing through the campus, the students still pursuing them, with the Irish and Italian cops pursuing the students. For the students, and I think even the marchers, it was all in fun. For the cops, however, it was their worst dreams come true—rich, WASP, Ivy League students pursuing poor, scantily clad, virginal Catholic girls—and they went berserk in a real police riot, cracking heads wherever they could find a Yale skull to bend their night sticks over. It was a classic rite of spring, replete with phallic symbols, fertility, and the greenness of the coming season, but it alienated Yale from a police force that it was going to need badly in a few years.

Satire was still the primary string to my critical bow, and for some time I had been teaching an undergraduate course in the subject, beginning with Greeks like Aristophanes and coming up to modern satirists like George Orwell and Nathanael West, author of *Day of the Locust* and *Miss Lonelyhearts*, which in my opinion are the greatest of American satiric works. A number of articles had emerged from this, and in them I was pleased to find the fragments of a developing theme that the great satirists of the Western tradition did not merely attack the particular failings of their own time but chronicled a universal destructive energy—Pope styled it "Dulness" and described it as "laborious, heavy, busy, bold and blind." Dulness perverts nature, manufactures bizarre and grotesque worlds, and moves toward a futile conclusion in which, instead of the air being cleared as in tragedy and comedy, waste and confusion reign and nothing is solved. Ben Jonson's master swindler, Volpone, and his greedy Sir Epicure Mammon; Swift's Gulliver; Orwell's pigs Napoleon and Snowball; West's "people who came to California to die"—these were, I found from reading my own articles, different versions of the greed and stupidity that in satire always move toward a breakdown of sense and order in which "universal darkness covers all."

I was delighted that these essays had some coherence, and I reworked them, added some, and gave them the title *The Plot of Satire*. The book was not printed yet, but I could submit the manuscript to the department for consideration, along with copies of the editions of *Volpone* and *Othello* that I had edited and various articles. Then the long wait began. Harold Bloom used an offer of a professorship from another university to get his tenure at once; three jobs now had to be divided among four people: Tom Greene, a comparative literature scholar, Dick Sylvester, an editor of the works of Sir Thomas More, Harry Berger, a Spenserian, and myself—all Renaissance scholars. The professors agonized over which of the four of us to sacrifice. They were deeply unhappy with the predicament and went back to the provost again and again, but he remained adamant: three, not four. In the end they decided to let Berger go, a most unexpected decision since Harry had been a much loved Yale undergraduate, and a most engaging person.

Fate seemed to hang over these tenure decisions, and it manifested itself first in the death of Harry's oldest boy, Tommy, in a car accident, with all the attendant guilt and blame—what could you possibly say to the family in circumstances where it seemed you were already profiting from their earlier misfortunes? Eventually the Bergers moved to California to the new campus at Santa Cruz, where over the years Harry became a kind of Spenserian guru, but his family sadly fell apart.

Dick Sylvester was saved because it was felt that his work on the papers of Sir Thomas More—Saint Thomas to Catholics—of which he was the general editor and mainstay, ought to be supported to preserve the tradition of scholarly editions at Yale. But after tenure, nothing ever went right for Dick: depression, the death of a young daughter from an infection, an odd car accident that smashed his elbow, cancer of the throat that killed him. When the little girl died, I went over to sit with him in his backyard, and he said that almost the worst part was knowing that he would get over it. I last saw him when he was dying, sitting at home in a dreadful room with the shades down, trying to argue with a teenage proto-hippie son in a torn leather jacket, indifferent to his sufferings, who had recently smashed up the family car but wanted to take it out again anyway.

It would be comforting to think that we struggled and suffered in some great war for truth and knowledge, but I suspect that some of us were merely lucky, some unlucky. The frankest of the Yale English professors, that old cynic Talbot Donaldson, told me that they promoted me because they thought that I would make a good chairman, though as it turned out I never held the job.

Left, Civil War Monument, Williams College
(Williams College Archives and Special
Collections)

Above, the Handyman's Special: house on Mill
Road, North Haven

Below, a student at Oxford, in the Old Manor,
1950: the author and his wife

Yale English Department professors, 1967. Back row, from left, Charles Feidelson, Charles Taylor, Maynard Mack, Alvin Kernan, Dwight Culler, Eugene Waith, Charles Prouty, Bill Wimsatt, Dick Sylvester, Martin Price, Dick Lewis, Tom Greene, Harold Bloom, and Norman Pierson; front row, Louis Martz, Joe Curtis, Ben Nangle, Gordon Haight, Ted Hilles, Marie Boroff, Fred Pottle, John Pope, Davis Harding, Ed Gordon, and Dick Sewall

Above, Black Panther
David Hilliard speaking
to a crowd in "Moby
Dick," spring 1970
(Yale Picture Collec-
tion, Manuscripts and
Archives, Yale Uni-
versity Library)

Left, students trying to
erect the tip of "the
Lipstick" in Beinecke
Plaza, spring 1970
(Yale Picture Collec-
tion, Manuscripts and
Archives, Yale Uni-
versity Library)

Kingman Brewster at a press conference, April 30, 1970, announcing university plans for May Day (Yale Picture Collection, Manuscripts and Archives, Yale University Library)

"In the middle of life's journey": the author in his office in the Hall of Graduate Studies, Yale, 1972

"The college above the golf links": Princeton Graduate College (*Archives of the University, Department of Rare Books and Special Collections, Princeton University Library*)

Right, Princeton University president Bill Bowen at a council meeting, Princeton, 1974 (*Archives of the University, Department of Rare Books and Special Collections, Princeton University Library*)

The Princeton administration, commencement ceremonies, 1977. From left, Ernest Gordon, dean of the chapel; Neil Rudenstine, dean of the college; the author; Aaron Lemonick, dean of the faculty; Al Rees, provost (Archives of the University, Department of Rare Books and Special Collections, Princeton University Library)

Left, in retirement, Princeton, 1990

8

Goodbye, Boola Boola

The bells began ringing in Harkness Tower in the late afternoon as I stood in the seminar room with my back to the tall window that looked down into the chapel in the base of the tower. We were working away on Lattimore's translation of *The Iliad*, discussing the incredible bleakness of the warrior's code that was concentrated in Achilles' fate, a short life with honor, or a long life without it. Someone opened the door of the seminar room and said, "Kennedy's been killed." We all looked at one another across the long table and, as the bell kept on tolling, got up without saying anything and walked down to the Branford courtyard where the students and faculty were milling around, not so much talking as keeping each other company and trying to grasp the enormous event. That it was momentous, we all felt, but in quite what way was not certain. More than thirty years later its meaning is still not clear, neither the facts nor their significance, but we knew somehow that it marked the end of an era and the beginning of another historical time.

We watched the endless funeral on TV in a house in the suburbs where, after tenure seemed assured, we had moved as the Cuban missile crisis flared up, when nuclear war came closer than it ever has. The massive old bluestones that formed the cellar walls seemed to offer some defense against the rockets that we more or less really expected. As our children, now four in number, got older, the downtown New Haven public schools became more and more unsatisfactory, and there wasn't enough money to send them all to the local country day school, the usual way of solving the problem. So we found an old eleven-room brick house in North Haven for $17,500, and persuaded Yale to give us a mortgage for most of it.

The house was a splendid old Greek Revival wreck from about 1820, standing behind a huge maple just off Mill Road. It was adjacent, unfortunately, to a single-track railroad on which a coal train thundered by once a day, past the Prince of Peace Rifle and Revolver Club, past Cottontail Lane where the local Peeping Tom lived, past the "Enclave" tract where the mechanic who cut his neighbor's wife's brake lines for a small fee plied his trade. From its stone cellar and hand-hewn log beams to the beautifully fitted joints of the attic frame, it was a magnificent derelict used up by an old Yankee farm family that had retreated from one room to another until they were living in the kitchen and one other room in a wooden wing. Broken glass had been repaired by covering it with another broken piece and smearing some cement around the edges; the French drains were long clogged and seeping into the yard; the furnace did not work, and the roof needed replacing. The cellar was filled to the rafters with accumulated junk, and there was dry rot in the unpeeled logs that supported the floor. Massive brick chimneys, each with four fireplaces, all long covered, were at either end of the house. The foundation on one side of the wing had collapsed when the gutter rusted out and the ground froze hard. A huge poison ivy vine covered the weather side.

If ever there was a handyman's special, this was it. It was overwhelming, in short, but it was also a house of noble proportions and great dignity. To preserve it seemed a worthy project, so we borrowed enough money to put in a new oil furnace and moved in, planning, in typical American Dream fashion, to work on the house in our spare time over the years. It was from the beginning, in a howling blizzard when all the heat from the new furnace escaped through an uninsulated attic, more than a family with four young children and an academic career could manage. The local lumberyard got all our money, our hands were always stained with paint, and, except for the oldest, Geoffrey, the children were less than interested in putting in a new fence cut exactly to match the original or scraping the old paint off the elaborate scroll-work and posts on the side porch. "Why can't we live like everybody else?" the younger boy, Alvin, constantly asked. Geoffrey, indignant at my nagging him, cut "I Quit" into the long grass with the lawn mower.

I continued to take summer jobs, teaching in the John Hay Fellows Program for high school teachers for two summers in Williamstown and one at Colorado College in Colorado Springs. The latter provided our first outing on the American Road, new style, with big motels, swimming pools, TV in the rooms, swag lamps, the haute cuisine of Moline and North Platte, and all on an expense account. It took us six days to get to Colorado in our red VW bus, with the children and the dog fighting over seats in the back.

I taught Shakespeare, and in trying to interpret *Lear* I discussed the various views of the concept of nature in the play: "Thou, nature, art my goddess." Smithers wasn't having any of it—"What's this 'nature' you keep talking about?"—and stubbornly refused to understand my explanations of what seemed to me obvious. This got under my skin and I lay awake at night thinking of absolutely conclusive demonstrations of the nature of nature, until one day on the way to class my eyes lighted on a small branch on the ground—Eureka!—which I picked up and took into class. "This," I said, holding it under the nose of the scornful Smithers, "is a branch, and it, like all other things, has a nature. Its nature is to spring back into its original position when you bend it." At which point I gloatingly bent it, and it broke in half.

Summer teaching had its excitements, but editing textbooks offered better pay. It was always a bit infra dig in the Ivy League to edit textbooks. You were expected to spend your time doing "research" and writing lasting contributions to scholarship, and there was always some feeling, even among the younger and poorer faculty, that true scholars did not overly concern themselves about money, no matter how broke they might be. But textbooks were tempting—they were one place where you could cash in on your knowledge, writing skills, and the Yale name. Brooks and Warren had made a fortune from their New Critical textbooks, and in his dedication to a collection of the masterpieces of world literature Maynard Mack had revealed, in Latin, that the work had paid the orthodontist to straighten his children's teeth.

I tried for the drama market and published *Character and Conflict*, a selection of great plays from the Greeks to the present, with accompanying essays of my own to describe various aspects of the theater—characters, setting, dialogue, plot. This was followed by another collection of plays, *Classics of the Modern Theater*, illustrating the development of modern drama from Ibsen to Brecht and Ionesco, without any editorial additions except for a general introduction. Both sold well over a hundred thousand copies, and I probably reached many more students through these textbooks than I did in my classroom teaching. But whatever the long-term results, in the short term they saved our bacon, putting a new roof on the house, repairing the chimneys, flooring the cellar, buying the second car I needed to commute to New Haven without leaving Sue carless.

For most of the sixties, trouble and disorder were in the air throughout the country, including its colleges, but until the end of the decade they did not seem to threaten the stability of the Ivy League. For us the early and mid sixties were a golden age. The undergraduates were well trained, intelligent, and very serious about education. The graduate students were of the same high quality, and in the post-Sputnik period the federal government poured vast sums into the universities to support research and graduate education in all fields, especially the sciences.

It was at this time that I taught a Shakespeare graduate seminar that seems to me, at least in retrospect, the high point of my teaching life. It began badly. Hoping simply to get to know the students' names and break the ice a little, I decided on the first day to go around the twenty-some students asking questions about such small factual matters as "How many plays did Shakespeare write?" "How many brothers and sisters did he have?" "Are their names at all suggestive?" (One of them, an actor, was, like the villain in *Lear*, named Edmund.) Catastrophe! These bright students knew no facts, or if they did they could not recall them. One student, a very fine one, thought that Lear had survived his play, and when I followed it up a bit—"Are you sure?"—he persisted, "Oh, yes." All I could think to say was, "Well, we can find out when we discuss the play."

A description of this same classroom scene from the students' point of view by Jim Maddox, later a fine scholar and teacher, in an introduction to a lecture at the Bread Loaf summer school, gives an idea of how differently faculty and students see things, and something of what a Yale graduate class was like in the late 1960s.

> The most extraordinary graduate seminar I ever attended was a seminar in Shakespearean Tragedy at Yale in the spring of 1967. It was extraordinary for two reasons. One reason was that Al Kernan was teaching it. The other was the quite impressive number of students in that seminar who went on to become widely known Shakespeareans themselves. In that seminar were Stephen Greenblatt, today perhaps the most eminent Renaissance scholar of his generation; Marjorie Garber, now at Harvard; Larry Danson of Princeton; Meredith Skura of Rice; Maynard Mack, Jr.; Keith Staveley, and so on, and so on. I've often thought back upon all the future Shakespearean eminence gathered in that one seminar room, and I think I know the explanation for it. The explanation grows out of the famous first meeting of that seminar—a first meeting that the alumni of the seminar still recall, and rechew in enjoyable rumination whenever they meet. There on opening day we students sat, rather smug, I'm afraid, because we were in our last semester of classes, and almost audibly stroking our beaks over our feathers

in the act of preening ourselves, when Professor Kernan walked in and sat down. He glanced at the roll. But instead of calling the roll he chose one name and asked the student the year of Shakespeare's birth. (Inside 25 students' heads in the room there was sudden, hot panic. Birth dates?) The student couldn't answer. But instead of passing on to the next name on the roll, Al stuck to the same poor, predestined student, like what we have this past year come to know as a smart bomb. "Well, how about Shakespeare's death-date?" Al asked. More ignorance. Well, said Al, perhaps you're more familiar with other writers. Pope's dates? Wordsworth's? Joyce's? By this point, inside 25 minds in that room was the same prayer: "Please, God, let me be invisible for just another hour and forty-five minutes, and I will spend the rest of my life at work in the hospitals of Calcutta." To make a long story short, he scared us to death, with the effect that we never, never came to seminar without the play under discussion virtually memorized. No more preening. This, I think, is why there were so many people in that classroom who are such eminent Shakespeareans today. Those scholars were not born to greatness; they did not simply achieve greatness; they did not have greatness thrust upon them. I'm convinced that they were terrified into greatness.

In the seminar meetings after that first class, Al desisted in part from the questioning of students. Mainly, he lectured, reading off yellow legal pads, the pages not even torn out, so that the reading was accompanied by a constant sawing motion as he turned the pages. It doesn't sound, in the telling, like a very effective way to teach a class. There was no flash, no glamour, not one of the geegaws of the great lecture-hall pleasers. With none of the usual classroom distractions to set it off, we sat there and confronted nothing in what Al said but a depth of thought and a continuous power of concentration upon Shakespeare's scenes that remains for me one of the grandest models of teaching I have ever witnessed. It was clear that we were listening to a man who had made every effort to record and convey to us, with the greatest articulateness and with no pomp, his hard and deep thinking about texts that seemed worth years of study.

This mirror of myself at work in class, praising as it is, surprised me for two reasons. First, I had not realized that I lectured that much. The give and take of the Socratic method seemed to me right for seminars, but perhaps the first meeting made it seem wise to fall back on my notes. Second, I had not quite realized that I maintained the distance from the students that Maddox's writing conveys; but it is true that intimate teacher-student relationships not only made me uneasy, they seemed unprofessional.

These and many other old ways of doing things may be said to have ended at Yale in 1963, when A. Whitney Griswold died of cancer and Kingman Brewster was selected by the trustees as the new president. I always remember Griswold, who was a historian, calling me one morning saying that he and his son had argued about whether the ending of Orwell's *Animal Farm*, where the pigs look at the men and the men look at the pigs and can't tell one from the other, had any particular historical application. Since he had heard that I knew something about satire, he would like my opinion. I said that I thought Orwell was glancing specifically at both the Popular Front of the thirties and the Russo-German nonaggression pact of 1939. He said he thought so too, thanked me, and said he would tell his son. I was flattered, and impressed that the president of Yale argued over the dinner table with his family about the meaning of books.

Brewster was a Yale graduate from one of the Plymouth Rock families, an aristocrat in appearance, tall and ruggedly movie-star handsome, in manner genial, urbane, amusing, always courteous. He was extremely sharp, not so much in a philosophical way—he seldom read books through—as in a political, lawyerly fashion, knowing what to say and when, when to take chances and when to be conservative, how much time to give to this cause or that person. Women adored him, and most men liked him too. His straightforwardness, his sense of humor, and his real interest in what people had to say suppressed the envy that the aristocratic type normally generates, and he became, along with others like Clark Kerr in California and Bill Bowen at Princeton, one of the spokesmen for the new kind of American higher education.

When Brewster became president, Charles Taylor was brought in as provost on the advice of Irwin Miller, one of the members of the corporation. Kingman and Charlie made an ideal pair. Charlie was also a Yale graduate, later a colleague of mine in graduate school, who had since been teaching Shakespeare at Indiana University, a few miles down the road from where Miller ran Cummings Diesel and was rebuilding the town of Columbus, bringing in the best architects in the world to build extraordinary modern churches and civic buildings. Returning to Yale was a great opportunity for Charlie, just forty, hardheaded, and capable of immense amounts of work. Ambitious for himself and for Yale, he initiated with Kingman a management revolution.

Yale had always chased Harvard and in the long run lost ground in the eminence of its faculty and the size of its endowment. Like all their predecessors and successors, Kingman and Charlie looked from the beginning for ways to catch up. Charlie understood that planning in the modern way, based on extensive and accurate information, was the key to success. The old Yale had grown up simply doing what seemed best in each case, accumulating customs and procedures along the way, and no one took much care to know who was where or what it cost. There was no accurate count of the faculty, for example, and it was impossible, in fact if not in theory, to find out how many professors of each rank there were and what was the average salary.

Buildings, space, their use, tell a great deal about an institution, and les mystères de Yale, like the fabled mysteries of the streets and buildings of Paris, were a good way of getting a sense of the old university that was passing. The Yale campus was strung out along city streets, from the hospital in the south to the science campus and the divinity school in the north, without any coherent plan. Entrepreneurs had found little nooks here and there in this loose expanse where they could get on with business without interruption. Universities, after all, were supposed to be places for eccentrics.

Behind the University Theater, a ladder led into the bowels of a subterranean squash court that had been divided into two levels by a noted lighting expert at the drama school and converted into a factory making theatrical lighting equipment. Hooked up inconspicuously to the university power circuits, this shop was worked by two gnomes who knew nothing of where they were.

A large brownstone building on lower Hillhouse Avenue, almost invisible behind evergreens, contained a wonderful collection of rare old musical instruments, but no one ever came there, and only the curator was somewhere in the quiet of the vast halls. A printing business produced and sold Chinese-language texts in the basement of an old university house on Hillhouse. If all the Yale basements had been flooded by turning on a giant valve at the noon bell, the underground university that ran out into the open would have matched the above-ground university in size and perhaps surpassed it in industry.

But you had to look up as well as down. Out over the roof of Jonathan Edwards College, up some iron ladders into a two-room aerie with a view of the roofs and chimneys of Yale, Jack Tworkov, the abstract expressionist painter and sculptor, nested for many years. At the corner of the Old Campus stood Bingham Tower. Entrance to its upper stories was reached by an antique elevator that creaked and ground its way slowly up to the top floor, a huge room with fine windows on three sides looking out on the New Haven Green, the Old Campus, and Chapel Street. Bookcases held an excellent German library, on the floor was an enormous dirty Oriental rug, and resting on the entrance desk was a visitors' book still open on a signature many years old. Everything was covered with dust, but a distinguished professor known for his studies of Martin Luther had been living there, sleeping in an anteroom and using the attached kitchen to prepare light meals.

On the floor below, numerous locked rooms when opened revealed a collection of dusty antiquities, busts, broken statues, fragments of mosaic, gathered in the twenties from Dura-Europus, an early-Christian Roman frontier garrison post in Mesopotamia, and left untouched for the most part since the death of the classicist M. I.

Rostovtzeff (1870–1952), whose dig had unearthed the artifacts. There is always a spooky quality about these abandoned academic projects, as if the workers, like Keats's villagers on the Grecian urn, had just gone off one day, never to return. There were other kinds of abandoned fragments of Rostovtzeff's excavation in Dura-Europus lying about, such as the uncompleted series of publications on the project. In the beginning, as is the way with these things, there had been great enthusiasm, and scholars had fought over the right to edit one volume or another, on the coins or the armor or the pottery. A few volumes had been published, but the rest had run out like a stream in the desert, until they disappeared in the sands of time.

Cleaned up and painted, with some elevator repairs, the upper two floors of Bingham Tower eventually made a wonderful set of offices and meeting rooms for Yale's distinguished comparative literature department, which was looking for a place to set up shop. It has by now been there for thirty years and has no doubt since constructed its own mystères.

The new provost hired a permanent architectural consultant and set out, project by project, to bring the campus together—to computerize the budgets, survey available space, rationalize the rules, admit women, and bring modern efficiency to every part of the university. There was an administrative restructuring too. Old retainers, often Yale grads who had collected around New Haven and turned their hands to whatever needed doing, were forced out, and new kinds of professional personnel managers, labor negotiators, and money people were brought in. The old personnel manager, with the solid Yale name of Griswold, who knew everyone on the staff by name, gave way to a real hired gun, about twenty-five, sharp as a tack, and every bit as painful. The old-timer who talked to the unions was replaced by a new-style professional negotiator who loathed unions and was in turn loathed by them. Here began some of the problems that sour labor relations to this day in New Haven. A computer science department was launched, and a new, very generous medical plan for the faculty and staff was initiated. The treasurer protested mightily that the university would lose its shirt to escalating medical costs, and he was right; but the provost overrode him, and another modern building, a health care center, was built on Hillhouse Avenue.

The new brooms swept too clean for many of those used to the old carelessness, and everyone felt some nostalgia for the old order. No doubt the new efficiency also contributed to the growing feelings of alienation of what was increasingly thought of as "management" from the faculty and students. The tenants of a new biology tower in the neo-brutalistic style rebelled when the very modern architect, Philip Johnson, included a "statue" made of old automobile parts welded together at odd angles. They saw this as a criticism of science and technology, and despite different interpretations of modern consciousness offered by the provost and his architect, the scientists demanded that it be removed. It was.

All this took money and time, enormous amounts of both, and there was never enough of either. Kingman didn't worry about money —it seemed not to be in his nature—but Charlie felt with great intensity that he simply had to find a big sum to build the new Yale, and he thought he had found it in a new way of increasing the annual return on the endowment. Yale, like most other charitable trusts, had always proceeded in the most cautious, old-fashioned financial way, spending each year only a prudent portion of the actual income (the yield) from its investments, plus some part of current gifts. The growth in the market value of the investments (the gain) remained untouched each year and provided protection against the inflation that had become a standard feature of the American economy. This way of reckoning income meant, however, that the amount available from the endowment for annual expenditures was very limited. McGeorge Bundy, who had become president of the Ford Foundation after helping Johnson fight the Vietnam War, decided that all colleges and universities should shift their investment policies to the "total-return" method (yield plus some portion of gain) of figuring income, which had by then become standard practice in business. He commissioned a Ford Foundation study that showed universities how to get around legal limits on spending some parts of the gain from restricted funds and wrote a letter to the major American universities recommending the total-return method as a source of financing growth.

Using this method of calculating income, Yale at one blow increased greatly the amount that could be "prudently" spent each year, and it further increased its return by shifting its investment policy from safety to growth. The new method of investing and figuring income at first produced many millions of dollars annually with which, among other things, Yale raised its faculty salaries by several thousand dollars at one swash, to the level where, as my wife always said suspiciously, "Professors could afford to get divorced for the first time." But then the market dropped and, as a result of a "smoothing formula," Yale found itself drawing down and spending big chunks of money from an endowment that was losing value, not gaining.

At this time began the perennial budget problems that have plagued Yale ever since, plunging it into crisis after crisis. Budget cuts became standard, year after year. Bart Giamatti, Brewster's successor, destroyed his presidency by refusing to give big raises he felt he could not afford to the support staff. Benno Schmidt, Giamatti's successor, resigned when the faculty refused to accept a reorganization plan eliminating a number of departments, including sociology, that his administration had put together to save the ten million dollars needed to restore the physical plant, which was falling apart because repairs had been delayed so long from lack of funds.

In 1965 Charlie offered me a job as associate provost, and I accepted with an understanding that I would continue to teach at least one course. I knew almost nothing outside my own department at the time, not even that three divisions — humanities, social sciences, and sciences — made up arts and sciences, and I was curious. I also thought that I might not want to teach forever, and that I might want to continue in administration, and this seemed a good way to find out what went on. I had an office in the Hall of Graduate Studies, a nice orange carpet, a real painting on the wall of a giant abstract hammer smashing a big rock, and a secretary, Holly Stevens, who was the only child of the American poet Wallace Stevens and was editing her father's works at the time. Her mother, the model for the head on the Mercury dime, was a great beauty and it cast a shadow over Holly all her life. The Stevens's house, according to Holly, was always deathly quiet, with three people in separate rooms reading books. When she gave me a copy of her edition of her father's poems, *The Palm at the End of the Mind*, I think I was flattered that she inscribed it "From one to another."

The duties of the new position of associate provost were not formally defined, and it was left that I would gradually find my own clientele and range of jobs in the course of doing what needed to be done. Some of what was needed, though not wanted, found me right away. The telephone jangled, and at the other end was a distraught faculty member, an old friend:

"Alvin, you've got to help me, at once."

"I'm busy right now. Can it wait until tomorrow?"

"No, no, no, right now."

"OK, let me try. What's the problem?"

"I was coming out of the Co-op with a bag full of books, when a cop stopped me and accused me of stealing them."

"Did you?"

"What difference does that make?"

"What did you do?"

"I ran, but he knew me and ran after me down Broadway shouting, 'Stop, Professor ——!' "

"Well, the Co-op doesn't usually pursue those matters if you call up and explain that there was some kind of a mistake, that you forgot to go through the checkout, and that you will be glad to pay."

"No, no, you don't understand. The manager is mad and says he is tired of the faculty and students ripping him off, and he is going to make an example of a professor, and take me to court. I'll be ruined."

"Well, call Milton DeVane [the professor's lawyer] and I will call the manager and see what can be done."

I hung up and got the manager on the phone, and he was indeed irate. He was fed up with the petty theft that was becoming common, he said, and he was particularly tired of faculty members who ought to be models for the undergraduates making a joke of the whole business of thieving. Well, he was going to open it all up in court, and maybe it would have some effect if he could publicly shame this professor, or get him a fine, possibly even some jail time.

The thing needed time to allow the manager to cool down and for some people whose views he valued to speak to him, so I suggested that he not file his complaint at once, which he was threatening to do, but give it an hour. There were big problems in this for both the Co-op and the university, I said. By now he had already cooled a bit and saw the point, and he agreed to wait an hour. I instantly telephoned a number of administrators and faculty members who were on the Co-op's board—Yale was also his landlord—and they agreed to call the manager and tell him that scandal was not going to do anyone any good, except the media, and that perhaps it would be better to settle for an admission of guilt, an apology, and payment, all by letter.

He did, and declared himself satisfied if the professor never entered his store again. But I was not. I felt bad about the cover-up, which was the old way of doing business, and even now I cannot bring myself to mention the name of the professor, though he has himself for years told the story as a great joke. The times were changing, though not in the way one might have hoped. A few years later the world roared with laughter and paid off with big sales when Jerry Rubin published a book with the title *Steal This Book*.

Life in administration was endlessly interesting for someone new to it, and it was also very busy. Being in effect the secretary of the budget committee took up four to six weeks every spring, when the budget committee—provost, dean of the graduate school, dean of Yale College, the comptroller, the computer center director, and myself—went line by line over every budget in the university: not only arts and sciences but all the professional schools, plus the library, athletics, and on and on. During my time the budgets were first computerized and, rather than the old typed sheets with lots of hand corrections, we got floods of blue and white computer paper. When changes were made by the committee, clean copies could be printed up by the next day, which was a great help in keeping things straight; but in the long run computers complicated the budget process rather than simplifying it, which is the usual way of computers. Whether it resulted in better administration, I cannot say.

University governance was still quite autocratic at that time. Chairmen and faculty members might argue, or even threaten to quit, but they accepted with very little question the authority of the university administration to make the final decisions on matters of the utmost importance. The leave policy for faculty was in disarray, and it was given to me to straighten out. I worked for a week or so putting together a generous and logical leave plan, which the provost and the deans approved. Then it was simply printed up and sent out as official policy. There were no complaints. The faculty handbook needed revision, and, presciently, I persuaded Bart Giamatti, then an associate professor on leave, to rewrite it, remove contradictions, and bring it into line with the policy changes made one by one over the past few years. He did so and a copy was sent to every faculty member. There was not a single audible murmur at that time, but only a few years later you would have closed the university by trying to operate in this way. The old trust in authority, and perhaps the old fear of it, as well, disappeared somewhere in the late sixties, as the relationship of administration to faculty, students, and staff changed from one of legitimate authority to one of management.

In 1966 Brewster decided that it was time to admit women to Yale College, in part because it seemed only fair, in part because young men wanted to go to school with the other sex, and in part because it made economic sense. For example, women tended to take more courses in the humanities than in the sciences, and since there were empty seats in humanities classrooms, though not in the expensive science labs, a number of women could be admitted without increasing the size of the faculty, the teaching plant, or the budget. But new dormitories and other facilities would be required. Yale lacked funds to build these new facilities and looked around for a way of doing it on the cheap. McGeorge Bundy is said to be the "third party" (unnamed in official accounts of what transpired) who suggested a merger with Vassar College, but Mary Louise Brewster was a loyal graduate of the prestigious women's college, and there had always been a close relationship between it and Yale. So why not, thought Kingman after a few drinks, go ahead and approach Vassar with a proposal that it leave Poughkeepsie and move its students, faculty, and, most certainly, its rich endowment down to New Haven? Ordinarily an idea like this would have died with the rising of the sun, but such was Kingman's optimism, persuasive power, and charm that he was able to get his trustees at least to listen to the idea. He opened talks with the Vassar president, Alan Simpson, and set up an office run by Eve Katz in the basement of Woodbridge Hall to coordinate planning for the merger.

Practical questions soon cooled the first flush of enthusiasm. Where would the Vassar students go in our already overcrowded dormitories? Would the Vassar faculty, solid but only modestly distinguished, be absorbed into the Yale departments, or kept separate, like the faculties of Barnard and Columbia? How would the Yale alumni respond, and how would the fashionable young women at Vassar—probably the most social of the women's colleges, in ways described in Mary McCarthy's popular novel *The Group* (1963)—feel about leaving the daisy chains and maypoles of their rural campus behind? The project seemed doomed, and how glad I was to be out of it, when a call came from Woodbridge Hall asking me if I would be willing to take on responsibility for dealing with the Vassar faculty, and at the same time to open with some Yale departments the question of how faculty issues would be handled. I could not say no, though I longed to, and thus began many long trips to Poughkeepsie to meet with the faculty of different departments and tell them about the pleasures of life in New Haven.

The assumption in Woodbridge Hall was that everyone connected with Vassar really wanted to become members of the world-famous Yale University. I knew that this was by no means the case, and I soon discovered that the Vassar faculty had well-founded concerns about what would happen to them in New Haven. They were very frank about it, much franker than I could be, and I spent long afternoons in ornate, overheated college lounges trying to answer their questions honestly but in a way that would not torpedo the merger:

> "Does the Yale faculty really want the Vassar faculty to join them?"
>
> "Yes, I think I can frankly say that those I have talked to [a very carefully screened group] are quite enthusiastic about the possibility. You have built a strong

faculty here and it can only strengthen, not weaken, the Yale departments."

"Look, let's be honest, most of our members won't disgrace the Yale departments, but we are more teachers than scholars, and we will seem like pretty drab country cousins. There will be resentment, and we will be left to the side, auxiliaries in most cases. Besides, we like it here, and many of our faculty are women, while the Yale faculty is mostly men. It would be an inhospitable atmosphere."

"There is always that possibility, of course, but the opportunities would seem to far outweigh the risks. Wouldn't many of you enjoy the challenge of these new arrangements and participation in the activities of a large research university with excellent students, a major library and labs, graduate students, better leave policies and salaries? Or what about the alternative? Move to New Haven but keep Vassar separate from Yale, except for allowing all our students to cross-register for courses?"

"No, that would be even worse for us. Our students would flock to the Yale courses, and few would come our way in return. Alongside the Yale faculty we would always look less attractive. Here, we are the only faculty and ours are the only course offerings. There really doesn't seem to be anything for us in the move except trouble."

"Well, let's look at what the change would mean, department by department, and see how each member would fit in, what skills would be duplicated, and which unique . . ."

And in this way the long, sweaty afternoons dragged on.

Things went not much better in New Haven, where Brewster was trying to deal with a faculty dragging its feet, a doubtful set of trustees, and a number of other big problems, like space. Simpson, anxious to be reassured about where he would be located if he were to move, came down one day from Poughkeepsie with his blue-ribbon committee to look at the real estate situation. Kingman really didn't have the faintest idea where the large amount of space that would be needed could be found, and there was not a dollar for new construction. It was such a painful subject that he preferred not to worry about it, but when Simpson, a sensible and helpful man, arrived he gave him a good lunch with quite a lot of wine and then a tour around campus showing him this building and that as if all were available. By the time a very large group of Vassar and Yale worthies came to the Yale Divinity School, a Georgian brick quadrangle with large interior courts up on Science Hill on Prospect Street, Kingman had decided that this was just the place, and in his booming good-natured way he led the group through the courtyard—brushing off the divinity dean, Colin Campbell, who came out, quite naturally, to see what was going on—pointing out one feature after another that would be just right for Vassar. This was all news to the divinity school, and windows all over the quad popped open and the heads of grizzled theologians hung out trying to hear what was being planned for them. It wouldn't have worked anyway: there wasn't enough room, even if Yale's original mission of preparing pastors to tend their flocks had been abandoned. It was a wonderful example of Kingman's shoot-from-the-hip style, and the remarkable thing is how few held it against him, and how often it worked. But not in this case.

Simpson was for the merger, but his view could not prevail against the faculty and the trustees who knew and liked Matthew Vassar's and the Smith Brothers' old Poughkeepsie. They voted the merger down resoundingly, though Vassar went on to transform itself into a college that admitted men as well as women, and in the process lost the mystique of high society and the strange accent that had been its distinctive mark. Perhaps it was inevitable anyway, since the women who once had gone to Vassar would increasingly go to the Ivy League men's colleges, showing that they too preferred to be where the other sex was.

Back at Yale, Brewster had the trustees if not persuaded at least willing to hold still for the admission of women. When the Vassar adventure failed he decided simply to go ahead, reassuring the Old Blues that the same number of men would be admitted as in the past, plus whatever women could be fitted in. There was no new money, no new building, just some expansion of space where possible, a few bathrooms for women, often still complete with urinals, crowding everywhere. Kingman's view was that if he simply did it, the money would follow, and in time the needed buildings would be built. The important thing was to do it, and he did, in 1969, but living conditions were rough for a time and the arrangements for women caused a lot of complaints, as I heard from my daughter Kate, who was a member of the class of 1974, the second to include women.

Some of the old ways of doing business hung on, of course, though they felt less and less comfortable. A secretary complained that the mail she had to open for a very distinguished professor contained explicit pornographic pictures. It would have been possible to ignore the complaint on the grounds of the professor's privacy (for the days of "harassment" had not yet arrived), but the employee surely deserved protection too, and I agreed to have a look to see how serious the matter was. After the offices had closed one day the secretary took me to the professor's office and removed from the files some very old-fashioned pornographic pictures of sailors in white jumpers, black shoes and socks, but no pants, rumps raised in the air, boyish faces turned morosely toward the camera. As I looked at the pictures, trying to keep them away from the secretary, she kept reassuring me, "Don't worry about me, I have brothers." Charlie Taylor and I talked it over and decided that it just wasn't serious enough to get into a very messy fight with a professor, and that it could be handled another way. I talked to the secretary and suggested that she not open any plain manila envelopes but send them in to the professor unopened, with the rest of the mail, without saying anything. This seemed to satisfy her, and nothing more was heard about it. In a few more years this kind of thing would be a civil rights case, and Yale would have been sued for not protecting the secretary and for interfering with the First Amendment privileges of the professor. I cannot help feeling that the old way of handling these things, though not ideologically pure, may have caused less pain for all.

I managed well enough as an administrator, and I like to think that I genuinely helped to run the university more fairly and more efficiently, but wanting more time for scholarship I opted to go back to full-time teaching after three years in the provost's office. The National Endowment for the Humanities provided me a grant for a year's leave in 1968–1969, which was fleshed out to full salary by Yale. I retired to a new office high in the tower of Sheffield-Sterling-Strathcona Hall to complete a contract I had with the English publisher Methuen for a history of the English theater between 1576, when the first professional theater in England was built, and 1613, the year Shakespeare retired from the stage. This volume was part of a series on the English theater edited by my old friend Clifford Leech at Toronto, and there were three other writers involved in my volume. I wrote my part during the year of leave, but the other writers were very slow. Mac Hosley in Arizona, who was doing the section on the stage, simply could not resolve to his satisfaction such questions as whether there had been an inner stage and what size the platform stage had been. These are unanswerable questions, it would seem, at least on the basis of the existing evidence, but Mac could not let go, and the whole project dragged until 1975, when my threats to pull out finally forced the publishers to go to press. When the book at last came out, the most favorable review of my section contended that it was the full flowering of New Critical criticism but that, unfortunately, the New Criticism was stone dead.

The advance on the book paid, however, for a trip to London, Rome, and Athens, for a week in each place in high style, for Sue and me, without the children. It was our first trip back to Europe since 1951, nearly twenty years, and we enjoyed theater, opera, museums, good hotels, and travel. Greece was the greatest experience: the Parthenon for the first time, early morning at Mycenae looking past the Lion Gate over the plain of Argos, the long walk at Delphi through the temples up the mountain, past the Pierean spring, where we stopped to drink, without becoming poets. Our driver was another Alexander, who like most Greeks felt that all things Greek were the best. On the road up to Delphi he pointed to some seagulls on a nearby dump: "Eagles," he said proudly. When I looked doubtful, he looked again and, determined to preserve the greatness of Greece, added, "Young eagles." Most standard tourist sights disappoint, turning out to be less than the promise of their pictures and descriptions. But at what may have been the very last moment when the sites were not crowded, Greece did not. Only the pyramids, graves, and temples of Egypt compare, in my experience.

When I returned to teaching in the fall of 1969, there was a feel of crisis in the air. The old academic order was obviously disintegrating everywhere, and as part of the change traditional ways of understanding literature seemed to be on their last legs. Lionel Trilling offered an explanation of what was happening and our responsibility for it in his book *Beyond Culture* (1965), and particularly in his essay "The Teaching of Modern Literature." He talked in this article about the great modern works that he and others had introduced into the curriculum of literature, Sir James Frazer's *Golden Bough*, Thomas Mann's *Death in Venice*, Nietzsche's *Birth of Tragedy*, Conrad's *Heart of Darkness*, Freud's *Civilization and Its Discontents*, Kafka's *Metamorphosis*. These are books, said Trilling, that "ask every question that is forbidden in polite society," and they were the books that all of us taught to our students in the fifties and sixties to get them to look critically at such standard optimistic ideas as progress and rationality, which they took for granted. Trilling was chagrined to learn, however, that students, instead of developing a healthy skepticism about our rationalist society, simply absorbed from these works a "bitter line of hostility to civilization," bought it without question, and accepted it as the new orthodoxy. "Don't trust anyone over thirty," baaed many of our students, ready to believe without question all that the books we introduced them to had taught about the ills of modern society.

Trilling's public acknowledgment of the failure to teach an Arnoldian view of literature—"the best that has been thought and said," the spirit of an informed criticism—was a shocking event. At that time Trilling was not only our most famous literary critic, he had in books like *The Liberal Imagination* (1950) established for literature a place of importance in education and in personal life. For him to despair of the entire project, to publicly declare it a failure, was catastrophic to many of us. In Dublin, Denis Donoghue, the leader of the academic critics there, called a meeting of all interested parties to discuss the implications of "The Teaching of Modern Literature" when it first appeared. But now the students we had taught to read these books were about to give us a lesson in what we had taught them.

9

When Do We Want It? Now!

The sixties were different from the fifties, more permissive, unstructured, increasingly subjective. A time with higher expectations of life, for which J. K. Galbraith might have coined the term "the age of affluence," had arrived to replace a generation raised in economic depression, disciplined by war, trained to submit to the given. Eager to right old wrongs and be done with old ways, students now were children of prosperity who were increasingly bored, narcissistic, and looking for scenarios in which to try out new identities and find new careers.

There were many on hand to feed these interests. "The times they are a-changin'," we heard, and there were prophets in the land with new lessons about drugs, revolution, power, and the irrational. There was a new music, too, with a fundamental, relentless beat and an overwhelming assault of sound that with electronic amplification blasted the ear and, reinforced by flashing strobe lights, obliterated Apollonian order in Dionysiac energy. Norman Mailer, the apostle of hip, in "The White Negro," told the young that normal middle-class life in America exploited them just as it did the blacks who were marching on Selma. Speaking for feminists and others who were done at last with the old repressive order, Germaine Greer announced that "the group fuck is the highest ritual expression of our faith."

Life Against Death: The Psychoanalytical Meaning of History, Norman O. Brown's book published in 1959, was enormously popular with students in the sixties. It summarized the project of thousands of other gurus in the years to come:

> For two thousand years or more man has been subjected to a systematic effort to transform him into an ascetic animal. He remains a pleasure-seeking animal. Parental discipline, religious denunciation of bodily pleasure, and philosophic exaltation of the life of reason have all left man overtly docile, but secretly in his unconscious unconvinced, and therefore neurotic. Man remains unconvinced because in infancy he tasted the fruit of the tree of life, and knows that it is good, and never forgets.

For Brown even sex itself as normally practiced was a form of repression, an officially sanctioned version of a much more general carnal desire, an attempt to channel too narrowly the broad delight in all kinds of erotic play that characterizes the free activity of desire in childhood. By way of one form of play, Brown privileged anality—homosexuality's beginning move out of the closet?—and at the center of his book is an anal-erotic interpretation of Jonathan Swift, the eighteenth-century satirist and divine. The good dean's coprophobia is reversed to read co-prophilia, and his famous poem "Cassinus and Peter," which ends with a "college soph" reacting in horror when he at last is forced to say that his beloved, "Celia, Celia, Celia, shits," is interpreted not as Swift's attack on the hypocrisy of mankind in concealing its basic animal functions—the standard reading of the poem—but as an advocacy of anal aesthetics and fecal revelry.

Timothy Leary, a former associate of Milgram and an experimental psychologist at Berkeley and at Harvard for a time, was also telling the young that conventional life and learning were dull behavioral patterns imposed by their elders to control them. Running a community of the turned-on in a mansion in Millbrook in the Hudson Valley, Leary was the guru of the drug movement, recommending to the young in books like *The Politics of Ecstasy* (1968) that they "turn on and drop out" of rat races like family and education. Many of our students followed the Pied Piper of Millbrook into the wild world—sometimes terrifying, sometimes reassuring—of kaleidoscopic imagery released by LSD, and the serenity of pot. These drugs for many called into doubt forever the authority of a world based on normative daylight sensory experience and the cautious structures of standard rationality. It was not only that the inner scenes opened up by drugs were so much more exciting than drab quotidian reality, it was that they were so powerful as to appear as revelations of further reality on which new societies could be built, new moralities come into being, new and more pleasing personalities take shape.

In some ways this was all the familiar bohemia of earlier times, the subculture of opposition that seems to be a permanent feature of modern, democratic, permissive, capitalist society. But now, hyped with drugs and amplified with sound, faces and voices spread everywhere by TV, bohemia went militant, attacking middle-class mores and undermining rationality by recommending extraordinary states of consciousness to the young. These revolts probably would not have come to much had not the civil rights movement in the South and the Vietnam War authenticated the distrust of authority at all levels and supported the radical position that a revolution was necessary to change things.

What began as ideas soon became actions unlike anything seen before on college campuses. Buildings occupied at Columbia. Shotguns at Berkeley, the National Guard at Kent State, rifles at Cornell. Students stoned not on alcohol but on LSD. The four-letter words of the free speech movement blasting from the loudspeakers in Sproul Plaza and then spreading into conversation everywhere. The daily marches of protest at the administrative buildings for some cause or other—

"Hey, hey, ho, ho, somebody's got to go." "What do we want? Everything." The sexual revolution found the campus fertile ground for free sex, and loves that had earlier not been able to whisper, let alone speak their names burst out of the closet shouting defiance to a world that had long suppressed them.

Change was everywhere. Hair became a symbol of a new freedom, clothing became costume and statement. It is difficult now when so much of this has become part of the campus "lifestyle," a term that seems to have replaced the older "character," to realize how overwhelming it was when it was new. I suppose that I found much of what was happening hard to accept because of the rigid authority that had been imposed on me in the wartime navy when I was the same age as the rebellious students. It wasn't, I think, that I envied them their freedom so much as that I had accepted the concept of a more or less unquestioned and unquestionable authority as the most reasonable way of running any institution. There is a story of an old man out in the English countryside who dropped dead when he heard that King Charles I had been executed in 1649, and my shock was similar when I saw an unbearded child protesting the draft wearing the green coat of a marine gunnery sergeant, complete with twenty years' worth of hashmarks and expert rifleman and pistol badges, over a white silk shirt with French cuffs! Everything familiar was mocked, everything that had been anathema was praised, and the students began to teach us many things we had not known about the freedom that we had always more or less assumed we were exercising to its fullest.

Many Americans viewing the marches and the costumes on the nightly news found it all titillating, but it was a direct challenge to the rational principles on which Western society was built, and university administrators like myself suddenly found ourselves in the front line of a great culture war, defending against assaults of the irrational. With its tradition going back to the training of Congregationalist ministers, a Yale education had always been a moral education, designed to produce, in purpose if not always in practice, a reflective individual, inward, thoughtful, controlled, and isolated, a living version of a Cartesian *cogito ergo sum* or David Riesman's "inner-directed man." Most of the faculty and administration still identified with this ethos, and probably most of our students still did also, but we had lost our ability to defend it against a group of militant students in possession of a deeply known, unquestioned, gnostic truth: that all power is corrupt and all those who exercise it are to be smitten hip and thigh by the zeal of the righteous.

Slightly veiled threats increasingly became a way of doing business, and a rough style of bargaining, which we did not deal with very effectively, involving a good deal of confrontation became standard negotiating procedure. The regular defense of faculty and administration was to treat outrageous events as if nothing had happened, showing the vandals that "they are not getting to us." We thought if we preserved our cool all of this would somehow go away. "Brewster, you're full of shit," someone shouted at the president in a meeting. Most of us pretended not to hear, though the chaplain, Bill Coffin, remarked afterward, "It's good for Kingman to hear what people really think." But things soon got a lot rougher than a few rude words.

The dean of the school of art and architecture, a political hotbed, was an old crony of Kingman's, his clown-prince, really, with absolutely no knowledge of art, architecture, or universities. He paid no attention to business, and Joe Lieberman, who would later become a U.S. senator from Connecticut, was put in the office to make sure that someone answered the phone. When he did, it was usually to tell callers the number of the provost's office. The A and A building was the modernist design of Paul Rudolph, all harsh cement slabs with broken corrugations, bleak expanses of glass, and to the Chapel Street side a rising column penetrated with holes of various sizes and configurations. Rudolph had designed the building while he was dean of the architecture school, and he once told me that the holes represented the sphincters of various close friends. That was modernist architecture, affront and snigger, and the students hated it, not only because it was uncomfortable and inefficient to work in, but because it was a depressing architectural environment, so they tried to burn it down. Just who did it was never established, but that it was arson there was no question: the smell of gasoline hung over the place for days.

Twenty-eight years later, when Rudolph died, the New York Times reported that the Yale art and architecture building had been burned in 1969 by students who thought that its "severe concrete design [was] a symbol of the university's antipathy toward creative life." There had never been any doubt that some unknown students had set the fire, but the charge of arson brought Vincent Scully, who had long denounced the coldness and inhumanity of modern architecture, out of an unwanted retirement to charge in a letter to the editors that there was no proof that the fire had been arson, and, somewhat unnecessarily it would seem, that students were not the only ones with access to the building, and that "those of us who have been associated with Yale students for many years regard them as incapable of such an action and unfounded declarations of their guilt as unpardonable slanders" (*New York Times*, August 12, 1997). The new liberalism is as alive and angry as ever, and as willing to deny plain facts; but the grim building still broods over the art section of the campus.

A particularly nasty confrontation occurred soon after the fire when a group of Latino art students imported some toughs from the Bronx to frighten the administration into giving them special treatment. A meeting was reluctantly agreed to, and Charlie Taylor lectured the group on how universities worked: reasoned arguments, planning, consultation, maintenance of good manners, the beneficent desire of the university to treat all its members fairly. The imports from the Bronx found this kind of talk ludicrous and made their feelings clear with many profanities. Charlie stiffened, and the scene turned ugly, with very real threats to hold him out the window and drop him in the courtyard below (no campus police had been brought to the meeting, "lest their presence be provocative"). A student photographer, a young man named Nick Doob, had been given permission to film the meeting, and for his own reasons Doob later made the film public, and the audience roared with laughter at the sight of the uptight WASP provost and shouted "right on" to the obscenities of the laid-back Latinos. I recount this painful story only to suggest how little at this time the university could count on some of its own to share in the defense of its traditional values.

The administration might have seemed to have had all the cards—certainly we had control of most of the money, and nominal authority in all other places—but the power was difficult to exercise. We could call out the campus police, or even the town police, though these still disliked Yale, and in a pinch even the National Guard. But the times were tricky. Above all else, the daily consideration was the real fear that the mass of neutral students would turn openly against the university. Every move we made to defend ourselves was said to be "provocative."

Conservatives later said that administrators everywhere simply lost their nerve in the late 1960s and gave the store away. But in fact we restrained ourselves, and held our tongues, with a great deal of effort — I remember always trying hard to keep quiet and not act, for fear of appearing "provocative," while being lectured by a group of very boring, ignorant, ill-willed, and long-winded people. Nor had we lost faith by any means that the universities were positive forces in American life and worth great effort to save. Indeed, one of the things that made the attacks on the universities in the late sixties and early seventies so maddeningly difficult to accept was that it seemed to the old guard that they had always been reasonable critics of establishment views, advocates of good sense and the search for real truth, and above all democratic in making it possible, despite snobbish vestiges in the institution, for bright and ambitious young people to make their way up in the world through education. We ourselves deplored the Vietnam War, lived in a frugal manner, treated other people fairly, were, in short, on the side of the angels. To identify us as another repressive authority figure woven deep into the structures of corrupt American politics and a greedy, imperialistic capitalism seemed grossly unfair.

We may have been right, indeed probably were. What we failed to realize was that it made no difference. History had overtaken us, and a new myth of the university, phrased most polemically in the work of Herbert Marcuse (1898–1979), was challenging our traditional view of things. Marcuse was a German Marxist from the Frankfurt Institute for Social Research who escaped the Nazi persecution in 1934, taught at Columbia for a time, then at Brandeis, and by the late 1960s was teaching at the center of student ferment, in California. No odder mixture than this old European Marxist ideologue and the golden, narcissistic, ten-hanging youth of southern California could be imagined, but the man and the moment were oddly made for each other. In a series of books and essays, *Eros and Civilization* (1955), *One-Dimensional Man* (1964), and *An Essay on Liberation* (1969), all very popular, and even occasionally read on campus, Marcuse mixed a heady brew of Freudian psychology, Marxist political economy, and green environmentalism to incite his readers to revolution that would lead to a utopian "human universe without exploitation and toil."

The enemy was the same one the Marxists had always targeted, a bourgeois capitalist system that exploited its workers, repressed the authentic, decent instincts of its citizens, and made imperialistic war against the poor and helpless everywhere in the world to provide markets for its goods. But Marcuse's enemy no longer operated in the crude fashion of Marx's time of primitive accumulation, when workers were starved in order to provide capital for growth. In the "affluent society" a power elite of politicians, professors, financiers, and generals had corrupted the people by producing a cornucopia of "commodities of satisfaction" that perverted the authentic instincts of life by encouraging greed, consumerism, competitiveness, and an inability to distinguish the shoddy from the well-made. No work of Marcuse's had more effect than the 1965 essay "Repressive Tolerance," in which he argued that the openness and toleration of American democratic society was in fact a masquerade for a fiendishly clever form of tyranny.

The proletariat in the Western industrial countries, Marcuse declared, had been so corrupted by high wages and decent working conditions—chickens in the pot and cars in the garage—that it no longer constituted an effective revolutionary force. Instead, the torch of revolt had passed into the hands of the disaffected young, particularly students, who were fed up with the old lies, the ancient repressions, the shoddy goods, the limits on pleasure and happiness. Their revolution was to be social and psychological, an attack on industrial pollution and a cleansing of the corrupted capitalistic consciousness.

Marcuse proclaimed a "Great Refusal," which he said was now taking place in the free speech movement at Berkeley, the student riots in Paris in May 1968—l'imagination au pouvoir—in Vietnam, Cuba, and Nicaragua, and everywhere on campuses across America. He identified every social tremor—miniskirts, rock 'n' roll, drugs, long hair, obscene language, minimalist art, draft card burning, graffiti—as one of the long-awaited signs of the revolution that the industrial working class had always failed to deliver. Instead of being, as they sometimes were called, noisy troublemakers, narcissists, the now generation, and draft dodgers, Marcuse offered students the roles of a new intelligentsia, the vanguard of the Great Refusal and the New Left. Rather than the self-sacrifice that earlier revolutions had required, the instincts would now revolt, sex would escape from exploitative pornography and commodity gratification to achieve a deep and satisfying, truly human eroticism, a triumph of the body, not the will. An instinctual barrier would rise against cruelty, brutality, and ugliness, safeguarding the release of the human, the tender, and the sensuous. Even the automobiles, the color TV sets, the clothes, the drugs, could be kept, for Marcuse's Marxism had made its peace with the machine and industrialism. Only by continuing to use technology and science could humanity reach that utopian state in which man escapes from the necessity of want and work. The ethos of the old meritocratic and scientific university—low pay, relentless hard work, long hours, a grinding competition for grades and tenure, and the gut-tearing business of pursuing an elusive truth could not compare to Marcuse's bright permissive vision, in which you could do what you wanted and be a hero of the revolution by doing it.

Charlie Taylor was on leave in the spring of 1970, going to Switzerland to study at the Jung Institute. He eventually became one of the leading Jungian analysts—a strange reversal, I always thought, for this most rational of men. I had agreed to be the acting provost from January to July in that fateful year. It was decided that Brewster would deal with the public problems that were building rapidly, while the provost would try to keep the normal academic business of the university running. I soon found myself involved in such matters as an urgent request for two new, very costly computers that had not been budgeted. I knew very little of computers at the time and struggled with the question of whether we really needed a machine for the new department of computer science and a big new number cruncher for the treasurer's office. In the end I compromised, of course, and found the money for the academic machine but told the treasurer he would have to come up with his own funds. It may well be, though I had no idea of it at the time, that the most important thing I did in the way of ordinary business as provost was to hire Paul de Man, with the far-reaching consequences that I will relate in the next chapter.

But more serious problems were coming. Some universities—Berkeley, Harvard, Cornell, and Columbia, among others—were living in a state of near siege throughout the late sixties, though so far at Yale there had been mostly just talk. But in the spring of 1970 the New Left found its cause on the New Haven Green, just outside Yale's Old Campus with its nineteenth-century Gothic dorms enclosing the original college building, Connecticut Hall, and its statue of Nathan Hale regretting that he had but one life to give for his country. In the Connecticut state courthouse on the north side of the green, Bobby Seale, the gangster drug lord and leader of the Black Panther Party, was being tried for the torture and murder of one of his local followers who had been suspected of being a police informant. The state charged that the man had been killed and his body dumped in a wood north of the city on Seale's order. The defense simply denied these accusations, said that Seale knew nothing of the murder, and contended that the whole business was contrived by the government to discredit and jail a man it considered a dangerous agitator.

The trial was a lightning rod for the many disaffected people, including Yale faculty and students, who by now suspected all forms of authority. A very weird cast of characters began to assemble in New Haven. Jean Genet, the French homosexual novelist, struggled with the police; William Kunstler, an old friend of Brewster's and a graduate of the Yale Law School, arrived to give a speech counseling Yale to surrender to avoid violence; Jerry Rubin urged the students to revolutionary action and Abbie Hoffman pushed his book; Big Man, editor of the Black Panther newspaper, breathed fire; and other local and visiting radicals demanded that the Bulldog and the Panther lie down together. By this they meant closing down the university, providing $500,000 for legal defense funds, and intervening with the state to free Seale. If these demands were not met it was suggested at various meetings that one student a day commit suicide until they were, that Brewster be kidnapped, that the library's copies of the Gutenberg Bible be sold, that the New Haven water supply be turned off, that rifles be stacked on the green, that the students "pick up a gun" to show their manhood.

Today it all sounds so crazy that most will not believe it, but people were out of their heads. As for us, what would you think if you were to hear for the first time someone like Tom Dostou, surrounded by his six-man bodyguard, speaking in a Yale hall, making threats like this: "I don't think any pickets or strikes will work. The pigs [police] are ready to kill. We've got to say that Yale will be electrocuted if Bobby Seale is brought to trial." Doug Miranda charged that "Yale is one of the biggest pig organizations. . . . We're going to turn Yale into a police state. . . . Fifteen Yalies have dropped out of Yale to join the Panther Defense Committee so far. Fifteen of the thousand leaders of tomorrow who have become revolutionaries, who will pick up a gun and walk into Brewster's office and say, 'Get out of the city.' " How could we know that it was only political noise?—certainly people seemed willing to say and perhaps do anything. So the university temporized. It provided halls for the radical groups to speak in, it paid for offices and telephones for them, it attended every meeting to which it was summoned, and it tried earnestly to answer the silly charges that were leveled at it, as if it half accepted the guilt that was being heaped on it. Above all it avoided "provocation," which is to say any strong defense.

Yale University may have been tagged by the radicals as an elitist, educational arm of a tyrannous and murderous state, but physically and psychologically it was in reality almost defenseless. Its physical plant sprawled across the city and was almost unguarded. Its long commitment to discussing all sides of an issue made it difficult if not impossible to lock its gates or turn off the endless inflammatory discussions that were held with the intent, as it was often put, to "shut the motherfucker down." New Haven, a blue-collar manufacturing city, had a long-standing grudge against Yale, an institution that paid no taxes, and the city police, especially after the St. Patrick's Day parade riot, were not much interested in our troubles. Our own campus police force was small and constrained by the policy of avoiding provocation.

As the excitement mounted, things began to get meaner. Letter writers threatened to kill the president and kidnap his children. Student strikers threw pickets across the entrances to classrooms and roughed up students trying to cross the lines. A Yale-owned store on Chapel Street was "liberated" by the Task Force for Social Justice in the Arts, and for once Yale fought back, filling the store during the night with the university's total inventory of toilet paper, in this way getting people out of the building who were not much interested in moving several truckloads of toilet paper. The climax was to be a big May Day meeting on the green, drawing people from all over the Northeast to protest the Seale trial.

Most of the community saw no great problem in anything that happened ("There is much to be said on both sides," many felt), and some thought that even arson and bombs were justified ("The wrongs have been great"). They crowded for entertainment into fiery meetings to cheer radical blacks, angry faculty, outside militants, and outraged students advocating nothing less than revolution and anarchy, beginning with the closing down of the university. Jerry Rubin, smelling excitement and opportunity, lectured the students about a heroic young man who had stabbed his tyrannical father with a butcher knife, drawing the conclusion that this was the only way of getting rid of patriarchy and repression. The audience laughed and cheered, with some jeering no doubt, but without any sense that there was danger in all this, or that even if it was all a joke it was the kind of bad, dangerous joke that should not be tolerated. The estimation of the situation as entertainment was not entirely wrong, for the revolution of the sixties and the seventies, particularly in the universities, where it mostly took place, was at least as much showbiz and hype as it was a serious attempt to overthrow the established order. But the carnival quality made it little less dangerous, and I found myself often thinking of Nathanael West's novel The Day of the Locust, which ends in apocalypse caused by a mob of citizens in Los Angeles—"the people who had come to California to die"—simply out looking for a little excitement.

But the administration, myself included, charged with responsibility for the university, took the whole business as we had to, with deadly seriousness. No American university had any experience with challenges of this kind, and it was not improbable to imagine buildings burned out and the university closed down, with all the attendant confusion. It was even easier and more probable to consider that we might well lose control of the university for a time, and that some kind of self-appointed "committee of public safety," using the more radical "guests" as enforcers, would take over and have to be removed forcibly.

Racism was a big issue in all the events of the spring of 1970, almost as big as Vietnam, and the two causes had been joined in the minds of many as related instances of the racist tyranny of America's rulers. It was critical for the Yale administration to have the support of its few black faculty members and students if it was to keep control of the campus. No group played its cards more carefully in this situation than the African-American group that wanted some very practical things: more tenure slots for black faculty and more money for African-American projects. A deputation of black students asking half a million dollars for the "communications arm" of their action group visited me soon after I moved behind the provost's desk. The amount was ludicrous, and intentionally so, but the negotiations had to take place with solemn faces, and I had to hear once more about reparations and the shame of Yale's long racist history.

All the black groups in the university sensed that this was their moment. To precipitate a crisis, it would have been necessary only for leaders like the philosopher Ken Mills, a man from Trinidad with a high Afro haircut that, to his annoyance, always leaned to the right, to present outrageous demands, and then when they were rejected to tell their followers to go on strike or take some other strong action. The undergraduates, so sacred had blackness become, would have followed instantly. Instead, the blacks chose to bargain, and early in the spring Brewster and I attended a meeting of the black faculty members to hear and respond to their demands that more blacks be hired, and that those already on the faculty be paid more and promoted more rapidly. It will seem incredible now, but I actually was so innocent that I gave them a little lecture on how the university was always changing, with one group after another coming to power. Their turn would soon come, I assured them, if they worked hard and became the great scholars and teachers the university existed to nurture. Their expressions ranged from amused to baleful. To my chagrin, Kingman, whose family had been one of those in possession of the university since its founding, and who didn't much care for the idea of ownership shifting about, asked me in a genuinely curious way as we were leaving, "Just what did you hope to accomplish by saying that?"

In my view none of the blacks trusted us or had any interest in identifying with the old Yale. But we controlled the money, the appointments, the prestige, and with enormous practicality they saw that Yale would be in place, and still rich, long after the Black Panthers and Stokely Carmichael were gone. There were genuine revolutionaries in the black group, but even they wanted to do business. Business did not mean endorsing the Yale administration or in any way taking sides against Bobby Seale; it meant neutrality, and the bargain was struck in a huge meeting of the faculty of arts and sciences—the faculty that really counted politically at Yale—late in April, with the May Day crisis fast approaching.

In order to accommodate the very large number of faculty members expected to attend, we met not in the usual faculty room in Connecticut Hall but in the more spacious Sprague Hall at the music school. Students gathered in large numbers in the street outside to cheer and boo the people going in to the meeting. Their roars to my fearful ears sounded like 1789, though they were in fact in a good mood, and not particularly radical that day.

The black faculty members entered late, as a group, and though it was obvious that a number of people who did not belong to the faculty were among them, no one thought that it would be helpful to raise a challenge. They filed in purposefully, and with solemn faces occupied a row of seats, well forward, that one of their members had saved for them. There were some very angry conservative faculty members present that day, like Jack Finkelstein, professor of ancient Near Eastern languages, who had left Berkeley after the troubles there and was here to warn against a similar capitulation. After Jack and others had had their say about the absolute necessity of holding the line, the black faculty presented their printed demands, nonnegotiable, in the fashion of that time. After reading them, Kingman whispered in a pleased way that there was nothing impossible in all this, and was so excited that he, gouty foot and all, actually leaped over a small flight of stairs leading up to the stage to get to the microphone and make a deal.

But all his wonderful energy and genuine goodwill led him into a fatal mistake in an attempt to set the scene for the bargaining. Without premeditation, I think, and I was sitting next to him—although the historian of the moment, John Taft, in *Mayday at Yale* (1976) speaks of a "prepared speech"—he rose and said among other things, "I am skeptical of the ability of black revolutionaries to achieve a fair trial anywhere in the United States." Since there was no real evidence that the trial was a setup, and because it was absolutely critical for everyone, and particularly for Yale, that it be as fair as possible — and furthermore be perceived by all as fair — to call the justice of the state into question was, particularly for a lawyer, which Kingman was, a dreadful misstep. In a news conference some years later, when he was leaving Yale to become the American ambassador to the Court of St. James's, he said that his remarks had been made "privately in a faculty meeting," and that they had been "misinterpreted and that what he had tried to convey was that it would be improper for the university to interfere in the Seale trial." But his audience took another meaning, and gasped, and in that instant the president lost the support of the conservative members of his faculty and many of the rich and powerful alumni, without gaining any support from the radicals, who were convinced that he was indelibly the spokesman for a corrupt establishment. He was never comfortable with either group again, and the remainder of his term was marked by the boredom and alienation of a man no longer at home in his university. When he left for London he was able to joke that his popularity among the rich alumni was so low that his resignation should be worth $100 million for the current fund drive, which was lagging badly in reaching its goal to stanch the budget deficits that had been running at more than a million dollars a year.

Meeting followed meeting during the spring of 1970, and the weekly assemblies of the Yale faculty were regularly scenes of high politics. Party lines were sharply drawn among radicals, liberals, and conservatives, and tempers ran very high. Radicals, including the highly excitable Scully, the great teacher who taught generations of students to look at and care about the buildings around them in their cities, John Hersey, the author of *Hiroshima* and master of Pierson College, and J. P. Trinkaus, known as "Trink," the master of Branford College, wanted the Yale faculty to go on record as condemning the trial of Bobby Seale. On one occasion it was actually proposed that the Yale faculty vote to declare him innocent, some believing, with that awesome sense of self-importance of many academics, that we had the power to do so. My own view, and that of many of my friends, was that the trial, whatever we might think about Seale's innocence or guilt, was the business of the courts and far beyond the competence of a bunch of professors. And if we began to meddle where we were not competent, we would antagonize the state of Connecticut, which granted the charter containing our exemption from taxes, grounded on the assumption that we were a nonpolitical charitable trust, and further enrage the people of New Haven who paid our taxes for us. But the actual vote was delayed only by some fast maneuvering, and in fact it never did take place. Intentions never lasted very long.

Another week the faculty was hunting down other scents. Now the great issue of freedom was whether the faculty should support the "moratorium" on teaching that a strike management committee was demanding. The long-standing requirement that a Yale student take two terms' study of a foreign language was dumped as a restraint on the rights of students to choose freely. Then there was a proposal that grades should be eliminated in Yale College! The grading system had been coming apart for a long time. The threat of being drafted hung over the heads of students in the sixties, but they were protected by educational deferments so long as they remained in "good academic standing." This in turn made the faculty reluctant to give students low grades lest they be drafted and sent to the jungles; and so began the decay that eventually destroyed the old grading system and with it the work ethic it had reinforced. Other colleges had already gone further. Stanford University eliminated D and F grades in 1970. Brown University, "intent on making transcripts reflect only achievement," not failure, began in the late 1960s reporting no grades below C on the transcript, and allowing withdrawals from classes at any time in the semester up to the last gasp. The Yale faculty decided not to eliminate the grading system altogether, as was proposed, because the students would still need grades for entrance to graduate and professional schools, but only to eliminate failure. "Since the grade of 'F' will no longer be recorded on a student's record," one of the professors argued with the kind of logic we heard a lot of in those days, "the faculty will give 'Fs' much more frequently than they now do, and this will be salutary for education."

The students were as muddled as the faculty. A group of fire-eaters broke into the middle of a large class one day and disrupted the lecture.

When hauled up before the discipline committee and asked to explain themselves, they said that they had not intended to disrupt the class, only to make a political statement. "Why, then, didn't you arrive at ten o'clock, at the start of the class, rather than ten-thirty?" "We overslept," said Smithers.

I continued while provost to teach a large lecture course on Shakespeare. A picket line was set up outside the building to prevent anyone from going to class, but some students would sneak in by various ways —a few even climbed the drainpipe and came through the window— to avoid confronting the pickets. Fed up with this kind of dishonesty, the outraged pickets appeared one day in my class, some of them armed with toy machine guns—referred to as "symbolic"—which they fired at everyone—"ack, ack, ack"—to accustom us to the violence that was going to be required to topple the ancien régime. They then tried to take over the microphone in order to conduct a seminar on Bobby Seale and the lack of justice in America. I couldn't just stand there and take it, nor could I quite turn on my heel and walk away—our usual dilemma. So I took a risk and said to the freedom fighters that since we all believed in democracy, why didn't we put it to a vote. They were puzzled but confident, and said OK. I asked for all the students who wanted to hear me lecture on *Hamlet*, the text for that day, to raise their hands. Out of several hundred students, all but one raised a hand. I could not, or would not, resist going on to ask, "How many of you want to hear a discussion of the Seale trial?" One hand alone went into the air. Total victory, savored to this day, and as the freedom fighters stalked out with their toy guns I provocatively shouted after them, "Why don't you stick around today and really learn something about alienation?"

Symbolism provided a mask for aggression more and more frequently. If the administration was "provocative," the students were "symbolic," meaning we couldn't do anything without giving offense while they could do everything without really doing anything. The students gathered daily for inflammatory rhetoric on the plaza of the Beinecke rare book library, built with the donors' profits from S&H Green Stamps, just outside the president's office in Woodbridge Hall. One day they brought a giant piece of junk sculpture by Claes Oldenburg. The base was a black plywood contraption that looked like the chassis of a tank or a self-propelled gun. Rising straight up from the base was a huge, upright lipstick with an inflated red plastic tip that made it look as much like an erect penis as it did a lipstick. But the tip deflated from time to time, and when it went limp it was entirely the wrong symbolism for revolution and sex militant. So a hard tip was inserted and from that day on it stood erect in the center of the university as a threat to the establishment. Like all modern junk art, this particular piece of statuary, though not very inflammatory, was considered by its very antitraditional qualities, and its threat of violent liberation, a gage of defiance thrown in the face of rational authority. Authority took it that way — Kingman loathed the damned thing — and for a time we surreptitiously removed it at night, but returned it when accused of provocation. The Lipstick sat there for years, until it was finally removed to one of the college courtyards, where it still sits.

But all was not symbolic. Cans of gasoline were found in the attic of Silliman College. After a speech by Abbie Hoffman in Ezra Stiles College, a crowd marched on the First New Haven National Bank chanting "The streets belong to the people," but they succeeded only in setting a few small fires near the green. Two bombs went off in the entrance of the hockey rink, the building designed by Eero Saarinen and known as Moby Dick for its resemblance to a whale, just after it had been emptied following a big rock concert. Violent attempts were made by some radical students and outside troublemakers to prevent fuel from being delivered to the power plant that supplied the university with electricity.

May Day would be almost a relief, but as it approached many began to feel that we should send the students home, lock up the campus, and enlist as many faculty and staff as possible to patrol the grounds to prevent damage. I took this view to Kingman, who after a long and serious discussion of all the possibilities rejected it on the grounds that it was worth a great deal of risk to show that Yale was strong and confident enough in its traditions of openness to meet any challenge to its central values, while continuing to maintain its educational mission of teaching and research. But it was decided that students would not be required to take final exams that spring, since it had been so difficult to study. Instead they could opt for a grade of pass in all the courses in which they had registered, without any further work, or they could study over the summer and take an exam for a letter grade in the fall.

Brewster was by no means unaware of the real dangers of his chosen strategy, and he took a number of precautions, such as setting up a war room near the green manned by Sam Chauncey and Jonathan Fanton; bringing trustees, notably Cyrus Vance and Bill Scranton, to New Haven to be witnesses and share in the decision making; and asking for a representative of the Justice Department to be on hand in case of trouble. Chauncey asked the New Haven police for help in intelligence gathering, and the chief requested a National Guard presence on May Day, which he himself commanded. It was decided not to request cancellation of the local Soap Box Derby, which was scheduled to roar down Hillhouse Avenue from Science Hill on May Day. Even if one of the cars was booby-trapped—by then this was the way we thought— and went off in front of the president's house, the bomb could not be very big.

The federal government was represented in the person of John Dean, who spent May Day in headquarters in a local building and in a helicopter overhead. When he later wrote about the Seale trial in his 1976 book Blind Ambition, it obviously was not, after what he had been through with Watergate, any very big deal. While in jail for obstruction of justice in the Watergate cover-up, one of the federal marshals wanted to talk to him about the time they had been together in New Haven:

> "You remember me?"
> "Up in Connecticut."
> "The big demonstration at Yale."
> "Oh sure."

"The memory pushed the claustrophobia back a few degrees," Dean went on. "He and I had shot the bull one afternoon back in 1970 when I was covering a pro–Bobby Seale demonstration for the Justice Department. He wanted to reminisce, but I was spent and nauseated."

May Day dawned bright and clear—and anticlimactic. Thousands of people gathered on the green and in the various college courtyards, but all were in a good mood. The National Guard was prominently lined up around the green and in front of the Grove Street Cemetery's neo-Egyptian brownstone wall and gate with a golden bee of eternal life buzzing the promising words, "The Dead Shall Be Raised." There were traces of tear gas in the air now and then, a few bare-breasted women—freeing themselves of the restraint of the patriarchs, some of whom were following them closely around to see that they didn't cause any trouble—and a bearded giant with "FUCK" written in bright red lipstick on his chest, but Armageddon, thankfully, it was not.

We waited nervously in the president's house on Hillhouse Avenue, where once the great elms had stood in long rows, now replaced by parking meters. Peace ruled that day, and as the people straggled back to their cars and gleeful faculty members like "Father Yale," George Pierson, descendant of one of the founders, stopped in to have a drink and congratulate one another, Kingman's telephone rang. It was Bill Coffin, demanding that the troops be removed from where they had been stationed throughout the day. Their presence was, said Bill, provocative. Kingman had asked for the troops, and was glad he had, and he was tired of the word "provocative." He replied gently, "Bill, it has been a long day. Why don't you just go home now and have a drink?"

So completely did Bobby Seale occupy the attention of the Yale people that Nixon's invasion of Cambodia, which exploded in protests on most of the college campuses in the country a few days later, caused scarcely a tremor in New Haven. There was only a certain amount of revolutionary energy, and once it was expended, further outrageous events could not get the students into the streets. It was a happy ending, but the revolution in American society and in its universities was only beginning. Martha Mitchell, wife of President Nixon's attorney general, probably delivered the judgment of the country on the disorder in the universities when, drunk and locked in her bathroom not long after May Day, she called the New York Times and declared that "the academic society is responsible for all of our troubles in this country. . . . The professors in every institution of learning . . . they are totally responsible for the sins of our children."

"Shall we have a band this year to lead the academic procession for graduation through the town green, as in past years?" Kingman asked, and Mary Louise Brewster responded, "Absolutely." So in our robes and furred gowns we marched to martial music in front of the courthouse where Bobby Seale was still being tried, up to the Old Campus and the Yale graduation ceremonies for 1970. The crowd dispersed quickly after the degrees were handed out, and as they left I heard someone say, "I hope I never hear the word *Love* again."

10

Question All Authority

"Question *all* authority," read a popular bumper sticker of the seventies, and all systems of order were questioned at every level in that decade.

The questioning took its most painful and personal form at the level of individual minds. There was in the seventies an outbreak of various mental problems that reached, at least so it seemed to me and many others, epidemic levels. My evidence was anecdotal, of course, for the "helping professions," despite the fact that their offices were crowded with patients, particularly the young, stoutly denied that there was a mental illness epidemic. If there was, they felt, it would be blamed on the taking of drugs by the young, and this would offer support for theories

179

of chemical causes for mental states, which would in turn under-mine the "talking cure" and its basis in the concept of character as the product of the individual mind on which the psychoanalytic "science" depended.

But in the world I lived in it was clear that something was badly wrong. Kingman Brewster's eldest son was living in a cave on Martha's Vineyard, a fashionable place, but still a cave. A friend took out a second mortgage on his house to pay for a year's psychiatric treatment for his daughter, somehow believing that she would be cured by the enor-mous cost of that kind of hospitalization. Harold Bloom's older son began a lifetime of grave troubles. Coming closer to home, and a less serious matter, but indicative still, my younger son was diagnosed as dyslexic by a psychologist who predicted that he would never gradu-ate from high school unless he attended the doctor's special school. My older son began hallucinating and hearing voices controlling him. I went into a major depression.

Perhaps Thomas Szaz is right that mental illness is a medical myth, not a biological disorder, only an extreme form of antisocial behavior. If so, then there is no need to look for a chemical cause, such as drugs, which many blamed for the madness that was in the air in the seventies, or some form of Cold War weltschmerz. It was only a deeper manifes-tation of the revolt against traditional social and political authority that had taken open forms in the sixties. One of the most popular books at the time on this subject, Ken Kesey's *One Flew Over the Cuckoo's Nest* (1962), pretty much made that point, though with a more liberal slant than Szaz, with its depiction of an asylum where those who are called mad are really sane, but harmless, while those who are sane are really mad, and vicious. The "scientific" backup for this widespread view was the work of the British psychiatrist R. D. Laing, who in his London clinic and in his famous book *The Divided Self* (1969) treated schizophrenia as the painful but eventually therapeutic response of a sane personality to a mad world and to dysfunctional families that tied individuals in the "knots" of conflicted responses.

How many times had I, like other teachers, without really understanding the terror I was playing with, talked glibly about "madness as sanity" in literary madmen like Hamlet and King Lear who stripped away the hypocritical pretenses of the world to look directly at the truth. But it was no longer so easy to believe that madness was sanity when Geoffrey began to hallucinate and hear controlling voices. We found our way to a hospital in Middletown run as a proprietary venture by some psychiatrists in New Haven to make money out of the epidemic of mental illness. There was a little counseling by clinical psychologists—the proprietors seldom came near the place—but mostly the patients were heavily sedated, zonked out really, with Thorazine and slept a good part of the time. In the psychiatric hospital's basement exercise room, surrounded by the tumbling mats and Indian clubs of an earlier therapy, the patients and their families assembled once a week to "talk things out." The text came not from Shakespeare—"to define true madness, / What is't but to be nothing else but mad"—but from Sartre: "Hell is other people." The reigning theory here was that schizophrenia—which was the favored diagnosis—was the disease of dysfunctional families (drug taking only intensified the symptoms), and therefore all the family had to search together for what was troubling the patient, and then, it was hoped, correct what was wrong. It was further thought good to bring the different families of all the patients together, or at least all that would come to that dreadful place, so that one family could share their problems with and learn from others.

And so, on cold winter Thursday nights, filled with guilt and resentment, we loaded our other protesting children into the car for the drive to Middletown, where we took our seats in a circle of folding metal chairs and shared the shame, the confusion, the anger, the fear of other families caught in this same trap, listening to the clinical psychologist query the patients:

> "Well, Tommy, what do you think really went wrong?"
>
> [A long silence]
>
> "I don't think anything is wrong, I just want to go home."

"What does someone in the family think—you, Sissy, do you think there is anything wrong with Tommy?"

[No answer]

"You other patients, you talk with Tommy, do you think there is anything wrong with him, does he have any problems that are like your own?"

[An even longer silence]

"Yeah, well I don't think his parents really understand him. His father's always trying to make him do things he doesn't want to do."

"Like what kind of things?"

"Well, you know . . ."

And then it petered out, to start up again, futilely, only to die once more. Here and there a parent, more often a mother than a father, would make a real effort to say something helpful by identifying some chronic but meaningless controversy—an argument over going to rock concerts overnight—but the son or daughter would usually blush and refuse to pick up the conversational baton. In a way the most defiant ones, whose parents usually were not present, were a relief. They joked about it all, thought taking drugs was fine, and when asked what they intended to do, how long they intended to stay in the hospital, replied cynically that they would be there until the insurance ran out. They were right. In the end we never knew what was wrong—what kind of answer could there possibly be to a question like that?—and so Geoff came home and we all toughed it out.

And then it was my turn. The work seemed to pile up. Even though I was no longer provost, there were still time-consuming special committees, like the one searching for a new rare book librarian, which I chaired. I was leading the effort to start a new kind of literary major (of which more later in this chapter). I was also by now the director of the division of the humanities, which meant involvement in all tenure decisions in the humanities. This was also the high point of my popularity with students, and I was directing as many as ten dissertations at once, many of them by brilliant students, but all the more demanding of time and care for their brilliance. My undergraduate lecture course in Shakespeare had more than four hundred students in it and was one of the most popular in the college. In addition, time had always to be found to read and to write, articles had to be turned out on a regular basis, and a book still had to be published from time to time.

My scholarly career had crested, but with it came personal trouble, the usual midlife burnout: deep depressions, exhaustion, a growing sense of futility, and a considerable amount of paranoia. Anyone who has experienced depression, and a great many have, will know how I felt. No one describes better than Sara Suleri, much later a faculty member at Yale, in *Meatless Days* (1989), the particular kind of depression that was endemic to New Haven: "It does not pretend to be a place where people eat or spend their leisure in wide spaces, uncloistered; it believes rather in the value of a dark interior. There are plenty of those about the town—dark buildings, twice-locked gates. . . . What cramped the town was the weight of unwritten volumes: they scored lines of unfinished writing on every second face that walked the streets, creating almost audible nocturnal sounds of a hundred machines at work, grinding to produce massive printouts of anxiety." With me it wasn't that there was anything particularly wrong, though there were plenty of things to blame, but rather just an inexplicable feeling of emptiness. It was an effort to walk across the room, and I felt alienated from everything I had once cared for intensely. I dealt with what was beginning to feel more and more like a crisis by smoking and drinking even more, eating too much, playing more violent squash, working harder. I began avoiding people, eating lunch alone with two drinks in a restaurant downtown, or in Commons, and found myself more and more often sitting in my office simply staring at the wall, my mind turned off completely, until it came time to get up and go to a class, to a meeting, or home.

I hoped that a leave would help, and in the spring of 1972 Sue and I went to London with the two younger children for a semester's leave. We rented a house in Knightsbridge that the Brewsters had stayed in the previous fall. It was a brilliant theater season and all four of us trailed out night after night to find our way to the Old Vic or the Aldwych, to see Tom Stoppard's *Jumpers*, or a revival of *Showboat*; *Richard II* one night, the musical *A Chorus Line* the next. The children went to a school in Richmond where Marjorie became head girl, holding the Bible for the morning reading by the headmistress, and both learned to eat bangers and mash and swim in a chilly pool. I worked at the British Museum preparing an edition of Jonson's *Alchemist* for the Yale Edition of the Plays of Ben Jonson, which Dick Young and I had started years before. At home I slept as much as possible, long hours of dreamless sleep, hoping to get some energy back, but waked more tired than ever.

Back in New Haven in the fall of 1972, not much improved, I was offered a job as dean of the graduate school at Princeton University. Hoping to keep me at Yale, Kingman made an offer more generous than I could imagine, but after long wavering I accepted the Princeton offer in the hope that a new location would break the dark spell. I liked Yale. It had treated me well, and I had grown up there intellectually. Furthermore, its ethos was right for my temperament: saving ways, a blunt approach to issues, and an uncompromising position on academic standards. But these standards were getting harder to enforce, and there was not a lot of joy at Yale. A new scene, maybe, would help. The Princeton graduate dean's job was a scholar's job, and you were expected to maintain your scholarly work while serving in it. There were secretaries and office help galore. The possibility of doing scholarly work along with administration of course turned out to be no more than a dream: all administrative jobs function according to the principle that work expands to fill up all available time. But I didn't know that at the time, and it looked for a brief moment like a way for me to use my interest in administration to provide an escape from the endless entanglements of New Haven and some space in which to live and work pleasantly. Still, I probably would not have accepted the offer, for all its attractiveness, had it not seemed a way to break the increasing hold that depression had on me by then. I had forgotten Delmore Schwartz's line from his poem "The Hungry Bear Who in Me Lives": "Wherever I go I take him with me and spoil everything."

And then, shortly after making the decision, I had a heart attack. I had been feeling worse and worse, and one night I could not shake off increasing chest pains. I had to go out late in a storm, and driving along I became so angry thinking about some problem—I can't even remember what it was—that I stopped the car, got out, and roared into the wind. This may have made Lear feel better, but it made me feel even worse. I turned around and went home and tried to ignore what I told myself were only gas pains, but they grew and grew until, finally, Sue drove me to the new Yale health center. I looked at the kindly doctor who was giving me morphine. "Is it a heart attack?" "Oh, yes," he replied, and a great calm came over me. Whether I died seemed not to matter; it had all been resolved. The pain stopped, and there was only a sense of inevitability and with it a release from responsibility.

I lay in intensive care for several days listening to the beeps and watching the monitor record my heartbeat in pulsing lines of light. If it stops, I am dead. People came to see me. Harold Bloom came rushing in to give me an advance copy of his *Anxiety of Influence*, arguing that writers had to rebel against their great predecessors and creatively misread their works in order to find their own voices. "Can I read it next week?" I asked Harold, with some irony. He heard none. "Oh, yes, dear boy, that will be plenty of time."

My children came to peer quietly at me, not knowing what to make of this strange passivity on their father's part. My doctor was a thwarted philosopher who wanted to talk about metaphysics while I vainly tried to get from him some mortality statistics for the first thirty days after a heart attack. Heavy smoking must have had something to do with the attack, but the Valium they drugged me with killed all desire for a cigarette, and by the time I came off the medicine I was cured of smoking—one way to do that difficult task. Kingman was his usual generous self when he came by, saying that his original proposal to keep me at Yale still stood and offering a piece of excellent advice: "Never take a big step when you are feeling down; wait until you are back up again."

Not everyone was glad I survived. After I returned to teaching I was sitting at my desk one day, still feeling very flat, when a knock came at the door. Disdainfully silent in class, even when directly asked a question, Smithers had asked me as a special favor to give him a grade of "Honors" in a graduate course he took with me, on the ground that he needed one high grade to transfer to the psychology department. Against my better judgment, but eager to unload him, I did so, only to find that he had used the grade to keep himself in the English department. When his case was discussed by the graduate faculty everyone turned accusingly to me and asked how I could possibly have given him "Honors." I couldn't quite admit how badly I had been suckered, but I was furious, and when he asked me for a letter of recommendation for a job—how could he take me for such a patsy as to try the same scam again?—I wrote a letter that said he was a very bright and curious person, which he was, but that his trolley was off the track, though in ways that might make for interesting teaching. I wonder now which of us was the maddest. The days were already past when it was possible to write an honest letter of recommendation with the expectation of privacy, and letters had become, in fear of lawsuits, so inflated that they were now worthless.

My letter was immediately copied and given to Smithers by one of his friends, who was a junior member on the appointment committee at Rutgers. The Yale English department's director of placement called me up to say that I could not write such a letter and that he was forthwith removing it from the file. Smithers was outraged and had been waiting for the right moment to denounce me. It came when he found me in my office after I had returned from the hospital; he came up to the desk, looked me in the eye, and said, "I wish you had died." I replied without thinking, "But I didn't, and I'll live to piss on your grave," and immediately felt a lot better.

Whether or not there was any connection, it was still notable that the breakdown of the normal sense of purpose and order in irrational mental states had its counterpart, strangely enough, in a radical theoretical movement now known as postmodernism that also eventuated in anomie. Looking back, it cannot have been chance that the social revolution in the universities in the sixties was followed by a philosophical revolution in the seventies that challenged the intellectual authority of professors, their books, subjects, and methodologies even as the sit-in and the demonstration had earlier challenged the traditional social authority of deans and presidents. Social and intellectual forms move together, and proponents of the new philosophy, like J. Hillis Miller, considered themselves from the start to be "intellectual freedom-fighters," announcing from the barricades that "a deconstructionist is not a parasite but a parricide. He is a bad son demolishing beyond hope of repair the machine of Western metaphysics."

From the outset the attack concentrated on breaking down the reality of language—"The primary function of written communication is to facilitate slavery," said Claude Lévi-Strauss—and therefore inevitably centered on literature, the "word-hoard" of Western culture.

> Language, and thought like the wind
> and the feelings that make the town;
> [man] has taught himself, and shelter against the cold
> refuge from rain. He can always help himself,
> He faces no future helpless.

So wrote Sophocles in *Antigone* in praise of language, along with community, housing, and thought, as the first line of defense against the extremes of nature. And, whether Shakespeare's "great feast of languages," or the terminal gabble of Samuel Beckett's waiters for Godot, literature has been populated with characters who have "eat paper and drunk ink," like the pedant Holofernes in *Love's Labour's Lost*. All the accents of the city are spoken with delight in Dickens's novels, and in Joyce, words are juggled until they create a new language. But now this word-hoard was subjected to "the hermeneutics of suspicion."

Words have long been troublesome even to those who use them best, like Laurence Sterne and Samuel Johnson—who spoke of "the boundless chaos of a living speech"—largely because of the power of language to make real concepts that have no material existence such as justice or race. But in the 1970s the validity of language was challenged with unusual vigor by the linguistic philosophy known popularly as deconstruction. Meyer Abrams gets it just right when he says that this and associated theories abstracted language "from the human world and relocated it in a non-human site" where "the human agents who produce and receive a literary work, as well as the reality that work is said, directly or indirectly, to refer to or represent, are all translated into products, effects, or constructs of language or discourse . . . to the impersonal dynamics inherent in the signifying system."

Deconstruction appeared on these shores at a conference held in 1966 at the Johns Hopkins University and titled "The Languages of Criticism and the Sciences of Man." The papers read there were later collected and published under the same title. At Hopkins the leading French theorists of the time, Jacques Derrida and Roland Barthes, met their American disciples, Paul de Man and Hillis Miller, and together they cleared the ground of a host of old theories of interpretation and traditional linguistic values.

"Logocentrism," the faith in words that allowed mental constructs to appear as reality, was the central deconstructive issue; and literature, fictional and verbal, inevitably became the *Schwerpunkt* where the linguistic devices used for constructing false or illusory reality could most obviously be observed at work. "Texts," the term that now replaced "poems" or "works," were "demystified" by robbing them of their historicity, denying them meaning in their own right, and asserting that there was no truth in them, in the sense of referring to any reality outside themselves. Paul de Man spoke, for example, of "the fallacy of unmediated expression" and warned of the dangers of submitting language "uncritically to the authority of reference."

Deconstruction went far beyond "problematizing" words to demonstrating finally an utter emptiness of language, the absence of any meaning whatsoever, or the presence of an infinity of meanings, all equally right, which comes to the same thing. "Linguistic discourse," it was pointed out, when looked at closely is always breaking down, crumbling into nothingness, revealing holes, contradictions, absences, infinite regress, tautology, nothing outside the text, presence where there is only absence, indeterminacy, *différence*, the need for "supplemention," and numerous other logical and ontological failures. All that was left after this kind of analysis were tracks and traces, an infinite regression of deferred realities, each giving a momentary illusion of substance to the other, but eventuating in the void. Every statement contained traces of its opposite—Freud's explanation of penis envy also contains vagina envy, or penis hatred. As empty sounds, or marks on a page, texts have no meaning in themselves, only the meaning assigned to them by the interpreter of the moment, and no interpretation can "achieve closure," since the words disappear in an endless regression of terms. What the words say—their content—is contradicted by the grammar and the rhetorical constructions in which they are arranged, and vice versa. Derrida, as Barbara Johnson sums up his purpose, showed "the ways in which [the philosophers'] own language resists and makes impossible the very certainties they seem most eager to establish."

Using language to do its daily business, the larger world thought it all seemed obvious nonsense. Words point to things. But inside the academy, deconstruction's challenge of language—emphasizing its difficulties rather than its successes, its artificiality rather than its referentiality, its undecidability rather than its precision, its emptiness rather than its fullness, its falsity rather than its truth—had extraordinary effects. Language, it now appeared, as Sophocles had perceived, was not merely some secondary notational system but a central pillar of culture, supporting all other value systems and making the world real and stable. Once its validity—its ability to make meaningful statements— was discredited, and texts were stripped of the control of their own meaning, then it became possible to use words in any way for any desirable purpose. Words, because they were empty, grounded in no reality other than themselves and other words, were said to be the means by which the wealthy and the powerful imposed their "hegemony" on others and made their self-serving ideology, their metaphysics, their world-picture, into "reality." Militant feminists were now free to treat the Great Books as phallocratic constructions of a hegemonic male culture. Radical Marxists, like Louis Althusser, declared them to be "part of the state's ideological apparatus, joining such institutions as the Family, the Church and the Army in enabling it to reproduce the conditions of its production." Michel Foucault declared all human activity, particularly the use of language, to be an exercise of power, a means not of finding truth but of implementing the political will. Blacks denounced the Great Books as racist. Multiculturalists found the intellectual canon Eurocentric and imperialistic. Gay and lesbian rights groups saw in the traditional literature the suppression of sexual freedom and the concealment of homoerotic energies.

Even skeptics like myself understood after a time of radical attacks on language that the old regime of Romantic literature had become in many ways a museum, filled with great works but removed from its human context to a world of hushed reverence, separate from normal human activity. What was needed, a number of us felt, if literature was to be saved from oblivion, was a more open, less idealized context for literary study that located the canonical works, *Oedipus Rex* and *The Aeneid*, *King Lear* and *Madame Bovary*, in the middle not of perfect art but of a continuing, ever present human activity of making up stories that give meaning to events and sort out the perplexities of human life. There was no intention, on my part anyway, to reduce the value of the canonical works of literature, only to put them in a more lively and advantageous context in which their brilliant achievement would shine all the brighter. Little did I know the long, long road we were starting down.

Clark Kerr tells us from experience that "there are no rewards to the faculty members who seek academic innovation, only the burden of long, drawn out, and often disappointing consultation," and by and large he is right. Faculties' defenses of their own interests, and the intricacy of the machinery of academic governance, make for a system in which no one has the power to make needed improvements, but almost anyone, no matter how benighted, can easily prevent any real structural changes. The peril to literature, however, forced some of us to try to put our academic house in order, and in 1971 a small group of Yale faculty members from different departments but with shared literary interests—Adam Parry in classics, Paul de Man and Peter Brooks in French, Peter Demetz in German, Michael Holquist in Slavics, John Freccero in Italian, and Hillis Miller and myself from English—began to plan a new course of study dealing not with any single national literature but with literature as a universal and general tool of culture.

Adam, whose father Milman Parry had in a somewhat similar venture used contemporary Yugoslav epics to show how their Homeric ancestors were assembled, went to Europe soon after our plans were laid. There he bought a powerful BMW motorcycle in Germany, and on the first day with it, going onto an autobahn, he tried to beat a bus coming down the main road. His motor coughed, and he and his wife Anne were dead.

Peter Brooks had run through the streets of Paris in the rebellion of 1968 when it looked for a time as if students could bring down a government, even change an entire culture. Mike Holquist was a student of

Dostoyevsky and well suited to understand not only the dark turns and twists of Raskolnikov but the warmth and generosity of Prince Mishkin as well. They were probably both more radical than I was. My own feelings were those of a tory-radical, trying to preserve the old values by finding a new way to demonstrate their continuing power and importance.

We began modestly enough with a course and a textbook. The course, "Literature X"—Brand X? X marks the spot?—was easy enough to start since it required only that our home departments provide the teachers for a jointly taught experimental course, which they were happy to do, as long as it didn't go too far. The textbook was designed to supply a set of readings for the course. Never was a textbook more inauspiciously named than *Man and His Fictions* (1972), for it appeared just as the feminist movement was beginning to build up a head of steam. The indignant letters poured in: "Where do you hegemonic males get off trying to claim fiction for the phallocracy?" "Why are there so few women writers in this dreadful book?" "This patriarchical nonsense will never sell a copy in my university." And, indeed, it did not—it was out of print in a few years—but it served well enough for a time as a basic text for Literature X, mixing Tarzan of the Apes with Conrad's Mr. Kurtz; Superman with Achilles; advertisements with sonnets; *The Thousand and One Nights* with TV soap operas, all in the interest of showing the range of fiction making or storytelling, exploring its importance to individual and social life, trying to define its working principles and locate its purposes high and low.

The students took to the idea, and it was all very lively, with Howard Felperin acting out the great apes' "dance of the dum-dum" from *Tarzan*; furious discussions of whether *The Story of O* was pornography and if explicit sexual descriptions had a legitimate place in human fictions; whether there was a distinction between outright lies and fiction. In time the course expanded to become the undergraduate major of comparative literature, where it has continued to flourish.

But more radical theorists than we were proceeded to a great dismantling of literature. Harold Bloom told us that the great writers of the past were the enemies of "belated" modern writers who, far from benefiting by standing on the shoulders of their predecessors, as had long been argued in traditional "influence studies," suffered debilitating "anxieties of influence" until they misread the earlier poets in light of their own authentic selves. Geoffrey Hartman and Jonathan Culler declared critics the equals if not the superiors of the poets and novelists. The authors of the great works of literature were stripped of their literary property and reduced to the status of "scriptors" who did not create their works but merely exploited the stock of ideas common to their languages and cultures. Heidegger's "Language writes, not the author" became standard doctrine, though language was itself now empty of any truth. Roland Barthes delivered the coup de grâce in a famous article, "The Death of the Author," where he wrote that, far from being the creative genius that literature had made him, the author was only a historical idea "formulated by and appropriate to the social beliefs of democratic, capitalistic society with its emphasis on the individual." Terry Eagleton summed it all up by saying that literature is not truth, or even fiction, but "ideology," one of the means "by which certain social groups exercise and maintain power over others."

For more than a decade the Battle of the Words was fought with extraordinary ferocity in journals and at conferences. Deconstruction was an aggressive theory, determined to show the futility of language and through that the fraudulence of the great and the powerful who controlled words. It came with an arcane terminology and an opaque style, which made it maddeningly difficult if not impossible to be certain what was being said. And when readers understandably gave up trying to fathom these tormented texts, they were accused of failing to understand the complexities of the argument, even though it was a first principle of deconstruction—can deconstruction have principles?— that the meaning of a text was in the reader, never the author or the text. Its enemies were driven to fury by deconstruction's sophistry, its slipperiness, its contradictions, its willingness to apply its nihilism to all views except its own. They were especially exasperated by deconstruction's calm assumption that any view put forward in good faith in an argument by its opponents was per se uninformed and ill founded.

There was, of course, a good deal of truth in what deconstruction had to say about the slipperiness of language and its too-easy ability to create words that have no roots in any reality. But there was nothing very new in this, and how could there be any meaningful discussion with moderns who, when the ancients complained about their contorted and desperate prose, replied with masterly chutzpah that no one understood anything well enough to be entitled to write clearly about it?

A dogmatic ideology, impervious to argument, deconstruction tended to reveal its underside more often in action than in academic debate. Nothing had, for example, been more sacrosanct in the old universities than the prohibition against plagiarism. In the fifties at Yale, plagiarism meant expulsion; at Princeton entering students are still lectured on the importance of not trying to pass off the writing of another as their own, and the honor code requires them to report any case of which they are aware. Every paper and exam must pledge the student's honor that the work is his or her own. But in the seventies, some faculty members took to showing up at disciplinary hearings and arguing in deconstructive terms that the students could not be guilty of plagiarism since there was in the first place no such thing as verbal originality. "We are all plagiarists," they would say, Shakespeare as well as poor Smithers, feeding off the words of others and the common texts that make up our culture. Besides, as Karl Marx had taught, "All private property is theft," and since there is no such thing as the author, he cannot own "his writings," which were written by "language . . . not the author." At the extreme of ingenuity, the argument went that even if the words in two texts are the same, the contexts are different, and therefore the later version cannot be considered a duplicate of the earlier. Jorge Luis Borges, who cleverly dramatized many of these postmodernist views, wrote a story about two absolutely word-for-word versions of Don Quixote that were nevertheless different because written by different people at different places and times.

This kind of sophistic argument destroyed the morale of simple administrators, always nervous about their relationship to the faculty anyway, trying to define and punish plagiarism; and over time, though no college has yet said that plagiarism is acceptable, most, aware that things are not as simple as they once were, have ceased to press the matter. At the same time, students moving through the electronic world of

Xerox and computer hypertext, able in the 1990s to get term papers on almost any subject on the Web, sometimes free, have increasingly lost the sense of originality and literary property.

Nor have students had much moral leadership on plagiarism. Senator Joe Biden of Delaware withdrew in 1987 from the presidential race when it was revealed that some of his campaign speeches used without attribution material from speeches by the leader of the British Labour Party, Neil Kinnock, going so far as to substitute experiences of Kinnock *pere* in coal mines for his own father's rather comfortable life as an automobile dealer. Politicians are untroubled by these things, and Kinnock embraced Biden publicly on their next meeting; but when it was revealed that Biden's plagiarism went back to his law school papers at Syracuse University, the outcry forced him to give up the presidential race, though not his chairmanship of the judiciary committee of the U.S. Senate.

In 1988–1989 Shervert H. Frazier, a distinguished psychologist in the Harvard medical faculty, was charged with plagiarism in a number of articles he had published in professional journals over the years. Frazier insisted that there had been no intent to claim others' work for his own, only confusion in his notes; but the Faculty Conduct Committee recommended his resignation. He gave in, considerably embarrassed, but many distinguished members of his profession strongly defended him and his practices.

Not only was plagiarism becoming less noteworthy, the very concept was on the wane, as in the case of The White Hotel by D. M. Thomas. The novel, published in 1981, tells the tragic story of a young woman born in Kiev to a Russian Jewish father and a Polish Catholic mother in the late nineteenth century. It begins with a stream-of-consciousness autobiographical poem about her unrestrained erotic fantasies of a stay in a Swiss spa and moves on to her analysis with Sigmund Freud, reported in the style of his early studies in hysteria. She becomes an opera singer in Kiev and marries the Jewish director of the opera, who is killed in a gulag. When the German army captures Kiev in the fall of 1941 she is the lone survivor of the mass murder of Jews in the infamous ravine of Babi Yar. Thomas lifted a description of the massacre almost word for word from a 1970 English translation of an account by an actual survivor, Elizabeth Erdman, but he never acknowledged what he had done, speaking when challenged only of an "indebtedness" that he felt he had openly and adequately recognized and refusing all requests for payment. When the TLS asked a number of experts to comment on what another time would have unhesitatingly called plagiarism, they were not at all sure it was any longer possible to define or condemn it, and spoke instead of how common, though unacknowledged, it had been in the past.

These examples of plagiarism may seem only the actions of un-scrupulous rogues, but facts were getting as slippery as originality in the world at large. Noted scientists cooked the books on their experiments to appear to make important discoveries in order to win Nobel Prizes. The distinguished president of Rockefeller University resigned when charged with publishing phony results in experiments, and he was not reinstated when a panel later cleared his name. Reporters— Janet Malcolm, for example—put in quotation marks words their subjects never actually uttered, then defended themselves when sued by saying that the quotes were legitimate since they were more or less what the subjects had said, or perhaps only implied. And the courts backed them up.

Scholars took similar primrose paths. At Princeton an assistant professor was recommended for tenure by his department despite charges by distinguished historians elsewhere that his book on German capitalists' support of Hitler misquoted and silently changed its documentary sources. The senior appointments committee turned the author down for tenure, which greatly angered some senior members of the department, who railed against "facticity" and "the tyranny of facts." Eleven professors joined to defend the author in an issue of *Radical History Review* (March 1985). Elsewhere a prominent Harvard historian, Simon Schama, described his books as "historical novellas" and "works of imagination, not scholarship," which include some passages that are "pure inventions," "purely imagined fiction" (*Dead Certainties*, 1991). Probably all historians, knowingly and unknowingly, include some imaginative material in their works, but that Schama felt it possible openly to boast that he did indicates the extent to which such concepts as fact and originality were losing their force in the writing world, slipping gradually away into nonexistence.

The ongoing devaluation of the word cannot be quantified, only illustrated, but the consequences for scholarship and learning went to the very foundation of the enterprise of higher education. What was at stake appeared starkly in a scandal of the 1980s. Paul de Man, who died of cancer in 1983, was very much a mandarin, a charismatic teacher of literature to the elite at Harvard, Cornell, Johns Hopkins, and Yale. In the later years of his career he was one of the leaders of deconstructive criticism, to which he brought an exquisite ability to tease opposing significations from texts. A very sinuous "boaconstructor," as Hartman called him, de Man tried to practice deconstruction and at the same time save his own subject, literature, by proposing that literature is the only "mode of discourse" that is self-consciously aware of the emptiness of its own linguistic medium, or, as he famously put it, "the vertiginous possibilities of referential aberration." Other kinds of writing naively take it for granted that words refer to things and make a statement, but literature, de Man argued, is the kind of writing that recognizes and dramatizes in its rhetoric all the traps that language puts in the way of its users. "A literary text," de Man wrote in "Semiology and Rhetoric," "simultaneously asserts and denies the authority of its own rhetorical mode. . . . Poetic writing is the most advanced and refined mode of Deconstruction." All the great writers, in other words, had been great deconstructionists; but surely this was a Pyrrhic victory, for it meant that in the end the great writers could only show the emptiness of language and the impossibility of any absolute meaning.

Born in Belgium in 1919, de Man immigrated to the United States in 1948 and, after working for a time in New York and teaching at Bard College, made his way through Harvard's Society of Fellows. One distinguished appointment followed another, and in 1970, as he was being wooed by Victor Brombert for the French department, I had the responsibility as acting provost of offering him a position at Yale. I wanted to impress him and had arranged for Brewster to stop by during the interview for a few moments and offer de Man a distinguished new DeVane professorship, which would free him from teaching responsibilities for three years and require only that he give a series of lectures each year on a subject of his choosing. A scholar's dream, seemingly, but de Man surprised us both by saying no, he really wanted to teach, it was the classroom that most interested him. I had never met him before, and I was impressed by his shy geniality, but it was his wariness, his care, his ultimate toughness that came through most powerfully.

He came to Yale in the fall of 1970, and in the next thirteen years he became a scholar of world renown and a teacher of extraordinary power, able by the force of his intellect and charisma to form extraordinarily strong bonds with his graduate students. One of his students said to one of his critics, "You really didn't love him enough." Alice Kaplan describes in her memoir, French Lessons (1993), how impressed students were with his every word:

> In the class, I wrote down de Man's examples, and even his asides; the key to the mystery might be anywhere. The man who began to look like his dog (an example of metonymy); how he taught for Berlitz when he first came to this country; jokes about marriage. The concept of "mise en abime" was a big deal. De Man explained "mise en abime" by describing a cocoa can with a girl on it holding a cocoa can with a girl on it holding a cocoa can. When does it stop? There are problems, concluded de Man, with trying to represent reality. The first step in any systematic literary analysis, de Man taught us, was to chart the polarities, the systems of oppositions in the language of a text.

De Man's death at age sixty-four was widely felt as an unmixed tragic loss; but in 1987 a Belgian student looking for dissertation material turned up a number of journalistic pieces written by de Man in the early 1940s, during the Nazi occupation of Belgium, for newspapers controlled by the Germans. It was a time when a number of old Nazis were turning up, not only the German philosopher Heidegger—strangely enough the lifelong lover of Hannah Arendt—but Klaus Barbie in France and Kurt Waldheim in the presidential palace in Austria.

De Man's pieces were by no means the crudest kind of propaganda, but they did follow the Nazi party line on crucial matters like racial characteristics, the necessity of putting the good of the state over the interests of the individual, the German role in civilizing Europe, and the necessity of accepting and working with the new Nazi world order. The Germans had won decisively in 1940, he believed, and "any future was likely to be a German future." One particular essay, "Les Juifs dans la littérature actuelle," published in Le Soir on March 4, 1941, argued that since the Jews had contributed nothing of importance to European literature, "on voit donc qu'une solution du problème juif qui vis-erait à la création d'une colonie juive isolée de l'Europe, n'entraînerait pas, pour la vie littéraire de l'Occident, de conséquences déplorables" [it follows that a solution to the Jewish question which envisages the creation of a Jewish colony isolated from Europe would not lead to de-plorable consequences for the literary life of the West]. Were the Jews to be sent to Madagascar, or some other place "isolée de l'Europe," de Man concluded, Western culture "would lose, all told, a few [literary] personalities of middling value and would continue, as in the past, to develop according to its own great evolutionary principles." Like many, de Man was comforting himself with Madagascar when the reality was Auschwitz and Dachau. A concentration camp used for gathering Jews for shipment to the East was already in place in Belgium when de Man wrote.

As knowledge of these early writings spread, scandal grew. Paul de Man's uncle, Henri de Man, to whom he was very close—he called him his father in a crucial letter—had been for a time a Belgian quisling of high rank, whose patronage probably made it possible for someone of de Man's youth and inexperience to get such an important journal-istic job. He perhaps used this same pull to avoid being sent in one of the numerous "voluntary" labor contingents from Belgium to the Ger-man factories. Further poking about resulted in a long article by James Atlas in the New York Times Magazine (August 28, 1988) reporting that fol-lowing the war de Man had gone to New York after being involved in some murky business dealings in a publishing venture in Belgium that had bankrupted his family. His wife and three children went to South America when he came to New York, and the family was never reunited. Nor did he support them. After gaining a teaching position at Bard College with the help of various New York literati, notably Mary McCarthy, he remarried, probably before divorcing his first wife, though they may never have been legally married in the first place. After a brief stint of teaching in a Berlitz school in Boston, he joined the prestigious Harvard Society of Fellows, where he was known as "a man of the left" and a member of the wartime resistance, but not one who talked of his experiences. There was an anonymous effort to denounce him as a collaborator when he applied for a passport, but in a letter to Renato Poggioli, the director of the Society of Fellows, de Man denied the charges of his accuser, saying that he had never collaborated with the Nazis. Poggioli accepted his word and the charge was suppressed.

And with this, de Man's European past disappeared altogether, apparently never mentioned by him to anyone. Alice Kaplan wrote her Yale dissertation on French writers who collaborated with the Germans, but despite her admiration for him she "didn't go to talk to [de Man] because I had no idea that he had given a minute's thought to the problem that interested me most—the problem of the fascist intellectual. He seemed the least interested of anyone on the faculty in that topic."

After the scandal broke, de Man's former students and colleagues remained passionately loyal to him, and the many literary people with a commitment to deconstruction denied at first that what de Man had written during the war was a very serious matter, or even if it was, that there was any connection between the young man's folly and his later work. At a conference in Alabama the faithful decided to get it all out in the open by publishing a two-volume work, the first volume printing de Man's wartime journalism and the second offering nearly five hundred pages of defenses. In the latter, "Les Juifs dans la littérature actuelle" was itself deconstructed by the father of deconstruction and de Man's close friend, Jacques Derrida, himself a Jew, to demonstrate that its linguistic contradictions and "semantic insufficiencies" allowed it to be interpreted not as support for but as a demystification of Nazi racist views and of "vulgar anti-semitism." But Derrida got to what was really troubling him and the other deconstructionists when he argued cunningly that de Man's theories about the absence of a definitive meaning in words and texts could not be taken as a defense erected in later life against the guilt of what had been written in youth, trying to erase what he had written about Jews by discounting the meaning of words. Anyway, he went on, ideas and life are distinct from one another, and you might as well attack Jean-Jacques Rousseau's views, on which de Man had written eloquently, about the innate goodness of man by bringing up the awkward fact that he forced his mistress to send all their children to a home for foundlings!

But de Man had critics who insisted that his later literary theories could not be separated from his earlier life but had to be seen as an elaborate strategy to deny that he had done anything shameful, or even that anything had happened. Jeffrey Mehlman, who had been a student of de Man's, argued that there might be "grounds for viewing the whole of Deconstruction as a vast amnesty project for the politics of collaboration in France during World War II." Or as Stanley Corngold, another de Man student, put it, "de Man's critical work [deconstruction] makes good sense, once it has been identified as his carapace and portable house. But to continue to teach it while pretending to forget its beginnings in Nazi collaboration is to play out a masquerade—a life that is, then, precisely only a text."

But motives are metaphysics, though we like to think they are plain facts, and despite the power of his personality, de Man the person finally escapes us. We can never know for sure his motives when he wrote for Le Soir and Het Vlaamsche Land, any more than we can be certain that his involvement with a theory that denied the meaning of words was an attempt to deny responsibility for having written in favor of the "final solution." Myself, I think he was a tough and complicated man who always knew just what he was doing and what he had done. But I don't think we can know for sure.

What we can be certain of, however, is that l'affaire de Man tells us in no uncertain terms of the power of words to endure and even to "speak with most miraculous organ." Deconstruction may have scorned what it calls "the myth of semantic correspondence between sign and referent," but de Man's early words stood fast. Not great works of art, but only brief pieces of trivial daily journalism, reading consumables written to earn a living and entertain a mass audience, propaganda designed to serve the political moment and personal need—still, de Man's words lay there in the dusty stacks of the library for fifty years, until their moment came. And when it did, the words themselves spoke clearly and authoritatively, however cleverly Derrida might deconstruct them.

The words "on voit donc qu'une solution du problème juif qui viserait à la création d'une colonie juive isolée de l'Europe" pointed straight to a real world where six million Jews perished in the Holocaust. The de Man affair further demonstrated that "correspondence between sign and referent," words and things, was, however loose and imprecise, far from being a myth. His rediscovered words brought back into being, as if the past had always been there waiting to be evoked by them, a flood of exact events and persons. The Belgian concentration camp and the shipments of Jews to it, the numbers in the labor battalions going to Germany and the dates of their departure, the German takeover of the Belgian media, the editorial policy and the writers for Le Soir, its nickname, Le Soir volé, the politics of de Man's uncle and his place in the government, exactly where de Man lived, how he got his apartment, his relationships with other members of the family, his effort to escape from Europe in 1940, and on and on. If there is one basic axiom of deconstruction, it surely is Il n'y a rien hors du texte—"everything is a text," everything, that is, is made up and unreal—but far from there being nothing outside of the de Man text, everything was out there, waiting to be called back into reality by the awesome power of words to retain and control meaning.

The de Man case removed deconstruction from the realm of pure theory and put it, protesting and wriggling, in a full living human context. It confronted deconstruction with the monstrous and passionately felt fact of the Holocaust and asked, Is this too only a text? Can its meaning be endlessly deferred? Can any "reading" of it, such as that it did not take place, be considered as correct as any other? The answers to these questions inside the academy have been unfortunately muted, and overdiscounting the truth of words has remained a bad habit. But the de Man case did mark the end of the taste for theory and, though it has sedimented throughout the academy, there was in the eighties a return to more directly political modes of change.

11

A Long Walk After Lunch

princeton and the later 1970s

In the fall of 1973 I took up a new position as the dean of the graduate school at Princeton and learned some things I didn't know about academic tribes. A friend who taught at Stanford saw the move from one Ivy to another as no real move at all, no more than the 150 miles between New Haven and Princeton; but that is a long 150 miles.

Students from the *Yalie Daily* swarmed into my office:

"Why do you want to leave Yale?"
"Do you think that the Yale budget is
out of control?"
"Why would you ever want to go to
Princeton?"

The Princeton newshawks who came up to interview me in New Haven understood that everyone really wanted to move to Princeton, but they were suspicious that this might be some kind of Yale plot against old Nassau:

> "What changes do you intend to make in the Princeton graduate school?"
>
> "Do you think the Princeton grad school is inferior to Yale's?"
>
> "In what ways?"
>
> "What's the difference between Princeton and Yale students?"

The students were right: Tigers and Bulldogs are totemic animals, and all colleges and universities are still tribes in which loyalty to and identification with the group are paramount values. All outsiders are viewed with suspicion at Princeton, even by its many Nobel laureates, particularly if they come from the hated rival tribe, Yale. At Yale it is OK to come from Princeton—it doesn't really matter that much, it's considered a natural step up—but you are likely to run into problems if you come from Harvard, and vice versa. At Princeton it is all right to come from Harvard, and vice versa, but not from Yale. There are many ways of describing the differences among the Ivy Big Three, but no one did it better that Bart Giamatti, soon to become the president of Yale, who told the following cautionary tale. If things went badly at Harvard, a national committee would be impaneled to discuss why Harvard was not first and how much money needed to be spent to make it first. At Yale, the faculty would meet, the professors would blame themselves, confess their failings, and vow to work harder. At Princeton, two men would go for a long walk after lunch.

There is much truth in this little story, at least as much as in the theory that each of these institutions bears indelibly in all its parts the stamp of its dominant religion, Unitarianism at Harvard, Congregationalism at Yale, and Presbyterianism at Princeton. What it may tell you is that things move more indirectly, perhaps even a bit more shiftily at Princeton, where the term "pre-bicker," originally used in connection with selection of eating club members, has great meaning, and a stranger like myself had better step cautiously and circumspectly.

We moved in the rain, one of those cats-and-dogs type of rains, coming down in solid sheets. Bill Bowen and his wife, Mary Ellen, came over to welcome us, along with other administrators, and to make sure that the dean's house had been refurbished to our specifications. It had, so much so that Walter, a perfectionist floor finisher who would not leave until every detail was just right, was still getting just a few things right, and we had to dodge him as well as the rain while we moved in, jumping from one piece of brown paper to another, being told that it would be several weeks before all the floors would be completely dry. The cat ran away at once to hide somewhere in the depths of the basement and not show up again for several weeks, while the younger children amused themselves getting ice out of the freezer door of the biggest refrigerator we had ever seen. There was a silver safe, to which the combination seemed always to be lost, and a suit of Chinese armor in the attic.

Bill Bowen had become the president of Princeton the year before, and he was building a new administration in which Neil Rudenstine, later president of Harvard, was the college dean; Sheldon Hackney, later president of the University of Pennsylvania and head of the National Endowment for the Humanities, was provost; and Aaron Lemonick, professor of physics, was the dean of the faculty. It was an all-star cast, and Princeton, in glowing financial health, was clearly about to begin a new era.

Princeton looked golden, in an idyllic small town, with a robust endowment that had been nurtured over the years by a number of Presbyterian financial geniuses and now was available to support educational experiment. Bowen was a master of saying the right thing— "You can make more difference here than in New Haven," for instance. He was an economist by trade, and he was all business. He was unhappy and depressed only when he had no problems to solve, the thornier the better. He took an almost demonic delight in system and in work, and as provost earlier he had devised budgetary programs that worked well.

He had also created, with the aid of the philosopher-politician Stanley Kelley, a system of campus governance that could handle with due process almost any question that might come up. An endless series of committees piled on committees, all elected by the incredibly complicated Irish single-vote system, absorbed an enormous amount of time but provided a representative elected body to deal with any issue, no matter how trivial or how grievous. Original sin could have been tied up in these committees and debated by those with opposing views for years. It was a vast democratic Rube Goldberg machine for producing legitimacy for academic policy, and it offered a surefire way to deal not only with legitimate problems but with nonnegotiable demands as well. If a problem arises, don't say no, or yes, send it to the appropriate committee, made up of elective members from all campus groups, including students, and let it work its way up—if it doesn't drop dead of tedium along the way—to the holy of holies, the Council of the Princeton University Community, composed of townspeople, administrators, staff, students, and anybody else who happens to come by. By the time anyone has spent several long and late, very late, evenings trying to explain their grievances to the CPUC (I still break out in a sweat on hearing those dreaded letters), they begin to see the virtue of compromise. By the time I arrived in Princeton the managerial revolution in administration was already nearly complete.

The Princeton Graduate School had been founded in the early 1900s by the classicist Andrew Fleming West, a scholar in medieval Latin. West had ambitions, and what he wanted more than anything else was a Gothic graduate college in the Oxbridge style, in which he would preside over a society of fellows like Arthur over the Round Table in Camelot. He located a donor, Isaac Wyman, a landlord in Salem, Massachusetts, but despite frequent pleas in his Dickensian office for early payment, Wyman would not unbelt before his time—"That, sir, is not my way." But at last he departed this earth and the rotund West was fabled to have run down the road to Trenton to get a copy of the confirming telegram.

He wanted his fiefdom separate from the college—"above the golf links" was the way he always spoke of the location, about a half mile from the main campus—and this brought him into direct conflict with the president of Princeton, Woodrow Wilson, who supported the idea of a graduate school (he had a Ph.D. in politics from the Johns Hopkins University) but wanted it located in the center of the campus where graduates and undergraduates could interact. West had craftily persuaded Wyman, however, to make his gift with the stipulation that the graduate college and the sumptuous dean's house, to be named after Wyman, be located above the golf links.

Wilson was furious and, saying that "you can fight the living but not the dead," departed for Trenton and the governorship of New Jersey, and in time the presidency of the United States. Biographers have seen in the Wilson-West battle an oedipal struggle that the president would later repeat in the fight with Henry Cabot Lodge over the League of Nations. West, in full possession of the high ground above the golf links, persuaded the schoolchildren of America to contribute their pennies to build a high, pinnacled tower, complete with gargoyles and carillon, in honor of Grover Cleveland, who was resting from his presidential labors in Princeton. Cleveland Tower formed the corner of the great Gothic pile that was now built, complete with paneled dining hall, minstrels' gallery, organ (donated and endowed by Henry Clay Frick), courtyards, library, resident master. In 1913 this palace of learning was opened with several brass bands, and representatives of a hundred major universities marched in their colorful robes, waved their banners, made speeches, and ate banquets for days.

West's determination to remove the graduate college from the main campus had lasting effects. The graduate school grew and flourished, but the university remained basically collegiate. When a survey was made, shortly after I went to Princeton, on whether the alumni favored founding a law school, the response was overwhelmingly negative. "You go to Princeton for a good college education, and then you go elsewhere for professional training," expressed the majority sentiment. Most of the undergraduates did not know there was a graduate school, and the Orange Key tour of the campus for visitors did not even mention the existence of the graduate school above the golf links.

The graduate college, with its gargoyles and spire, was known irreverently to generations of students as Goon Castle. Chiseled into a flagstone in the courtyard were the words of Polonius to his son Laertes:

> This above all—To thine own self be true
> And it must follow as the night the day,
> Thou canst not then be false to any man.

The words from *Hamlet* sound fine to the ear of an amateur, but taken in context they seem like an older version of "I'm all right, Jack." There is much too much of being true to yourself in this play, and it most often takes the form of getting and keeping whatever you want by whatever means lie near to hand. I was about to order out the jackhammer when a second thought made me reflect that a recently arrived Yale professor arguing a fine point of literary interpretation of a monument by the original dean would not perhaps be the best way to spend what little credit I had, so I held back. There was also a bronze statue of Dean West seated in his flowing robes in the main court. In later years the students developed a kind of soccer known as deanball, in which various angled shots were bounced off the dean's flowing robes and his large bald head and stomach.

Everyone had a go at the new dean as soon as I moved into my office, hoping that I would commit myself to something without consultation and that the administration would then back me up in order to save a new dean. Mostly the faculty wanted graduate students—"the Einstein of the next generation" was how they were usually described—admitted to this or that program. Some very grand professors, Tom Kuhn for one, were not above testing a new dean by loudly demanding more students, and more fellowship money for them, of course. The chairman of the Slavics department, which had earlier been stripped of its graduate program, came by to tell me that "You cannot do this to a sovereign department." A mother wrote in Byzantine terms to say that she thought her daughter, a graduate student, was being ill treated because they were Unitarians, while those in power here were ruthless Trinitarians.

The active revolution on campus and in the larger American society seemed by 1973 to have come to an end. Nixon had decided to declare victory and pull out of Vietnam, leaving it to the mercy of Hanoi, and the battle between left and right moved on to Watergate. But the struggle for higher education had not ended: it was simply being fought on new fields with new tactics. The idea of "rights" was loose on the campuses as in the rest of the land. Whatever someone wanted had now become a "right" established by nature, guaranteed by the Constitution, and enforced by the courts; and whenever anyone, faculty, student, staff, disliked a decision, they had learned to question the process by which it was arrived at, going to court if necessary.

Bad cases may not make good law, but they do make good illustrations of the direction things are moving in. I was soon subpoenaed to testify in a trial in Trenton in which the university was defending itself against charges by a former graduate student who had failed to pass the qualifying exams for his doctorate—in Slavics, of course. The failed student had gone off to law school and there had decided that Princeton, not he, was the culpable party in his failure. He reached this conclusion by arguing that if his professors had prepared him adequately for his exam, as it was their duty to do, he obviously would have passed; his failure was therefore prima facie evidence that the preparation had been deficient, and he was entitled to damages.

That the lawyer who tries his own case has a fool for a client is another old legal adage, but Smithers broke this rule and lost his case. He had brought huge mounds of documents to the courtroom and argued them tediously and pointlessly, despite many warnings from the judge, and as he began sadly to remove them from the courtroom after the jury had ruled against him, the judge called out: "Just a moment, Mr. Smithers. I have told you many times while the trial was proceeding that you were in danger of contempt, but you failed to heed my warnings, and in the interest of getting the case tried, I have let you proceed. But now the case is concluded, and I sentence you to thirty days in jail for contempt of court. Bailiff, take him away." Smithers was hustled down the hall, protesting as he disappeared, "But I don't have my toothbrush!"

In some ways this kind of legal activism may have been a good thing, checking the tendency of administrators and faculty to be careless and high-handed about matters of the utmost importance to the students, such as their degrees, and failing to spell out rules fully and clearly. But at the same time, and not so good, it played a large part in redefining the relationship between the university and its students in negative ways. What had previously been thought of on all sides as a friendly, even a familial relationship of indulgent but stern parents and bright but careless children—together, a community of scholars— began to turn into an adversarial relationship. It was now called both a patriarchy and a hegemony, and in this telling the universities were cast in the role of exploiters, with the students, and more and more often the faculty, as the victims brainwashed by the establishment.

Two statues define the change. Princeton's notorious *Christian Athlete*, a serious-looking, handsome bronze youth with a football, was hauled away in the night as a prank, never to be seen again. Later a statue of Abraham preparing to sacrifice an insubstantial Isaac was created for Kent State University to memorialize the students killed there by the National Guard in 1970. Kent State refused to accept it, however, and it somehow found its way to Princeton and was placed behind the chapel, where it still stands as a testimony to the willingness of the older generation to victimize the younger in the name of an abstract law.

We seemed in the seventies to have settled into a culture war that, like the Cold War, went on and on in a less intense but in many ways a more wearing manner than a hot war. A very determined female graduate student arrived at my office to protest being failed in a general exam:

> "You cannot bring that tape recorder into this meeting. We are simply having an informal discussion of a problem."
>
> "How about if I don't put it on the table but over on your desk?"
>
> "No, not on the desk, nowhere in this room!"
>
> "Here, by the door?"
>
> "Never, never, never, never!"
>
> "Let your secretary take notes."
>
> "Well, OK, but let's get on with the discussion. And no tape recorder!"

But when the discussion got nowhere she decided that she would sit in the office until she got justice. The campus cop only wanted to be told what to do: "Do you want her out of here, Dean?" Put that way, I wasn't sure I did, thinking of what the student newspaper, the unspeakable *Daily Prince*, would make of it. All administrators soon learn to loathe the student newspaper above all things, and within the year I learned the hard way simply not to talk to them. If you did they would happily attribute to you, in quotes, whatever they wanted you to say, and you then had the impossible job of explaining to other administrators and faculty that you really didn't say it. And so I sat down again to talk with the student, and after a while, to my surprise, she got up and walked out. Time for dinner, I think.

There was a lot of dislike hanging around such incidents, and what once had been unthinkable now became commonplace. An angry black student who was coming up for his qualifying exam, and who on the basis of his course work to that point had little chance of passing, began screaming obscenities at secretaries in the politics department, making threats, sending the chairman advertisements for life insurance, and firing a rifle in the woods near the student apartment building where he and his family lived. Arriving at the office at eight in the morning you were likely to find a group of troubled white fathers and their crying wives demanding protection for their children. Public safety required the student's immediate removal, but this was not so easy as it once had been. Before he could be dropped from the graduate school or dispossessed it had to be established by formal proceedings that he had indeed done what he was charged with, and establishing anything in the required full legal sense was becoming more and more difficult. The student had taken a degree from the Yale Law School, and he now made the most of his training to lengthen the meetings of the discipline committee. Witnesses were called and cross-examined, depositions taken, rules analyzed. It turned out, of course, that like most universities we had very few written rules, and those we had were often illogical and contradictory. We had proceeded for years by traditional agreement and arbitrary authority, and now we were, like the rest of America, being forced to define and defend our procedures. The university lawyer, Tom Wright, was replacing the deans as the arbiter of student discipline, and "due process" as established by the courts and interpreted by Tom was replacing the inadequate rule books as the measure by which our procedures were judged.

In the meantime there were frightened families who had to be protected, and the only way to do that was to station a campus policeman in the housing twenty-four hours a day until the disciplinary committee made a recommendation. As the hearings dragged on, the student missed the deadline for taking his qualifying exams—which, wanting to stay in graduate school, was I think at least in part his purpose. The politics department recommended that he be dropped and his fellowship cut off. There had been earlier delays, and there was no reason to think that he would ever pass the exams, one of the basic hurdles in graduate school, but here again it was no longer possible simply to talk to him and send a letter saying he was dismissed. He sent us the letters, endless, irrational tirades couched in the jargon of the law, all duly registered at the post office and delivered with a return receipt requested.

The executive committee of the graduate school, a group of faculty stalwarts, was pressed into service to give him still another day in court. He appeared in a long brown leather coat, wraparound shades, and a brown bowler hat, sat at the end of the table, and started the proceedings: "Hey, whaddya motherfuckers want with me." All we could say, again and again, was, "You have to pass your general exams to stay in graduate school, and despite several extensions you have failed to do so." At the end of hours of wrangling and listening to a lot of obscene language, I felt that due process, at least by academic standards, had been provided and told the student that he would hear from me about the committee's decision. As he left, still arguing, one of the older committee members walked out with him, and as they went into the other room I heard him saying, "I understand you're a Yale man. I'm a Yale man myself." In the end, after another barrage of registered letters, he was dropped from the graduate school for failure to pass his generals; because he was no longer a student he wasn't eligible to live in student apartments, and we were able to evict him. He stayed until the last moment, never letting us be sure that he was going to move out peacefully, and then departed in an instant, leaving only a symbolic box of trash in the middle of the floor.

But if there were *formidables* among the graduate students, there were also the usual hapless creatures. One went on Halloween to an instructor's apartment to take the children out trick-or-treating. Dressed as Batman—was there some fatal attraction of Gotham City for Ivy League graduate students?—he took the children on the third-floor elevator, where another small girl got aboard and proceeded to pee on the floor. The elevator stopped at the second floor, where she got off, and then descended to the ground floor, where the door opened on one of the important professors in Batman's department, waiting for the elevator with his wife. There stood the student dressed like a bat, in the middle of a large puddle of urine, holding two small children by the hand. "Good evening, Professor ———, and Mrs. ———. How are you tonight?"

There were bigger problems, however, than angry or unfortunate students. Since World War II, the federal government had been pouring money into science, providing not only for ever more expensive laboratories but supporting the graduate students who worked in them. Grants and contracts also provided indirect costs of as much as 60 or 70 percent of the contract funds to support other university "indirect costs" such as libraries, administration, and janitorial services. The National Institutes of Health, the National Science Foundation, the National Endowment for the Arts, and the National Endowment for the Humanities poured additional billions into other areas to support leaves, research, publication, travel, conferences, programs, centers. In the 1950s, after Sputnik, fear that the United States was falling behind the Soviets in space led to the National Defense Education Act and the generous funding of graduate students in all fields, not just the sciences. In time, too, the federal government would guarantee student loans, which made it possible for the colleges and universities to raise tuition much faster than the rise in income and thereby pay for new buildings and staff.

There seemed to be no reason to look this gift horse in the mouth, or anywhere else for that matter, since earlier federal money gave the government no authority to meddle with the internal operation of the universities. In 1945, for example, in the authorization of the G.I. Bill, the U.S. Statutes at Large, volume 58, part 1, section 288 specified that "no department, agency, or officer of the United States, in carrying out the provisions [of the G.I. Bill] shall exercise any supervision or control, whatsoever, over any State educational agency . . . or any educational or training institution." But things had changed and the universities were surprised when in the sixties and seventies government, by statutes, executive orders, and departmental regulations, began to impose elaborate requirements that constituted an uncoordinated process of academic engineering. Universities' government funds were threatened if they failed to conform to certain practices decreed by some unknown bureaucrat. By now most of the universities were taking so much money from the government that their budgets would collapse if the tap was turned off, and even small colleges that accepted no government funds were forced into compliance by the threat of denial of tuition loans to students.

ERISA—it was the time of the acronym, this one for the Employees Retirement Income Security Act of 1974—for example, imposed costly pension fund regulations and decreed that the insurance mortality tables showing that females live longer than males could not be used to set retirement benefits. Conversely, males benefited from a diktat that their insurance rates had to be based on the longer life expectations of a pool that included females. Classrooms and dormitories had to be made usable by the handicapped, and new construction had to fit the needs of what were somewhat grimly called "the challenged." "Do medical schools have to admit the blind?" was the subject of a court case, and there were arguments about whether readers have to be provided for blind students in the absence of a library in Braille. In any institution accepting federal funds, student letters of recommendation had to be open, though the students could waive their rights, and in a number of states, including California, letters supporting faculty appointments and promotions had to be made available to the candidate upon request. With effects as yet unknown, but in an academic job market already catastrophically depressed, no one after 1994 could be retired from the universities on the basis of age.

Different treatment based on race, class, gender, sexual preference, age, or handicap was heavily discouraged in social organizations, however loosely connected to the university, in sports, in clubs, in student bodies and in faculty. The colleges were required to make public their graduation rates and campus crime rates, and the Department of Education tried to impose affirmative action standards on the accreditation process that previously had been administered by the colleges themselves.

Most seriously, of course, colleges and universities taking federal money were required to report on the racial and sexual mix of both their admissions and their faculty hiring and makeup. Quotas were never imposed de jure, but various "good faith" affirmative action programs described as "goals" and "timetables" had to be developed, filed, implemented, and regularly reported on. They covered hiring, promotion, compensation, and dismissal. These were monitored by the Office of Federal Contract Compliance Programs and the Equal Employment Opportunity Commission in the Department of Health, Education, and Welfare, and its spin-off, the Department of Education. Every appointment form had to carry information about race and sex, and every faculty member had to file with the university a statement of his or her race, which another regulation said it was illegal to request.

Once the regulations, the sanctions, and the monitoring agencies were set up, the program soon became self-driven as each university, anxious not to attract the attention of the federal regulators, modified its recruiting, promotion, and salary-setting procedures to give special attention to women, minorities, and other special groups. The government and the media argued, of course, that these are only long-delayed social rights such as "empowering" the handicapped, doing justice to women and minorities, making higher education available to all, broadening the educational perspective from a Western bias to a multicultural awareness of the entire world. Phrased in this way, it is difficult to argue against these causes and values, and I will limit myself to pointing out that it is equally obvious that government regulation has been entirely a *social*, not an *educational*, project. Nowhere along the way was there a single move toward actually stiffening educational requirements or improving teaching. That the teaching terms should be longer, that foreign-language requirements should be imposed everywhere, that government fellowships or loans should depend on high academic standing, that a writing requirement be made universal, that tenure standards should be raised in departments getting government grants, these were not causes that interested the legislators and the bureaucrats in Washington and the state capitals, or the special-interest groups in the universities that were their constituency.

They were concerned only with using the universities as a means of bringing about social changes, and, in fact, the causes that the students tried to force on the universities in the sixties by activism were largely put in place by government in the seventies and eighties by fiat. Politics was substituted for education, and politics seeks political ends, not educational ones. This is the mark of politics everywhere. When it becomes involved with social activities, welfare, environment, art, or education, it does not approach the questions in terms of what is best for these activities, or what will work, but in terms of what is politically most useful. The two approaches to experience, politics and education, are fundamentally at odds, and can tolerate each other only to a limited degree. One, politics, feels it is in sure possession of the truth and uses education as the ideal means to put its ideology into effect; the other, education, at its best, is always questioning and seeks truth by the close consideration of the evidence, skepticism toward any established position, and testing of all possibilities.

There were indirect consequences to government regulation as well in the politicized American university. Administration became larger and more bureaucratic in an effort to meet the requests of its many different constituencies and the reporting requirements laid on it by the steady increase of federal and state laws regulating the activities of the universities. Legal bills grew astronomically in a climate in which the courts encouraged all who feel that their rights have been infringed—and there are lots of such people around the modern campus—to take the university to court, or get an out-of-court settlement to avoid nuisance and expense. A number of intense special-interest groups appeared who viewed their causes as paramount national concerns and insisted, with a raspy rhetoric, that the university purge itself of its sins and force the world to do likewise.

There was no better view of the workings of the politicization of higher education than in the graduate school fellowship budget. Major graduate schools live and die by the amount of money available to compete for students. There are only a few really outstanding students in a given discipline in any single year, and all the major graduate schools compete ferociously for this handful. By the seventies the most distinguished graduate schools in the country, including Princeton's, were supporting almost all of their graduate students, trying to attract them by offering full tuition fellowships plus a stipend, at this time up to about four or five thousand dollars a year. After federal NDEA fellowships and Ford support for graduate students ended, the money to support graduate students came from university funds, but, to a larger degree than was ever acknowledged openly, it also still came from the government, though by a more indirect route. All the science and engineering students were still paid tuition costs, plus a stipend, and summer money by various government research and defense agencies, through the professors, who carried the students on their contracts as research assistants. The government not only supported the science students, it paid charges the university levied for indirect costs, which were used to support students in areas other than science.

We tried to find a way of shifting some of the costs to individuals by means testing the students and tailoring their fellowships to need, but the project floundered from the first. Most of the incoming graduate students, age twenty-two to twenty-five, had no income or funds of their own, and by now they believed that their intellectual abilities made them national assets properly supported by the institution. Certainly they themselves expected to bear no part of the cost of their graduate education. When we asked their parents to supply us with information on their income, some did, many with understandable reluctance, but many others protested loudly, saying that they had already supported their children through expensive undergraduate educations and that they had no intention of paying for several further years of graduate school.

But the most powerful resistance to means testing came from the departments and the professors. To have a core of first-rate graduate students in a department is absolutely critical. On them depends the quality of the seminars, the level of the dissertations, the research of the professors, and in the long run the reputation of the department. Ironically, studies later showed that we always have been poor at identifying the quality of graduate students at the time of admission, and that the rank list of entering students has little correspondence to their success in graduate school or in the profession. Even worse, the completion rate of all entering students is very low, barely over 50 percent in the humanities, a little better in the social sciences, and about 60 percent in the sciences. But the departments are desperately committed to their judgment of the entering students—so much depends on it, after all—and they more or less refused to have anything to do with the information we furnished them about the financial situation of those students. Each department had a fellowship budget, and without regard to whether the father could pay or the child had a trust fund the faculty put their maximum fellowships on the students they wanted most to attract.

In these circumstances a dean who wished to preside over a distinguished graduate school could not afford to risk his all-important federal funds, both direct and indirect, by refusing to follow the ukases that came from Washington in a never ending stream, dictating procedures in areas like admissions, appointments, promotions, and degrees — areas that had only recently been thought the sole province of academics. Perhaps the most serious result of all these many pressures on sensitive places was that ill will and distrust began increasingly to cover the campus with a smog of suspicion.

The faculty room in Nassau Hall is one of the great rooms in America. Built in the mid–eighteenth century, beautifully finished with paneled oak, elaborate molding, and high, broad windows, it runs lengthwise from the lobby of Nassau Hall, down between sets of rising pews on each side of a table, to a dais where the president sits to conduct faculty meetings. Here the Continental Congress met while the British occupied Philadelphia, and here they received George Washington to thank him for his military service to the new nation. His portrait by Charles Willson Peale hangs there, as do those of the past presidents of the university, including Aaron Burr the elder (father of the well-known vice president of the United States), James McCosh, and Woodrow Wilson. Princeton, being a comparatively small university — four thousand undergraduates, fourteen hundred graduate students in the seventies — has only a single faculty containing all the ranks of the professors in the few professional schools as well as those in arts and sciences. The provost and the deans have their appointed seats in the faculty room, and the dean of the graduate school, enacting Dean West's separation from the college, had the first seat below the dais, on the right-hand side, in the second row. The other major administrators sat in order of rank in the first row. In those days we all reported directly to the president, not through the provost, as later became the case, and meetings began with the president asking each of us in turn, "Have you anything to report, Dean So-and-so?" Sometimes you did, and sometimes you didn't, but to sit there as the sun sank outside the western window, burnishing the leather and soft wood, looking at the serious faces of great men like

Lyman Spitzer, the astronomer, or Lawrence Stone, the social historian, or Ansley Coale, the population economist, was to feel that, whatever power had passed to the politicians, you were still present at one of the great places of Western education.

It was anthropology that gave me my worst day in this noble setting. The junior faculty of that small new department and its students were engaged in a noisy and bitter revolution against the chair, Hildegard Geertz, the wife and collaborator in Java and North Africa of the most distinguished American anthropologist of the time, Clifford Geertz. The Geertzes had just come from the University of Chicago, he to the Institute for Advanced Study, and she, in one of the husband-wife deals that were just beginning to be commonplace, to the university. In many ways the revolt was against Cliff and his "thick reading" of cultures as if they were complex literary texts. The assistant professors in the department had recently begun with him a lifelong argument in the name of postmodernist theories that the anthropological investigator could not overcome his own bias long enough to say anything objective about another culture, and that to describe the poverty or ignorance of more primitive societies was to become a collaborator of imperialism.

The rebels found the opportunity to further their quarrel in the graduate courses proposed for the next year for anthropology. During the turbulence of 1970, the Princeton faculty had voted, among numerous other concessions, to give graduate students the right to approve the graduate courses offered by their department. Having voted this remarkable requirement, the departments simply forgot the whole thing and went on offering whatever courses the faculty wanted to teach. But the anthropologists had not forgotten, and in 1974 several assistant professors who were leaving the department and a number of graduate students who were also departing refused to approve the courses that the chair and a new professor, Jim Fernandez, a white knight arriving from Dartmouth, wanted to teach.

We were processing the courses in the usual way for the graduate catalogue when I was informed that they could not be offered because they had failed to meet the student-approval requirements voted in 1970. I was astounded—flabbergasted is not too strong a word—to hear that a group of people leaving the department could block the courses the people who were remaining thought it best to teach. It was maddening to be caught in this bind, but to touch it was dangerous. Long tradition required that all new courses be approved by the full Princeton faculty, and I fully appreciated the risk of bringing before them courses that had not been approved in the legal way, no matter how silly and how seldom used the rule of student approval might be; but I wanted to show the faculty how ridiculous this rule was, how it interfered with reasonable educational procedures, and how obstructive certain people had become.

For reasons I still do not understand, two distinguished faculty members (both from the department of East Asian studies, not anthropology), had decided to make a cause of the matter. Both were conservatives, not radicals. Their leader had distinguished himself in earlier debate by remarking to another faculty member who was proposing some surrender to supposed student demands: "Sir, you are licking a boot that has not yet even been raised in your direction." These two positioned themselves at the faculty meeting on either side of the hall, in the upper tier of seats, like two vultures sitting on the canyon edge. When my turn came to report, I explained to the faculty what had happened, and then said that I thought it was important to approve these new courses and asked them to do so on the grounds that the intention of the rule had in no way been to give power to those who were leaving the university to block the programs of their successors. I believed, I went on, that the courses had been voted on, positively, by the only voters with an interest in the matter, the faculty that would be teaching next year. I asked for a favorable vote.

The professors looked grave, the dean of the faculty put his notebook over his head, the presiding officer for that day, Sheldon Hackney, asked for comments, and the two vultures began denouncing me in turn. This was, they insisted, some kind of dark plot to subvert the rules of the faculty, a power grab on the part of a graduate dean from a strange university who did not understand the broad democratic ways of Princeton, an attack on the liberties and fundamental rights of the students, the act of an administrator with no feeling for the traditions of Princeton and the welfare of those students who had been entrusted to his care. This was, said the more vocal of the professors, rising to the height of his oratory, an act worthy of Hitler—I do not exaggerate—and as despicable as the assaults of the Third Reich on humanity. He may have overstepped a bit here, since there was a titter, but no one really wanted to cross him: he was considered too dangerous. When it finally came to a vote, about thirty-two were in favor of accepting the new courses, against about thirty-seven. Some vigorous negotiations got the courses passed at the next faculty meeting, and I consoled myself with the view that at least I had brought into the open certain things that needed some sunlight.

But when you pick up the tar baby it is not so easy, as Br'er Fox found out, to put it down. There was something like a blood feud between the departments of Near Eastern studies and East Asian studies. Soon their quarrels were somehow in my office, not the professors themselves but their proxies, which is how things work at Princeton, leaving you constantly wondering whether you are imagining sly moves and countermoves or whether something is really going on. The first problem came in the form of a letter from a disaffected graduate student in Near Eastern studies (he had not been invited to parties to meet important people, et cetera) informing me that a recent dissertation by an Egyptian student had been written by a team of American students paid for by a grant held by a professor of sociology in Near Eastern studies, Morroe Berger, and that it was my duty to look into this flagrant violation of rules. My first action was to dispatch one of the associate deans to impound the official copy of the dissertation from the library, only to have him report that it could not be found, which sent my anxiety level right to the top of the tube. The chairman of Near Eastern studies, Avrom Udovitch, was on the telephone instantly—how did he hear?—but knew nothing about it. The director of graduate studies, the endlessly pleasant and helpful Charles Issawi, came to the office at once with the departmental copy of the dissertation, which I instantly locked up, but told me he knew nothing of the matter, having only recently taken the job. Berger, the director of the dissertation, was located, and he and I had a long talk, not a long walk, after lunch, during which I decided he was an honest man trying to deal with a genuinely important academic problem.

It was, he explained to me, of the first importance to put some

American-trained Ph.D.s into the universities of the Middle East, not only because they could help with the research of our faculty, but in order to raise standards in the local universities. But, he went on, almost all of the students brought to Princeton from those countries had great difficulty in writing English, the language required for all dissertations, even if they spoke and read it fairly well. One of these students might do very well in classes and put together a good argument for his dissertation, but as written English it would never meet required standards. So you could either pass dissertations that sounded illiterate and put them on microfilm, as was required, for all the world to see, or you could provide help with the writing. Morroe had worked out a scheme in which the student would write a dissertation that would be judged solely on its intellectual merits, and then he would use grant money to employ other students in the summer to polish up the writing but not the scholarship. This is, I believe, the kind of problem that defines the meaning of real administration. Berger was cutting corners, no question, but the dissertation was, at root, the student's intellectual work, and the purpose of the entire arrangement was to spread and improve knowledge.

It took me some time to reach the student who had made the complaint, and when I did he refused to meet with me on the grounds that he was leaving the country for a year of research. I explained that this was a very serious matter, that it was important that he give me details and that he make a formal charge rather than simply writing what amounted to an anonymous letter. I wanted to smoke him out, find out why he had written in the first place, and put him in the middle of the formal committee hearings that were going to have to be held. I was sharp with him, he was evasive, and he instantly disappeared abroad. Later this incident was noised about as another example of my lack of feeling for students. The university copy of the dissertation did turn up: it had fallen behind a file cabinet on which it had been shelved. At least this is what was said, but by then everything seemed suspicious to me. I put together a committee, they talked to everyone, and they recommended that I not rescind the degree that had been given the Egyptian scholar, who remained blissfully unaware on the banks of the Nile of the cruelty of the allegories back in New Jersey. I accepted the recommendation but warned Berger that he was going to have to find some way of helping his students that looked less like buying a degree for them.

This kind of thing keeps you on your toes, but there are few who thrive on it. The aftereffects of my heart attack, severe chest pains under stress, never disappeared, and one day I came to on the floor of the toilet in Nassau Hall, holding on to the bowl, pressing my head against the cool porcelain. It was rather pleasant there, and I stayed for a while thinking about what to do. My predecessor, and the dean of the faculty at this time, Aaron Lemonick, once remarked with considerable wisdom that to make changes in the rockbound ways of a university was a matter not of bold strokes but of constant nudging over a long period of time. Or, as Woody Allen once put it more comically, "Success is 80 percent a matter of showing up." But this meant years and years of putting out fires, arguing with cranky students, dealing with hostile faculty members. I lacked the patience, and after a term of it, it was clearly time to go, but where?

Yale already had my successor in place, the English Shakespearean George Hunter, but the department and the provost, my old friend Hanna Gray, were willing to take me back on generous terms. Bill Bowen wanted to keep me on the Princeton faculty, and he was willing to do what was necessary. It is a heady experience having two major universities bidding for you, and I hesitated a long time before deciding that having made the move from Yale I really didn't want to slink back. So I stayed in Princeton, we bought a house, I stopped being a dean and went back to being a professor, and everyone perked up a bit.

A year's leave had been one of the inducements, and I used the second half of it to go to London. I found a house in Highgate, settled in at the reading room of the British Museum, and walked long wet miles every day. Not wanting to involve myself in any Anglo-American controversies, I spoke only when necessary, which turned out to be surprisingly rarely, and the rest of the time simply nodded, or paid silently, or pointed to the item I wanted. It was extremely restful, and since I had neither telly nor radio, for a time the human sound came to me only as a kind of distant general noise. In the evening I had a hot bath, with a long cold gin, and then, after a modest meal, regularly went to the theater. It was a fine season in 1978, one of the last before the traditional skills of

English actors and directors began to disappear in wild interpretations and American-style talking-into-the-armpit acting. It was a particularly good season for Gilbert and Sullivan, and I must have seen ten or twelve brilliant D'Oyly Carte productions. One of the great moments in the theater for me came while sitting in the top gallery, 50p. at Sadler's Wells, looking down on the stage at the Major-General's daughters in *The Pirates of Penzance* dancing in a circle and singing, "Let us gaily tread our measure / Life is but a fleeting pleasure." From above they looked like a great wheel, and the parasols they carried and twirled made still further wheels on the wheel, as if all life were caught up in spinning circles. To me, fortified with a whiskey from the bar, it seemed a revelation.

In the morning I crammed into the tube with other wet raincoats and umbrellas and made my way to the British Museum, where after reading the morning paper I made my way to the great central reading room, arriving early enough to get one of the blue leather desks, under the great dome above, where Marx and Lenin and Shaw had worked. George Gissing had called it "the valley of the shadow of the books," and it was not always the inspiring place that its defenders, trying to prevent the move to the new library at St. Pancras, have made it out to be. A large number of the seats were filled by regulars, as the air was with snorts, coughs, harrumphs, odors of wet clothing, and vigorous blowings into handkerchiefs. It was a place of cranks as much as scholars, and they paraded up and down the aisles on the way to the dingy tearoom, whispering or calling out in loud, imperious voices that asserted British authority over the realm of letters.

My own business in the library was to write a book about the end of the institution of Literature, with a capital L, that had been built up over the past two centuries, in a time when writing had become a profession and its products a commodity sold in the marketplace. I conceived of literature as an "imaginary library" constructed by many people and many books over a long period of time, and while by no means all the books that made up the imaginary library were shelved there, this was the appropriate place to write this book, for if any place stood for the world of letters it was the reading room of the British Museum. And, just as plans were being made to move the British Library to a new multicultural-style building up by the railway station at St.

Pancras, near where the whores plied their trade, so the high Romantic and modernist conception of Literature was disintegrating. The canon of great books, authors and their powerful imaginations, the formal perfection of the literary text, and the belief that literature was a central pillar of culture—these foundations of Literature were all crumbling.

Fine poems and novels were still being written, but somehow they no longer became Literature. Four of our major novelists had, I believed, explained what had happened. Saul Bellow, in *Humboldt's Gift* (1973), Norman Mailer, in *Of a Fire on the Moon* (1969), Bernard Malamud, in *The Tenants* (1971), and Vladimir Nabokov, in *Pale Fire* (1962), each explored the disintegration of one of the central Romantic literary values: the genius-author in Bellow, a mysterious and humanly meaningful imagined reality in Mailer, the "wholeness, harmony and radiance" of the literary text in Malamud, and finally, in Nabokov, sustaining communication between writer and reader. By looking at these novels in close detail—New Critical rhetorical analysis was still my primary methodological tool—I hoped to get at what was happening to Literature, its causes and its effects.

The Imaginary Library was published in 1982, to respectful reviews, but though the conservative right and the radical left were by then both shouting that literature had fallen apart, for different reasons, my elegiac tone did not catch the attention of any large group of readers. For a book of this kind it sold well enough, fifteen hundred copies, about half to libraries, and I see it quoted now and then, but interest in this kind of literary criticism was on the wane.

I returned in the fall of 1978 to teaching in an English department that was as uneasy about me as I was about it. Soon after first arriving in Princeton as a dean I had received two thick letters, posted in Washington, D.C., and signed only with the number 768. Both of these letters welcomed me as the person destined to let light into the dark Gothic halls and open up the unspeakable secrets of the English department. Tales were told in the letters of the changing of grades in the middle of the night, of personal vendettas that drove students out of graduate school, of falsified letters of recommendation that prevented people from getting jobs, of exams set on impossible dates, and of unjustified failures. Politics was not involved, the writer assured me, in those olden days, only personal likes and dislikes, ego, and academic power struggles. How was I to know whether it was true or not? What could I do if I thought it was?

I could do nothing, of course, on such flimsy evidence, but there was, I had to admit, a furtive quality about the Princeton English faculty, as if they knew secrets that could not be spoken, and wisps of ancient wrongs did seem to hang about the corridors of the Gothic building, McCosh Hall, where the department was housed. When some walls in the English office were torn down in the eighties, the words "W P Hope, Evelyn Thaw, 1907, Acquitted, Hunt. Gaunt" were revealed daubed in black paint on the old plaster. Word must have come while the wall was being put up that Harry Thaw had been found not guilty of the murder of the architect Stanford White, the onetime lover of Thaw's wife, the former chorus girl Evelyn Nisbet. It was the O. J. Simpson trial of the early 1900s, with a defense team that had imported a lawyer from California who was said to be the illegitimate son of Napoleon III. White was accused of having doped Evelyn in order to seduce her, and the revelations on the stand of his treatment of other women made the most distinguished American architect into a national villain. The U.S. House of Representatives passed a resolution declaring his "loathsome and licentious acts" to have had "a demoralizing influence on the youth of the land." The 1907 trial ended in a hung jury, and a second trial in 1908 found Thaw not guilty by reason of insanity, which was almost certainly the case.

The scrawl on the inner wall in McCosh may have given hope to "Hunt. Gaunt," but White was a great artist and a very genial man who had not had anything to do with Evelyn since she married Thaw, while Thaw was a most unpleasant fellow who whipped girls in brothels. Evelyn made the point when, years later, running a dive in Biloxi, she remarked that she had on the stand exposed the sensational details of her sex life to save a dreadful man she hated from jail for killing a wonderful man she loved. The verdict had nothing to do with Princeton, unless it was the unlikely fact that the Princeton Club rented the deceased White's townhouse, but to me the hidden words sounded like some dark Edgar Allan Poe curse on the English department, at long last revealed.

Princeton had once been famous for its men of letters. Edmund

Wilson and Scott Fitzgerald had been undergraduates there, and the Second World War had brought writers like Thomas Mann and Herman Broch, working at the time on *The Death of Virgil*, to town. William Faulkner strolled the streets for a time and seduced the faculty wives. Allen Tate in 1939 had started a creative writing department, into which he soon brought the critic Richard Blackmur and the poets Delmore Schwartz and John Ashbery. T. S. Eliot was at the nearby Institute for Advanced Study for a year, where Jacques Maritain also practiced his arts.

Eileen Simpson, in her memoir *Poets in Their Youth* (1982), describes the literary scene during and just after the war, when these writers attracted to the university visiting poets like Robert Lowell and Randall Jarrell, and budding poets like W. S. Merwin were undergraduates. These people shared an extraordinary sense of the importance of poets —Lowell once remarked, quite seriously, that it was a good thing that Jarrell had written about World War II or else we would not have known about it—and they were also still of the generation of Romantic *poètes maudits*, suffering severely from madness, alienation, guilt, and monstrous hangovers. The whole thing, Simpson wrote, remembering her Fitzgerald, ran on huge amounts of alcohol: "Never had there been so many parties—afternoon parties, evening parties, house parties, long long parties with short strong drinks. . . . Lunchtime daiquiris, before-dinner martinis, late-night stingers. For John [Ashbery] who awakened guilt-ridden and exhausted from a battle with demons, a 'brilliant' martini became the cure for a hangover, a nightcap or two the cure for insomnia." For a time, drunk and outrageous, Schwartz, with Saul Bellow as his assistant, taught as a replacement for Blackmur, off, according to Bellow, to lecture on Henry James in Damascus.

But the glory had long departed by the time I arrived. Poets have always been contemptuous of professors in English departments— "some professor followed us to dinner at Lahiere's," said Simpson dismissively—but now there were only professors. E. D. H. (Dudley) Johnson, white-haired with handsome, hawkish features, and totally Ivy Leagued, was a specialist on nineteenth-century novels and art. The *Daily Prince* gave an annual award to the best-dressed man on campus, in the days before coeducation, and one year they made two awards, one to E. Dudley and the other to H. Johnson. Carlos Baker, the most courtly and generous of men, was best known for his official biography of Hemingway, made possible by the Princeton connection with the Scribner family, Hemingway's publishers, who had started Princeton University Press and had long been active in its affairs. During the course of working with the Hemingway papers, Carlos came to loathe the man, and being an upright person he could hardly bear to go on with the work. In time he finished, but the result portrayed Hemingway in such an unpleasant light that the family was upset, and so was the literary world. By the sixties, Hemingway was the American writer, and to describe the national hero as egotistical, ruthless, vulgar, untrustworthy, vengeful, and generally despicable was not what people wanted to hear.

Both of these men were fine scholars, in the casual way the old order prized, and they found themselves uneasy with the different kind of professors who took a more professional view of the department. To these men, research was more important than teaching, the course of study more factual than moral; appointments and promotions were made on the grounds of publication and scholarly reputation, not teaching, social graces, and congeniality. Louis Landa, a scholar of eighteenth-century literature, was the chief of this group, and he was matched by the great Renaissance theater scholar from Chicago Gerald Bentley. Ged was engaged in the monumental task of writing the many-volumed Jacobean and Caroline continuation of E. K. Chambers's *Elizabethan Stage*. It was a lifetime's work, and Ged spent every moment he could in the Public Record Office in London, poring over and copying, in the days before Xerox, lengthy extracts that had to be checked for accuracy again and again. He would leave immediately after his last class in the spring and return to the departmental office directly from the plane, dropping his bags on the floor, just in time to teach his first class. He was a great scholar of the old historical persuasion, convinced that his drudgery would produce an ordered view of the facts about Renaissance actors, theaters, playing companies, and stage practices that would be useful forever. Just before I retired, and he died, I reminded my graduate students in a course on Elizabethan theater that Professor Bentley still came to the library to work every day. They had never heard of his books, though they were on the bibliography I had given them, and they were uninterested in the scholar.

The dominant figure in the department, highly professional in his interests but a maverick in his theories, was the Chaucerian scholar Durant W. Robertson. A distinguished historian, he had long ago fastened upon the idea that until the eighteenth century all the great English writers were Christians before they were anything else, and that therefore their works had to be read as Christian allegories. Robertson was himself a nonbeliever, but he held his literary-religious doctrines with all the zeal of an Augustine—*The City of God* was one of his central texts—turning the bright, bubbly Chaucer into a stern moralist, and the broad-minded Shakespeare into a tractarian writing against sin. If you want an intellectual following you need a system, some specific way of approaching and interpreting a text, preferably with a lexicon of its own and some conversion mechanisms, and this Robertson had, but he was troubled by a sense that his enemies were everywhere, working against him ceaselessly.

He had started teaching at Yale before the war and had been ridiculed by the New Critics who were just coming into ascendancy. His archenemy at Yale, the equally aggressive Talbot Donaldson, taught Chaucer as a good-humored man of the world with a lot of tolerance for human foibles. They had never met until one day at a conference Talbot talked for a long time to a man he didn't know and then, when the conversation ended, asked someone, "Who is that interesting fellow in the white suit?" White suits were "Robbie's" customary uniform, a tribute to the old South. "Why, that's Professor Durant W. Robertson" came the answer, at which Donaldson rushed back, sought Robertson out, and said, "Oh, Professor Robertson, I am so sorry, I should have known you, but we have never met. I hope you will forgive me," and on and on, making, as Talbot, a man not given to apologizing, reported, a real ass out of himself. Robertson looked at him coldly as he babbled on, and then said, "And who, sir, are you?"

The department regarded me with suspicion, thinking that I had the ear of Nassau Hall and that whenever I disagreed with a decision I went to my friends in the administration. They did not realize that once you leave an administrative position you are no longer a player in the game, and busy administrators waste no time on you. If they want your opinion, they will inquire, but mostly they do not, and I was happy to walk the wide way around Nassau Hall on my way to work in the morning and home in the evening.

12

The New Technology Calls
All in Doubt

television, books, libraries, computers

There is a close connection between the various movements, political, social, and intellectual, that changed higher education in the latter twentieth century, and these forces were symbiotic with a technological revolution as well.

Scholars have long argued that the most fundamental discovery in information storage and communication was the invention of the written phonetic alphabet in the sixth or seventh century B.C., and that the stylus, the printing press, and now the electronic byte were only different methods of recording alphabetic writing. This argument commands respect, but the appearance of each new recording method has brought with it such extensive social disturbances and institutional rearrangements, particularly in education, as strongly to suggest that the appearance of a new way of storing and transmitting information brings profound cultural changes. Historians generally assume that Johannes Gutenberg and movable type in the fifteenth century cracked the old medieval world apart and played a central part in creating the modern world with its widely distributed, cheaper, uniform printed materials. Less well recorded, but equally radical, was the earlier transformation of Athens in the sixth and fifth centuries B.C. from an oral to a manuscript society, from the recited poems of Homer to the written philosophy of Plato, with effects that are dramatized in the Socratic dialogues.

And now, in the latter twentieth century, the transition from a print to an electronic society has been accompanied by equally profound cultural disturbances. The extent of the change first appeared in television. At the outset many professors, myself included, refused to allow it in the house, hoping to preserve conversation and reading; but in the long run it was impossible to resist. The children wanted it so much, since all their friends had it and talked about it, and we could watch football and baseball, or even the Army-McCarthy hearings. And, perhaps the most insidious persuader of all, parents could prop the children in front of it before supper, giving husband and wife time to have a drink together and talk about the day without interruption. On weekends, too, we could sleep later while the children amused themselves for hours with cartoons and advertisements for candy and toys.

So there it was in the house, finally, a big square black metal box with its rabbit ears standing on top, and in some ways it was a medium of the starkest and most unforgiving truth. "If there was one thing the piercing eye of the television camera was able to convey to the people," says David Halberstam in The Fifties (1993), "it was what was authentic and what was artificial." Halberstam was talking about the Kennedy-Nixon debates in 1960, when Nixon lost the election in effect because the huge number of people watching the spectacle saw him as pale, sweating, and horribly nervous, in contrast with a cool and self-possessed Jack Kennedy, made up effectively, perfectly at ease and in complete control of the situation. Whether this was reality or another piece of showbiz remains open to question, but there is no doubt that again and again in the early decades of television it did reveal reality sharply. It was particularly effective in opening up the problems of blacks in the segregated society of the south, particularly in the Montgomery bus boycott and the Little Rock school integration crisis. It helped defeat the opportunism of Joe McCarthy and his henchmen, Roy Cohn and G. David Schine, and it revealed the power of Mafia crime families in hearings conducted by Senator Estes Kefauver. On the "tiny screen" Fidel Castro took over Cuba, Nikita S. Khrushchev pounded the table in the United Nations with his shoe and promised to bury America, Timothy Leary recommended drugs, and the French army was defeated by the Vietnamese at Dien Bien Phu. In the sixties, television would bring the Vietnam War into the American home.

It was all real enough, but as reality was absorbed into TV it was reworked by the medium. The time between innings in baseball, and after punts in football, to take obvious examples, expanded to allow for advertisements. In the civic life of the nation the politics of issues was transformed into a politics of images, in which charisma became all-important and no point that required more than four words could be made effectively. Events on the news were so dramatized, cut, ordered, framed, interpreted, that they too became art forms, but an art of the false and unreal. An entire ethos gradually emerged in the melange of ads, political announcements, sports, sitcoms, westerns, and public service programs. TV was good natured and laughed a lot, but it was intolerant of anything much out of the ordinary. It was anti-intellectual, taking things at their most democratically obvious. It was family centered, presenting in ads and dramas a pompous and foolish but hardworking father, a shrewd but retiring mother, and a bunch of loud, go-getting children. It was relentlessly materialistic, dedicated to acquisitiveness, and while the family came first, firstness consisted of getting more and bigger cars, dishwashers, clothes, and houses. Any deviation from the great middle-class way was as ruthlessly exterminated on TV as the crazy gunslingers who were cut down without pity on the streets of Old Dodge City every Saturday night by a flinty Marshal Matt Dillon, to the admiration of the whore with a heart of gold, Miss Kitty, wise old Doc, and the "forwardly challenged" Chester.

Television is the technological actualization of Plato's cave, a mass medium controlled by advertising and playing therefore to a mass market, throwing on the screen almost totally false images of the world. Falsity is built into a Pavlovian device that works by telling its subjects how free and individual they are even while conditioning them. The degree to which it has trivialized and vulgarized American life has yet, I think, to be fully understood, but the outlines are clear to anyone who looks. Americans are a different people than they once were, and what they are has largely been made by TV.

Television is at odds with education in ways that can be seen most distinctly in a comparison with literature. Literature, as much a product of print culture as bardic poetry and Homeric epic were of oral, tribal society, has always been a book-centered Gutenberg institution—try to imagine literary studies without books, a library, or reading! "Oral literature" is really an oxymoron, at least until the orally composed text is printed. But now, as the printed book gives way to electronic media as the most efficient and attractive source of entertainment and information, literature increasingly seems located in the intellectual rustbelt.

Print and literature encouraged the close analysis of a text, reading it again and again to produce subtle, sophisticated, ironic interpretations. The Great Books gave permanent form to literary art, crystalline, perfect, complete, and unchanging. Literature was considered a revelation of the deep workings of the human mind, a ritualization of permanent truths about the human condition, in words of the greatest expressivity, an ornament to its language and nation, a source of knowledge for society at large, and a benefit to all individuals who read it with the care it required, which it repaid many times over.

Where a dense printed text, like one of Shakespeare's works, encourages complex interpretations, the TV image is direct and uncomplicated: what you see is what you get. People accustomed to this way of getting information are not very interested in the complicated books and ways of reading that are central to literature. Nor are they likely to continue to accord to printed books and reading the cultural importance that literature has been able to take for granted in the past. Where literature was elitist, TV is democratic. It obviously does not favor authors as print did; fifty years of television made not one writer, or even one director, famous—it has made only stars. Its works are ephemeral, seen for an instant on the screen and then, except for reruns, gone forever, never to live long lives on library shelves. Its substance is the visual image and orality, not the more abstract printed word, and it therefore does not encourage the intellectual complexity — irony, ambiguity, paradox — or the elaborate structure of ideas that is characteristic of printed books. Although the products of television can, of course, be closely analyzed and complexly interpreted by Gutenberg people accustomed to print modes of close reading, they do not often get this kind of interpretation because they do not ask for it or need it.

In the 1980s the print-based university was still very much with us, and it was at its very best at Princeton University Press, where I was a member of the editorial board and later one of the trustees. There was a pleasant, somewhat old-fashioned air about the Press. We were given not a gold coin but two new twenty-dollar bills at the beginning of each meeting we attended. PUP emphasized book design and was one of the few American publishers that had its own printing plant (which it has since sold), and its high-quality work made us all feel a little closer to the history of books and the days when the bookseller and the printer were still closely related. PUP had been founded by a Princeton graduate, Charles Scribner, and since then it had been overseen by one or another of the members of this distinguished family of publishers.

When I served, however, times had changed, and the chairman of the board was Harold McGraw, notorious for having beaten back a hostile takeover of his company, McGraw-Hill, mainly a publisher of technical books and trade magazines, by American Express. Harold was a great friend of mine and of the Princeton Press, but he represented a new kind of publishing. Once when I sat next to him at dinner, trying to make conversation, I asked him which of the many books his firm had published he took the most pride in. He might well have said the edition of the Boswell papers that McGraw-Hill had financed and printed over many years at a considerable loss, but he said nothing. As the silence deepened I slowly realized that he probably couldn't remember any of the books his firm had published: this was not his line of work. I was indebted to him for paying for the publication of one of my books, on the effects of print, but he was essentially a man of high finance. He gave me lunch one day in the dining room at the top of the

McGraw-Hill building in Rockefeller Center, a room decorated in the style of a colonial tavern, complete with fireplaces and wooden doors that opened on nothing but air for sixty floors down.

Being on the editorial board was familiar but interesting work. There were four of us, one professor from each division of the university, and we met once a month with the editors to consider the books they were recommending for publication. The number of manuscripts submitted rose steadily—from 740 in 1972 to 1,129 in 1981—and the number accepted rose comparably, from 83 in 1971 to 118 in 1981. The board members did not read the manuscripts, unless there was a particular interest or problem, but made decisions on the basis of the reports of two or three outside specialists and the recommendations of the editors. Herb Bailey was a fine director, very knowledgeable about print and publishing, and editors Jerry Sherwood, Sandy Thatcher, and Joanna Hitchcock were sensible and smart. Ed Tenner, the science editor, was a brilliant man who later wrote an excellent book, *Why Things Bite Back: Technology and the Revenge of Unintended Consequences* (1996), on the downside of new technologies, which comments very nicely on the subject of this chapter. The faculty members of the board, such as the historian of print Bob Darnton, the astrophysicist Jerry Ostriker, the mathematical physicist Art Wightman, the specialist in Japanese Earl Miner, were all prime scholars as well as people with a professional interest in print and printing, so that a meeting was usually a high-level seminar on a wide variety of topics and a broad discussion of publishing. This was one of the few academic committees that people actually enjoyed, and it made you feel that you were part of the long and very highest tradition of learning and the printed book.

But it was a changing tradition. There were too many books being written by scholars seeking only promotion, and there were too many being published, at Princeton and elsewhere. And was there, after all, such a great difference between the books we published and those we turned down? Reader's reports, on which so much depended, were not always the unbiased and careful work of experts they were supposed to be but often the careless products of whatever mood busy people happened to be in when they wrote them. And after a time it was impossible not to see that there were ruling fashions in scholarship and publishing as in everything else. We took turns chairing the editorial board, and after his four-year term Darnton delivered a wonderful spoof on trendiness in publishing:

> Don't submit a book. Submit a series. . . . If you must propose a book, make it a book about birds [Herb Bailey was a dedicated ornithologist]. . . . If you can't come up with a field guide to birds, choose one of the following subjects: William Blake; Samuel Beckett; the nobility of almost any French province between the sixteenth and eighteenth centuries; a new theory of justice; a translation of anything Japanese. . . . The press reader must be able to say in his report, "This study combines hard digging in empirical data with a significant contribution to theory."

In his good-natured way Darnton was saying that the worm of custom had bored deep into the apple of book knowledge, and its progress was revealed with each new batch of manuscripts: books about how we lost China, about Greek rhetoric, about who was responsible for World War I, about whether John Ruskin went mad seeing circles or squares, about John Maynard Keynes in Bloomsbury, about the morality of dropping the atomic bomb, about whether Roosevelt knew about the Holocaust, about slavery, Romanticism, parapsychology, the ice age and the dinosaurs, medieval religious and social thought, the art of the fin de siècle, the French Revolution, the Russian Revolution, revolutions, the causes of poverty, race relations, the totalitarian state, Freud and Jung, mercantilism, and on and on.

It all ought to have been reassuring—scholars exploring the multiple aspects of this great world—but in a way it was also dispiriting. It produced the same mixed feelings that a great library does: what a treasure house of knowledge, on one hand, something about everything; a library of Babel, on the other, an infinity of books saying everything imaginable about every conceivable subject, a quagmire in which all certainty is lost. In an endless line, the books argued now one side of a question, now its opposite: that Marx, not Nietzsche, is the true prophet of postmodernism; that nurture rather than nature, or vice versa, determines character; that all truths are relative, or that some of them are absolute; that all wars are unjust, or that there is such a thing as a just war. You will supply your own favorite overworked dilemmas, but we will in the end come to the same place: a growing suspicion that the Preacher was right when he said, "Of the making of many books there is no end; and much study is a weariness of the flesh."

We were near the end of the golden age of print, and hard times were beginning to be felt in the libraries. Libraries, particularly the great collections of the research universities, are visible monuments of the printed book, and at every level of operations they began in the eighties to be in deep trouble. Columbia University decided in 1990 to close its prestigious library school—except, presciently, for the rare book section—on the grounds that the professional study of books and their management no longer had a place in a research university. And in the twelve years before that, fourteen other library schools, out of a total of fifty-three, had closed, including those at the University of Chicago, the University of Southern California, and Vanderbilt University.

It was discovered—an omen of things to come, as it were—that large numbers of books were disappearing before our eyes from the shelves of the older libraries. The fact is, a recent report concluded, that "all book repositories are self-destructing time bombs." It had long been known that the pulp paper made after about 1870 disintegrates over time because the alum-rosin that helps it take ink evenly combines with moisture to form an acid that breaks down the bond between the pulp fibers; but now the "shelf date" had arrived, and the libraries were faced with the fact that "40 percent of the books in major research collections in the United States will soon be too fragile to handle." The deterioration can be halted by a difficult process of deacidification, and some of the books can be saved by being microfilmed. But these remedies are so labor intensive and therefore expensive as to make it possible to save only a relatively few of the endangered books.

There seemed to be no good news for the libraries, which are particularly vulnerable to the economic squeeze. Prices of printed materials continued to outstrip both the general rate of inflation and the rate of growth of library resources. Journal prices rose by 400 percent from 1970 to 1990, and books by almost 40 percent from 1985 to 1990. Despite more than a 300 percent growth in library expenditures from 1970 to 1990, acquisition of books and monographs declined by 30 percent, while the amount of published material worldwide that libraries needed to acquire increased by as much as 50 to 100 percent. Despite cuts in purchases, cataloguing arrearages continued to mount. Even if libraries continued to acquire new materials at the present rate, much less at the rate they might wish to, they were faced with building new space at a cost of tens of millions of dollars, with associated ongoing maintenance and operating expenses.

Book publishing was in no better shape than the libraries that bought its products. Indeed, the two, like drowning swimmers, were intensifying each other's problems. In spite of the challenge of electronic information, the book is not about to go away. About eleven thousand titles were published in the United States in 1950, when commercial television first appeared in quantity. By 1970, thirty-six thousand books were printed, and by 1979 approximately forty-five thousand. The rate of increase continued into the nineties. Publishers' income during this time rose even faster, from $500 million in 1950 to more than $7 billion in 1979. But prosperity was only on the surface, for during the same time the average sale of single titles of trade books dropped below twenty-five hundred, and the standard university press monograph by 1990 sold only about five hundred copies, almost all to libraries. Both trade and academic publishers responded to the drop in sales by escalating prices and doubling the number of titles published, which pushed sales down still further—stagflation. And the returns from the bookstores reached landslide proportions. Just to add to the difficulties, the federal government began taxing unsold inventories of published books in a way that makes it uneconomical for commercial publishers to keep printed books in stock past the end of any tax year (thus the perennial difficulty of getting textbooks needed for classes).

As sales of academic monographs dropped below five hundred, which was regularly the case with literary criticism titles, they went below the break-even point, and smaller university presses like those at the University of Florida, Rutgers, and Penn State eliminated weaker subjects altogether. Other university presses cut back severely, looking for "quasi-trade" books that would sell in the five thousand range. The presses at Ohio State, Northwestern, Penn State, the University of Iowa, and other places were warned that they could no longer expect the university subsidies that had kept them in business. Publishing was in trouble everywhere, but scholarly publication particularly felt the strain, and careers that had depended on it suffered greatly. By 1997 Columbia University Press began "publishing" some of its monographs only on the World Wide Web, printing copies from the database only when an order was received.

The decline of print was felt not only in literature but throughout the educational system, which from the little red schoolhouses to the great research universities had been built on the printed book and universal literacy. What was wrong? Most obviously, something had gone amiss with the linked skills of reading and writing. A survey conducted by the Census Bureau in 1982 found 13 percent of American adults to be illiterate, and the New York Times reported that "the most widely held estimate is that from 23 million to 27 million adults, nearly 10 percent of the nation's population, cannot read and write well enough to meet the basic requirements of everyday life" (September 7, 1988). Among those who can read but choose not to, the so-called aliterate, various surveys show that something like 60 percent of adult Americans never read a book of any kind, and a majority of the remainder read no more than one book a year.

The results began to show up in the universities between 1963 and 1995, when the average verbal scores based on reading skills on the SATs declined from 478, an all-time high (on a scale of 200–800), to 424. The average math scores fell but not nearly so much, from 502 to 466, suggesting that reading is in more trouble than figuring. "In 1977, a blue-ribbon panel commissioned by the College Board concluded that the decline was the result in part of the increased ethnic diversity of the test-takers, but also of lowered expectations, less homework, the proliferation of nonacademic courses and grade inflation" (New York Times, August 28, 1996). But no one in modern America likes to admit what really happens, and great efforts have been made to cover up the decline. Failure, after all, is only getting the image wrong. Princeton decided over the protests of some of the faculty, including myself, to allow the students themselves to decide whether they needed to take a remedial English course, to which they had previously been assigned on the basis of their work on a graded writing sample. Though writing skills, as well as reading skills, were noticeably dropping in the college, far fewer elected the course; "argal," fewer needed help in writing.

Using the same kind of logic, the College Board, which administers the SAT exams, in 1995 decided to "recenter" the scoring, meaning that anyone who previously would have scored 424 on the verbal test would now receive a 500, and a perfect score of 800 would be given not only to those who answered all the questions correctly but to those who formerly would have received a 730. "We don't define perfect that way," said Bradley J. Quin, head of the program, when asked if giving someone a perfect score for a less than perfect performance would not misrepresent the facts. But Diane Ravitch did not blink the facts: "One need only read the proposed 'National English Standards,' developed by the National Council of Teachers of English and the International Reading Association, to see the incoherence in the field of 'language arts.' If English teachers believe that grammar and proper syntax are unimportant, then it is not surprising that their students would perform poorly on a test of standard English. What is the practical result of recentering? The College Board has turned the deplorable performance on the verbal test into a new norm. The old average was a standard that American education aspired to meet; the new average validates mediocrity" (*New York Times*, August 28, 1996).

In my last years of teaching an undergraduate lecture course in Shakespeare, even with very intelligent students, I found myself looking for ways of getting around the fact that they had not read the texts, or had read them with almost no comprehension. Easy enough in the lectures — you simply filled in the story, read and explained key passages; but in the discussion sections I had to devise the method of picking a central scene, assigning students parts to read in it, having them play the scene, and then, only then, talking about what it meant. One student complimented me, he thought, by saying at the end of term that I had made the plays sound sufficiently interesting that he hoped that he would have time to read them someday.

The literacy crisis is a fundamental threat to traditional higher education but particularly to literature, and postmodernism indirectly recentered the literacy crisis in remarkable detail, by offering strange new theories of reading. Reading, our critics agreed, is a very difficult matter. Phenomenological "reader-response" and "reception-aesthetic" types of literary criticism characterized literary texts as incomplete and riddled with gaps, making reading a "problematic" activity, not an exact skill, thus providing room for a multiplicity of interpretations, no one of which is right or "privileged" over any other. Harold Bloom, by way of another example, told us of reader-poets who must mis-read earlier texts to avoid being influenced and deprived of their own authentic voices by their predecessors. Reading badly is, paradoxically, reading well in the world of Bloom. Structuralists preferred "writerly" over "readerly" texts—that is, books in which readers project their own concerns into the texts rather than subjecting themselves, in the way literate people once did, to "authoritarian" texts and authors that determine meaning. Hermeneutics, a general theory of interpretation, posits that meaning is never in the text but always in the theory of interpretation applied to it. Deconstruction assumes nonreferentiality and a basic indeterminacy in all language, and a consequent semantic instability in any text, making reading always uncertain and relativistic.

The simultaneous appearance of a literacy crisis that threatens literature and a literary criticism that apologizes for decreasing reading skills by explaining how hard, if not impossible, it is to read what is printed is still another demonstration of how the various components—social, technological, moral, theoretical—all move in the same direction.

Cause and effect are tricky business, and it would be hard to say that the electronic revolution caused the literacy crisis, though it is difficult not to suspect electronics when we learn that the television set is on seven hours a day in the typical American home. At first, electronics looked the way all new technologies do, only adjuncts to the traditional operations of the university, new and more efficient forms of typewriter, slide-rule, and mimeograph, rather than revolutionary ways of doing and conceiving things. But their effects reached deep into academic life in ways that Professor Morris Zapp, the antihero of David Lodge's novel *Small World* (1984) describes for a novice teacher:

> There are three things which have revolutionized aca-
> demic life in the last twenty years, though very few
> people have woken up to the fact: jet travel, direct-
> dialing telephones and the Xerox machine. Scholars
> don't have to work in the same institution to inter-
> act, nowadays: they call each other up, or they meet at
> international conferences. And they don't have to grub
> about in library stacks for data: any book or article
> that sounds interesting they have Xeroxed and read it
> at home. Or on the plane going to the next conference.
> I work most at home or on planes these days. I seldom
> go into the university except to teach my courses.

Since Zapp's time e-mail and the Internet have created a multi-versity as large as the world and nearly finished emptying the library and the professors' offices. Money was required for these changes, and during the flush times of the eighties the cornucopia opened and provided for the first time free use of long-distance telephone lines, secretarial help, expenses for travel to conferences, stamps and stationery in abundance, funds to pay for professional meetings, frequent leaves, and support for lectures by visitors in such numbers that they became a plague. The Princeton English department chairman had a fund that gave him forty thousand dollars a year to distribute as he saw fit, to support scholarship, paying the dental bills of ailing professors, and providing, on one remarkable occasion, all the meals for the graduate students in English for the entire month of July in the Annex, a local restaurant.

The contrast with older times was enormous. Then you had to beg letterhead from the departmental secretary and arrange ahead of time to make a long-distance call, establishing that university business was involved. If you had to deliver a paper, the university would pay tourist-fare air travel, but no other expenses, for one conference each year. In the early seventies when I was the director of humanities at Yale, with a large volume of correspondence, I had to plead for some secretarial help and was given, as a special favor, a few hours a week of the time of a typist in the graduate school. I scrounged an old dictating machine and took the belts to the secretary, who would type them as she had spare time in her schedule. Almost all professors, even the most distinguished, still did their own typing, unless they had a grant from some outside agency, and these were almost nonexistent in the humanities.

In the eighteenth century Alexander Pope described in *The Dunciad* a transformation from a manuscript to a print culture. He correctly foretold that print and the values it encouraged would destroy the old system of polite letters and the society of which it was a part, but he was wrong in his concluding prediction that the triumph of print would restore barbarism and the universal darkness of printer's ink would cover all. Instead print produced a new culture, including an educational system based on the reading and writing of printed books and centered in the library. There is no reason to think that the electronic era will not be similarly responsive to human needs, but what it will produce will be different. My argument, here as elsewhere, is not that bad is replacing good but rather something new replacing the old.

Some say, of course, that the database and CD are only new ways of publishing books, in the end more efficient than the scribal manuscript and the printed book. Modems will give us, it is said, entry at last to a complete union catalogue, elaborately indexed, that will provide instant access to all the books ever printed, which will be stored in a super database that will be the library of the future, as available to scholars in Dolts' Corners as in Cambridge. On the other hand, there are apocalyptic *Dunciad* views that the electronic age will be one in which "the growing impoverishment of language will escalate through a series of vicious cycles. Curricula will be streamlined and simplified, and difficult texts will be pruned and glossed. Fewer and fewer people will be able to contend with the masterworks of literature or ideas. Joyce, Woolf, James and the rest will go unread, and the civilizing energies of their prose will circulate aimlessly between closed covers. Whatever exchange of ideas there may have been in our society will wither away except among the echelons of the professional academics. The gulf between the academic and the man on the street, already wide, will become unbridgeable."

But electronic technologies have not so far destroyed institutions so much as remade them, in the way that television has already transformed such important activities as politics and news, even religion—which is increasingly becoming televangelism. When we look at the transforming power of electronics on society's other major institutions, can we doubt that education and learning will be similarly affected? The change is already well under way. Gutenberg concepts that no longer seem real in an electronic world—like copyright, plagiarism, creativity—are already becoming vague. The ambiguities, ironies, and complex structures of thought fostered by printed words are beginning to seem increasingly superfluous. Where the fixity of the printed book encouraged the conception of masterworks and permanent human truths, databases and hypertexts—in which one thing mixes easily with others and information expands exponentially—and television programs that flicker past, never to be seen or heard again, make Gutenberg ideas like originality, form, and permanence seem the quaint notions of another people.

At the deepest level, the steadying ballast of educational institutions is their governing concept of the nature of truth and falsity. And the computer, which is now used everywhere and for every purpose in the modern college and university, brings with it a distinctly different concept of truth than the printed book carried. Information, we might say, has replaced knowledge, and the difference was at once apparent even to nonspecialists like myself when we shifted from the typewriter to the desktop computer in the eighties. After a typed text had been corrected a few times, further changes, particularly moving big blocks of material, became impractical, and when it was printed it was locked into typographical fixity. But making changes large and small, moving big chunks about, and endless revision were the normal way of working on the word processor; and though the text might eventually be printed, even then it would remain available on disk for subsequent modification and reuse. If not printed, it could still be distributed online and endlessly adjusted to meet objections and take advantage of new developments. Other comments would gather around and become part of a new hypertext file. Small changes, perhaps, but they have the effect of making a writer (not to mention a reader) feel that a text is an ongoing interactive process, a set of endless possibilities never exploited or finally realized. At the same time the amount of information available in databases and on the World Wide Web, doubling in size every six months, has created an overload in which single facts are lost in the immensity of informational space. With these changes, the whole world of book-based knowledge monumentalized in the library began to shift and to metamorphose into a fluid movement of information and data. We can perhaps get a sense of the information society's ever-changing surplus of bits and bytes from the database run by the *New York Times*, into which the daily edition is dumped every day after the paper is printed, elaborately cross-indexed, a vast information bank searchable in full text on-line. If this is the future, then the computer brings us not the solid certainty of facts that it promised but a relativity of information that we are also seeing in our politics, theory, social causes, and educational system.

13

No Obligation to Be Right,
Only to Be Interesting

teaching as power and politics,

princeton, the 1980s

Everyone breathed a sigh of relief when 1984 ended without the totalitarianism that George Orwell had foreseen in *Nineteen Eighty-Four* coming to pass. Deconstruction may have brought something resembling "memory holes" and "newspeak," but in America "the death of the author" did not take place in the gulag. Instead of Orwell's world of poverty and perpetual shortages, Reagan's America was a world of booming markets, surplus goods, and new freedoms, where power was exercised not by electroshock and truncheon but by public relations, television, protests, and image control. And when the Russian empire imploded in the late eighties, the competition between democratic and

246

totalitarian principles seemed to have been decided absolutely in democracy's favor.

But while Marxism may have failed in Moscow, class conflict thrived on the American campus, where gender, race, and class politics increasingly drove academic debate. If the seventies had been the time of radical theories, then the eighties were the time when politics began increasingly to replace professionalism in the universities. Government lent powerful reinforcement to the new concept of a university with regulations and funding that favored social justice over knowledge or merit. Women and minorities could now openly use their subjects to argue for the purposes of their cause. New class divisions appeared in faculties where the institutional reputation was now established by the presence of academic "stars," and the books of the new "demoversity" were balanced by doing much of the teaching with "off-the-ladder," poorly paid, part-time help.

Women, backed up by governmental affirmative action programs and the courts, took the lead in demanding new remedies for old injustice. Higher education had long been primarily a masculine institution, but now women demanded equality in hiring and salary levels. The men didn't like it very much, realizing that a feminized university was going to take away their "old boys' club," and there were, and still are, pockets of resistance, particularly in the sciences. But the majority of male faculty members had a guilty conscience on this matter, particularly after most schools had gone coed, and faculty women soon began to appear in larger numbers. This was particularly true in the humanities, and especially in literature, fields that over the years had attracted more women and fewer men into graduate study, to the point that they were already well on their way to becoming "women's subjects."

Princeton's English department offers an instructive example of how things went in an elite Ivy League school. A distinguished feminist from Rutgers, Elaine Showalter, author of *Women's Liberation and Literature* (1971), became head of the department, and Sandra Gilbert, author with Susan Gubar of *The Madwoman in the Attic* (1979), was a chaired professor. The defining feminist appointment, however, in a department that was soon to become primarily female, was that of Margaret Anne Doody, who arrived from Berkeley, where it was said that the department threw a huge party on the night she accepted the Princeton offer. It was not her scholarship or teaching that had worn out her welcome—far from it, for she was a premier student of eighteenth-century literature, and as a teacher she soon had almost all the Princeton students, no matter what their fields, writing dissertations with her. She encouraged them to work with her, something that was considered infra dig in the old days, but she also, in a way women do more easily than men, paid attention to them personally, invited them to parties, spent endless time listening to them. They loved her, and "writing with Margaret" soon became the way of saying that you were working on a dissertation.

A Canadian woman and a product of an Oxford women's college, she was a donnish feminist of the old Helen Gardner stamp, a writer of learned detective stories such as *Aristotle Detective*, unmarried and willing to let you know straightway what she thought about masculine silliness. Her old-fashioned, schoolmistressy kind of feminism seemed, however, far less threatening than the thin-lipped disapproval, narrow-rimmed glasses, tight-bound hair, and feral gaze of some more advanced feminists. It was Margaret's ability to delay a decision forever that made strong men weep, and sometimes women too. Insisting on her rights, she established her authority over all matters in her own and adjacent fields, such as a desperately needed appointment in earlier-eighteenth-century literature. Then, however, she would be unable to make up her mind and would shilly-shally until the year passed and the time-consuming work of identifying candidates, bringing them in to lecture, taking them to dinner, and so on all had to be done again the next year.

Her scholarship showed what the "feminist approach to literature" could be at the very best. *Frances Burney: The Life in the Works* (1988) was a fine biography of the eighteenth-century novelist—who was no longer to be called "Fanny," or "little Miss Burney," as that archetypal male Dr. Johnson, and many a male since, had patronizingly done. The interest of novels that had been long underrated was raised by showing in them a theme of the greatest social importance, the bitter sex war underlying the polite surfaces of society in general, and a fierce hatred of intelligent women for the men who controlled them.

The move of women into English took place not just at Princeton but across the country, and while doctoral degrees in literature declined sharply in number nationwide from 1966 to 1993, the percentage of women receiving Ph.D.s in that field went from 29 percent to 60 percent of the total in the same period. In other subjects the increase in female faculty was not quite so large, but the trend was definite. Between 1966 and 1993 the percentage of doctoral degrees in all disciplines conferred on women went from 11 percent to 38 percent. The increases were much greater in some areas than others, and by 1990 more than one-third of the members of humanities and social sciences faculties were women.

Affirmative action, the term for the broad social and governmental movement to redress old grievances, in practice helped women more than any other group, but it also very much included blacks, Latinos, Asians, homosexuals, various third-world groups, particularly those from former European colonies, and last the handicapped. Tenure appointments and control of budgets were the primary goals of this loosely organized movement, united perhaps only in its shared dislike of the traditional DWEM (dead white European male) political and educational establishment. But establishing their particular cause as a university subject was important too, for it raised the social status of the subjects seeking recognition. A department of Latino studies was felt to confer on Central and South America a long-denied parity with Europe, for example. Courses in gay and lesbian history and writings were believed not just to reveal the experience of these sexual orientations but to give dignity to, bringing into the open and forcing acceptance of, sexual practices that society had until recently preferred to keep in the closet and designate as perversion.

Under pressure from these groups, politicization of the university accelerated, and every appointment, every tenure decision, every expenditure of funds became a power struggle. Sit-ins, marches to "take back the night," denunciations, threats, strikes, legal suits, use of the media, all became standard devices for insisting that more African-American professors be hired—even though they remained in short supply—or that Latinos be given minority status and included in affirmative action plans, or that rape crisis centers and women's studies programs be funded. Every group seeking change learned that you could get what you wanted by pressuring the authorities, and even Jewish groups, who normally, because of their great success in higher education, defended meritocratic practices and opposed special treatment for any group in admissions or hiring, found that they could get Hebrew studies and Holocaust centers by playing the political game.

To speak openly against any of these "minority" causes, for any reason, became increasingly uncomfortable. The feelings on campus about these matters were so strong, the resentments so fierce, the tendency to choose up sides so pronounced, the memories so long, the knives so sharp, that anyone with doubts tended just to shut up. The intensity of feeling can be heard in the remark by the radical feminist Susan McClary that Beethoven's Ninth Symphony is filled with "the throttling, murderous rage of a rapist incapable of attaining release." Most feminist scholars would laugh at the exaggeration of this statement, but it still gives some idea of the powerful feelings that were at work behind the feminist and minority issues. To think and act the right way became known as political correctness, or "PC," and though the radicals insisted that there was no party line on campus, it was generally understood that it was unwise to oppose any of their plans directly. In this way small groups of activists acquired power on campus far in excess of their numbers, and they began to turn tyrannical. The university administrators under these pressures, not hearing from more conservative elements in the faculty, tended to give in to preserve the peace and, since it was a time when large amounts of money were available from inflating tuitions and high return on investments, simply to buy their way out of trouble.

Opposing views were at sword's point, and a most depressing incident at Princeton about this time illustrated just how charged the academic atmosphere could become, how mixed-up the tensions between male and female, heterosexual and homosexual, young and old, traditional scholarship and politicized modern interpretations, right wing and left wing; how much, I am tempted to add, personal values had entered into and inflamed professional concerns. There were personal quarrels in the old days—academics are always a contentious lot—but there was also at least some attempt to keep discussion on a professional level and to leave more heated disciplinary matters to the deans. But now it was a dog and cat fight.

In the spring of 1989 the campus was filled with wicked gossip, and the *New York Times* reported the Princeton "administration's refusal to oust a professor accused of criminal sexual advances on a student" (May 11, 1989). Dorothy Rabinowitz, a reporter for *New York* magazine, "motored down," as some members of the English department liked to say, from New York to interview the leading figures in the growing scandal. They seemed eager to tell all, and they were, if the resulting article is to be believed (no one challenged her account), remarkably frank. A full story appeared under the title "Arms and the Man: A Sex Scandal Rocks Princeton," in *New York* magazine (July 17, 1989), from which the following information is taken.

An unnamed new graduate student described how a senior English professor, Thomas McFarland, had taken him home from the opening departmental party and forced him, a virgin, he said, onto a couch, holding his hands behind him. The professor had been undeterred by powerful imprecations: "Sir, I do not approve of this. I'm a Catholic. And I'm a Republican." Unfazed by the sacred word, Tom supposedly replied brusquely, "I'm a Republican too. I'm voting for George Bush," and proceeded with the work in hand. When McFarland told him to take off his sweater, the student remembered his mother undressing him for bed, and when McFarland dozed off he said the Lord's Prayer. Eventually he escaped and after a few hours' sleep went to the home of Showalter, then the director of graduate studies, who put him in the hands of the university rape counselor, who passed him on to the dean of the faculty.

McFarland was equally eager to tell his side of the story, and he pulled no punches. The whole thing was, he insisted, "a trivial incident," and he had trouble understanding why there was so much excitement about it. The student had after all, according to his account, "courted [him] rather aggressively." "If I hadn't been drinking, I wouldn't have looked at him twice anyway." You have to understand, he went on matter-of-factly, "I like to *dominate*. It was a tussle. That's what it was. Usually with boys, they want to wrestle to show their *macho* credentials. I've never liked anybody who wasn't heterosexual. Most of the people I've liked tend to be of an age when they would be students. All the great loves of my life have been students." But Princeton, McFarland went on, was a loveless place: "One reason I've always hated Princeton is that I've never found love here. At the end of my first year here, I just put my head down on my office desk and started weeping. I hadn't found anybody to love, that's why." Friends at City University of New York, where he had been teaching before he came to Princeton, had warned him, "You're not going to like it there. Princeton is not what you think." When he returned from a year on leave he "realized there wasn't a single person in this place I wanted to see enough to go and knock on his or her door. I can't tell you what a *melancholy* feeling *that* was." I was troubled by this since I was one of those he didn't want to see, though we had been friendly for a long time: both conservatives, both old-fashioned scholars, both products of the Yale graduate school in the same years.

This was the beginning of grim scenes played out on the inner stage of Nassau Hall, where a new president unfamiliar with Princeton had yet to settle in. When charges were first made, the dean of the faculty had "quietly suspended" McFarland, simply notifying the department that he would not be teaching that year. But as the controversy grew and it looked likely that there might be further sanctions, perhaps even dismissal, McFarland did what had by then become standard procedure: he got a very tough and efficient lawyer who began talking about due process, evidence, no witnesses, one man's word against another's, and the dangers to the university of scandal and suits. After listening to the lawyer, the dean decided that, as he had presumably originally intended, at the end of his suspension McFarland had to be reinstated in the English department; but in angry meeting after angry meeting the professors of English, led by the redoubtable Margaret Anne Doody, who had become the point woman in the matter, refused absolutely to accept him as a colleague again or to let him teach classes in the English department. A question of moral conduct, which in an earlier time when the authority of the administration was stronger, and the professors less politically active, would have been kept out of the faculty arena, was now thrown into the fiery furnace of departmental politics. The temperature was very high, and "friends" from the department came around to try to persuade McFarland to get out of town, warning him, he told Rabinowitz, "I fear for your life if you go back to that department."

There were many reasons, McFarland felt, why he was pursued so relentlessly in the department. Besides homophobia and the "loveless" Princeton ethos, there were now scholarly jealousy and academic politics. He was a traditional scholar of Shakespeare and of Romanticism, a member of the Wordsworth Dove Cottage crowd, and an editor of some of Coleridge's most arcane writings. In the past, Rabinowitz reported, he had not hesitated to scorn his colleagues' views:

> McFarland sent his senior colleagues a memo caustically describing the qualifications of new people the department was considering hiring. It said, in part, "The candidates seem excessively weighted toward not very serious women." Looking down the list of the candidates' dissertation topics, McFarland wrote, he saw only mock sociology, mock anthropology, grandiose forays into feminist theory, and "almost nothing connected in any promising way with English literature. . . . I do not like to believe, indeed I cannot believe, that this is the best being offered by American graduate education in English."

Now, McFarland felt, his colleagues were taking their revenge on him for his frankness and high professional standards.

But Margaret Doody would have none of it. In this kind of sensationalist journalism no one comes out well, and in Rabinowitz's hands Doody the schoolmistress became "a blonde in her late forties," her voice a sound that "could summon the dead to attention—a penetrating instrument that rises and falls in precisely calculated degrees," a moral prude, a militant feminist trying to put down an aggressive male, a narrow-minded crusader against vice. Still, she was allowed to speak for herself, and she denounced vigorously what she considered "a breach of trust and a violent assault upon a student." "Teaching is a responsibility," she went on; "a human being has been put in your charge. You have the utmost responsibility not to damage him." She was not, she insisted, being simply homophobic: "What we are talking about here is violence. It does not matter what the gender preference is. It's true that some professors for a very long time have seen students as a box of chocolates for their delectation. I think this is a wicked attitude, and I think it should cease."

Four senior English professors resigned in protest at the possibility of McFarland's return. Actually three of them had already decided to go to various schools in California for personal and professional reasons, but in these bizarre circumstances they thought they might as well maximize the effect of their departures by saying they were protesting the way the administration was handling the McFarland affair. The fourth, Doody, really did leave Princeton for Vanderbilt because of what she considered the spinelessness of the administration. But whatever the real motivations, the resignations stirred the kettle even more vigorously. The undergraduates threatened to picket if McFarland was returned to the classroom, and the graduate student who had first brought the complaint set about filing charges in court. So the university used the ancient technique of buying McFarland out, making a "settlement agreement," as it was called, paying his annual salary of about eighty thousand dollars for, it was said, eight years.

The anti-McFarland movement was hoist by its own petard. They were the ones who refused to have him back in the department, after all, thereby forcing the buyout. They were the ones who spread the news throughout academia that made it impossible for McFarland to get another job, ensuring that he would have years of leave on full salary. But they did not blame themselves, of course; they transferred their anger to an administration that in their opinion lacked the guts simply to fire someone they considered a rapist. Sex, homosexuality, male versus female, scholarship, appointments, teaching, personal lives, and academic business had all gotten badly mixed up with one another to create the kind of mess that tears faculties apart.

This sad business lightened only a bit when the affair was loosely fictionalized (at least so it was widely believed) in a book that appeared a few years later from the pen of Joyce Carol Oates, the best-selling novelist who had by this time taken up a faculty appointment at Princeton. While not a member of the English department, she had been deeply interested in the McFarland affair and must have shared the widespread feeling that the settlement, far from settling things, looked like lining McFarland's jockstrap with chinchilla. In her spare time Oates, who had an overproduction problem, turned out mystery novels under the nom de plume Rosamond Smith. In 1990 she dedicated to Emory Elliot, the chairman of the English department (one of those who had resigned and left for the Happy Valley), a story of murder at the Forest Park Conservatory of Music in Connecticut titled Nemesis. The heroine and central character is Maggie Blackburn, a fictional version of Margaret Doody (Margaret plus "burn" for Fanny Burney?), a lady of exquisite moral sensibilities as well as a fastidious concern for dress. Young Brendan Bauer, talented but poor and less than self-confident, a stutterer recently resigned from a Jesuit seminary, arrives at the welcoming party for his class at Maggie's house, where he is picked up by Rolfe Christensen, an older Pulitzer Prize–winning composer, taken home, gotten drunk, and raped. Christensen is a lout, a dandy given to wearing a jacket of a poisonous green, a drunk, greedy, a roller of big cigars, a homosexual who has seduced and destroyed young men all his life. He drives a flashy car, is filled with himself, and is so uncaring as to leave a window open at Maggie's house, killing her two canaries. In seducing young men he prefers strong-arm methods of the kind young Bauer describes: "He hurt me bad . . . he's very strong . . . he's big, heavy . . . must weigh t-t-two hundred th-thirty pounds . . . played at strangling me . . . laughed at me . . . said I wanted it too . . ."

When Christensen is murdered with poisoned chocolates—"It's true that some professors for a very long time have seen students as a box of chocolates for their delectation"—Brendan is immediately arrested, but shortly afterward another faculty member who has been appointed the administrator of Christensen's estate is also murdered, bound with the same length of electrical cord that was used in Brendan's rape and on Christensen. There is an unsuspected murderer loose, and who should it be but the provost of the conservatory, Calvin Gould, who had himself been seduced by Christensen years before when he was a young pianist and had his career ruined. So justice is at last done, the rapist eats one chocolate too many, the evil administrator who knew what was going on all the time, and was married to his sister—Oates fancies the incest theme—kills himself when Maggie finds him out. All a spoof, of course, laughing at the conventions of the murder mystery as well as the follies of the academy, but bitter laughter in these hard times.

The distinguished medievalist Durant Robertson, upon retirement, had glumly predicted that bringing women into the department would also invite the conflicts found in the McFarland case. But women are no more irrational and unprofessional than men, and many of them in my experience are much more clearheaded. What was new in the McFarland case, and the many battles fought across the country in the same bloody manner, was not the personalities of women or blacks or homosexuals but the injection into departmental affairs of political and social concerns. There were no longer any restraints on the expression of the strongest and most personal kinds of feelings, and radical decisions were made that had formerly been subdued by professional beliefs about what was decidable by a department. The outcome of the McFarland affair might well have been the same under the old professional dispensation, or maybe the old boys' club would have protected him, but it certainly would have been managed in a less painful and destructive fashion. I tend to think that a good thing; others will say that it is better for everything to come out into the open, but all will agree, I think, that it was a new way of doing faculty business.

The breakup of universities into special-interest pressure groups was accelerated by the appearance of a wider academic class system than had been known before. This was ironic, since the new activism absolutely denounced class differences. Faculties were always hierarchical, but increasingly a group of "stars" appeared at the top, while at the bottom a teaching underclass began to appear in numbers never known before. This trend was not so apparent at elite universities like Princeton, though more and more of the teaching there got done by graduate students. Elsewhere large numbers of teachers found themselves turned into an intellectual proletariat as universities cut back on junior staff to save money and to avoid having to deal with radical young men and women clamoring for tenure. Entering the academy in the late eighties, many new Ph.D.s became part-time teaching help, paid by the hour or the course, without benefits and off the tenure ladder. The trend has continued, and, according to a Modern Language

Association survey, by 1996–1997 only 37 percent of the 1,106 new recipients of English doctorates obtained tenure-track jobs, down from 46 percent three years earlier, while 38.7 percent accepted non-tenure-track posts. The remainder got no academic jobs of any kind. English was the major disaster area, but other fields of study were not much better off. Across the country more and more teaching is being done by "gypsy scholars" who are sometimes paid as little as four hundred dollars a course. The number of hours they can teach is capped so that the university will not have to pay medical or retirement benefits, and they are forced to work at second and third jobs to earn enough to live. As the job market for new Ph.D.s has continued to shrink, many have not even been able to get part-time work, and a group known sadly as "independent scholars" has appeared.

For the "stars" things were very different. Most American faculty members had earlier stayed in the classroom, the library, and the study, publishing not for general interest but as "a contribution to knowledge," as the old formula for the doctoral dissertation had it. Gradually, however, more and more scholars began to consider themselves public intellectuals, able to speak on matters of importance and interest to the mass audiences that read newspapers and magazines, listen to radio, and watch TV. Kenneth Clark could define civilization in terms of its art, Carl Sagan elucidate the cosmos, and Marshall McLuhan explain the social and psychological effects of the media. Joseph Campbell could interpret the mythology of Western culture, Noam Chomsky lecture the politicians on Vietnam, Allan Bloom open up the failure of Western education, and Stanley Fish debate political correctness and multiculturalism on TV with the conservative Dinesh D'Souza.

The role of the public intellectual, like the eighteenth-century philosophes Denis Diderot and Jean-Jacques Rousseau, was more familiar in Europe than in America until recently. Sometimes associated with the university, as Hegel and Theodor Adorno were, sometimes not, like Thomas Carlyle, Max Weber, Gabriele D'Annunzio, and Jean-Paul Sartre, the primary business of the intellectual is to produce ideas and generate world pictures that interest the public and make sense of things for them. There had been American intellectuals before, such as Ralph Waldo Emerson, Thorstein Veblen, and Walter Lippmann; and the twentieth century fostered in New York a group of people who saw the production and assemblage of ideas as a useful social role. Mary McCarthy and Lillian Hellman seemed born to be intellectuals, and Sidney Hook, William Phillips, Clement Greenberg, Philip Rahv, Dwight Macdonald, Lionel Trilling, and Alfred Kazin took like ducks to water to thinking about things of which they had no practical experience and telling others how to think about them.

But now every American college professor also suddenly seemed to have found a prophet's rod in his book bag, and even quite ordinary professors, like myself, began to work up their memoirs and to present their writings about medieval iconography or voting patterns in nineteenth-century Cincinnati in ways that suggested mystery, novelty, and scandal. Robert Nisbet accurately described what happened in the following way:

> The professor [became] not only teacher and scholar but also political intellectual, man of power in party and government, research enterpriser on a large scale, priest in the religion of individuality, therapist for all student needs, reformer, revolutionary when need be, and humanitarian supreme. And with this concept of himself goes the professor's concept of the university's role as the supreme institution in American life—as privileged aristocracy indeed, owing little, owed much—instead of the last enclave in our society for a detached, honest, and critical assessment of society, as a setting for the scholarly imagination in all areas.

In two novels, Changing Places (1975) and Small World (1984), the British writer and professor David Lodge created a character, Professor Morris Zapp, who was the epitome of the new model professoriat. Zapp was an English professor at Euphoric State, a satiric image of Berkeley, who knew everyone and everything, traveled constantly to conferences, drove fast cars, slept with his students, drew a large salary, and loved publicity. His scholarship, as described in Changing Places, was as voracious as his appetites:

Some years ago [Zapp] had embarked with great enthusiasm on an ambitious critical project: a series of commentaries on Jane Austen which would work through the whole canon, one novel at a time, saying absolutely everything that could possibly be said about them. The idea was to be utterly exhaustive, to examine the novels from every conceivable angle, historical, biographical, rhetorical, mythical, Freudian, Jungian, existentialist, Marxist, structuralist, Christian-allegorical, ethical, exponential, linguistic, phenomenological, archetypal, you name it; so that when each commentary was written there would be simply nothing further to say about the novel in question.

Stanley Fish, a professor at Berkeley in the seventies, was the model for Zapp and freely admitted it, rightly perceiving that while rapaciously opportunistic, Zapp was also lightning-quick mentally, good-hearted, and extremely effective. Fish had begun as a Yale graduate student in the early sixties working with Talbot Donaldson on a very old-fashioned subject, the poems of the early Tudor court writer John Skelton, famous for jangling verses called "Skeltonics." He soon perceived that Skelton was not the wave of the future and wrote a book, Surprised by Sin (1971), on Paradise Lost. Using a variety of "reception-aesthetics," Fish argued that the poem was constructed in such a way that the reader experienced "fall" in numerous fashions, metrical and rhetorical, as well as in the story. He also began to take up and explain in a clear and effective way the various new critical theories that were announcing themselves at the time, always staying just ahead of the fashion, in books with catchy titles like Self-Consuming Artifacts (1972), Is There a Text in This Class? (1980), and There's No Such Thing as Free Speech, and It's a Good Thing, Too (1994).

He moved to Duke University in the 1980s, where he built an English department notorious for its trendy radicalism—it included Frank Lentricchia, "the Dirty Harry of criticism"; Fish's own wife, Jane Tompkins, who tells us in her memoirs that after a time, believing that no one "really" knew anything, she refused to assign reading or subject matter to her classes; and a fierce polemicist known elsewhere as "the Iron Butterfly." Looking always for pastures new, Fish went on to practice deconstruction in the Duke law school—who would have thought lawyers needed any help in complicating texts?—and inevitably wrote a book on the subject, *Doing What Comes Naturally: Change, Rhetoric, and the Practice of Theory in Literary and Legal Studies* (1989).

Fish boasted that he would always be the highest paid professor of English in the country, and he let everyone know when he broke $100,000 in the mid-eighties. He was the star of the lecture circuit, present at every conference on hermeneutics, deconstruction, postmodernism, phenomenology, and new historicism; it was said that he commanded $5,000 a lecture, nearly as much as G. Gordon Liddy of Watergate fame or Henry Louis Gates, the spokesman for the conservative wing of African-American studies. He was perfectly at home in the new age of jet planes, credit cards, and rapidly changing theories, and admirable in his cool mastery of that world. But the smoothness of it all was troubling. The ease with which he moved from one theory to another, the amused way in which the consequences of believing this or that were so accurately described, the trendiness of the conference-circuit topics, had the effect of making literary study seem to be a commodity that could be shopped around in whatever way might be useful to build a more lucrative career.

Fish spoke for the new academic intellectuals when he claimed to have been relieved "of the obligation to be right" and added that the time "demands only that I be interesting." He later "repudiated this declaration" when he came to reprinting it ("Interpreting 'Interpreting the *Variorum*,'" in *Is There a Text in This Class?*), calling it "the most unfortunate sentence I ever wrote," but other academic stars had no second thoughts about the transformation of education into a variety of entertainment. When African-American professors like Leonard Jeffries at CUNY denounced Jews and argued that Western culture originated in a black Egypt, or Camille Paglia said that sex was no fun if the danger was eliminated, there was the smell of ideology, but there was also a sure sense of what would attract TV and newspapers. The Modern Language Association, once the grayest of cats, turned its annual meeting into a white-male-bashing gala where the titles of the sessions, formerly on such staid topics as "Nature in the Romantic Poets" or "Symbolism in the Poetry of Arthur Hugh Clough," vied to be outrageous and inflammatory. "Jane Austen and the Masturbating Girl" was matched by "Teaching as Transgression" and "The Dialectics of Cannibalism in Recent Caribbean Narratives." Papers were called for on "Before Sade: Early Modern Pornography and Literary Culture. How does the production and dissemination of pornographic texts (mis)shape the literary marketplace, and vice versa? Is there any 'cultural capital' associated with obscenity?"

In this world of burgeoning careerism, self-advertisement became an art form, and in the eighties "vitas" began to be longer than Horace once thought. All lectures and book reviews were included, and even lists of manuscripts read for publishers began to creep in. Fellowships and prizes were noted, even if the professor had only applied or been nominated for them: "Short-listed for the ACLS." Participation in panels at conferences increased the length of the vita, and in time no professional act or occasion seemed too trivial to mention.

The vita was the visible symbol of careers that now began in graduate school, where students saved all their seminar papers on computer, sometimes "publishing" them on their home page on the Internet, and sent them out to a multitude of specialized journals that sprang up to provide power for their editors and a place for tyros to publish. Narrowing specialization was the key to the flood of journals—"The John Gay Newsletter," "Gower Studies," "Cross Dressing"—and it was the central feature of the academic career. Subjects were broken down into smaller and smaller pieces, and people made their way in the world by becoming "experts" in one of the bits. A professor at a small community college in California might turn out to be the world's biggest expert on what happened in Hitler's Berlin bunker or how juries voted or Edgar Lee Masters. Once the subject was identified, a "networking" cadre grew up around it—"the Masters people," they would be known as—lectures were exchanged, an annual bibliography put on the Internet, conferences arranged, a journal started, contacts made with European and Asian groups, and international meetings held from time to time. You no longer delivered your paper at one of these many conferences organized to provide travel and networking occasions for academics, you circulated it beforehand and then attended "plenary" sessions where only a few stars actually read their papers aloud.

Celebrity became as critical to careers as knowledge of languages once had been. It didn't much matter whether the publicity was good or bad, scandal in academe was like blood in the water to reporters and anchors on the evening news. All you had to do was be bold enough and get a good lawyer. Professors began to think of themselves as extraordinarily interesting people who were no longer bound by the long-standing ethical practices that had been thought to make university teaching a profession. A time of changing sexual mores, the 1980s tested the old professional standards prohibiting sexual relations, even with consent, between doctor and patient, lawyer and client, professor and student.

I was on the college discipline committee when a poet was brought up on charges by one of his undergraduate students that he had seduced her by taking her to his digs, giving her raspberries, and providing a wine of the same color. She had later decided that this was very wicked—particularly, for some reason, the color coding—even though she had herself opened her chaste treasure to his importunities. Backed up by friends and wrathful parents, she had gone to the dean and asked for justice. The dean was nonplussed. Not only was student-teacher sex commonplace by now, it was no longer at all clear that the college could legally get away with treating as an academic crime an act that, taking place between consenting individuals of legal age, the courts did not consider to be a crime, or even a misdemeanor. There was, in fact, no explicit prohibition in the faculty handbook of sex between professors and students, since it had never been thought to be needed. But the dean was wily, and in the faculty handbook he found that while it might not be forbidden to screw students, it was forbidden to do anything that disrupted the instructional process. So the dean charged the poet with interfering with education and sent him up to the discipline committee. Here the poet insisted, at the great length that was now taken to be the mark of due process, that he and the girl were in love and if he could only see her everything would be all right. But she had had a complete change of heart and appeared before the committee to speak with loathing of "that awful old man" (he was in his thirties) who had taken advantage of her, when she had thought—and this was what really stung—that her teacher considered her a good poet and wanted to help her. After many hours of hearings the poet was found guilty of disrupting education, and the dean suspended him, with pay, for the two remaining months of his contract, not allowing him to teach the few remaining meetings of his poetry class. Only the appearances of the old authority system were left.

It used to be that you would never know the truth of these matters—and perhaps you still don't—but in this age of "teach and tell" it was inevitable that the poet, Michael Ryan, would sooner or later exploit the incident by using it in a book. And so he did, publishing *Secret Life* in 1995, described on the cover as "a searing memoir, superbly crafted." The cover picture was a close-up of a hand reaching through a crotch, probably female, and digging fingers into a soft belly just below the navel. The picture is probably keyed to John Donne's famous lines from Elegy 19, "To His Mistress Going to Bed": "Licence my roaving hands, and let them go, / Before, behind, between, above, below." Ryan's title takes off from the nineteenth-century porn classic *My Secret Life*, and most of the book is a modern version à la Joyce of a Catholic boyhood, complete with angry nuns, masturbation, a drunken father, and child molestation. Ryan portrays himself as obsessed with sex as the result of being molested when he was five by a neighbor just back from the Korean War. This, he says, in turn made him into a molester who sought endlessly to escape his own sense of being depraved by depraving others. The Princeton freshman who brought charges against him, he says, "was only one in a long line of students with whom I re-enacted my own sexual abuse, from the other side, as the molester, as if I could escape its unhappy imprinting by being Bob Stoller [the veteran] and not myself." He even penetrated his dog, he says, to act out his own shame at being penetrated.

By the time he arrived at Princeton in the late 1970s, he was, as he describes it, a sex fiend who thought of nothing but bodies, male and female. He cruised the rough bars of Trenton picking up men, he was the terror of students' parents and local husbands. "I like seductions," he gloats, "especially with students" because "I had power over them. Although I was teaching only two courses, Marcia was getting three grades from me, the third being her senior thesis on John Donne." Teaching was only the means of aggression: "I was her molester. To be invaded, to be confused about where the other person ends and you begin: this is what it feels like to be molested. It is an assault on the nervous system." All this is Donne vulgarized.

Still, he paid off: "I had turned in her grades (two As and an A+)." After this girl threw him over, he found more, filled with self-loathing, he says in his book, taking risks to punish himself but unable to stop because he was transforming himself from the victim into the victimizer. When finally caught and hauled up before the discipline committee, he felt that he was being unfairly treated (though in the book he admits to lying in his testimony), and it took him ten years to see that what he had done was wrong: sexually wrong, that is. He never acknowledges in his book that there was anything professionally or morally wrong with trading grades for sex, or with using his power as a teacher to exploit his charges. He seems never even to have heard of such things as professional ethics. Transfiguration comes to him, he feels, only years later when a student, who has propositioned him, tells him that she had been molested by her father as a child, and he wipes away her tears without feeling her up.

As time went on, predatory sex in the classroom became bolder. Jane Gallop, in *Feminist Accused of Sexual Harassment* (1997), argues that effective education requires sexual interaction between teacher and students. Speaking of two male professors who were on her dissertation committee, she boasts, "Seducing them made me feel kind of cocky and that allowed me to presume I had something to say worth saying." Once she became a faculty member, sex with her own students, male and female, became matter of course. "At its most intense—and, I would argue, its most productive—the pedagogical relation between teacher and student is, in fact, 'a consensual amorous relation.' And if schools decide to prohibit not only sex but 'amorous relations' between teacher and student [she had been sued by two of her female students for harassment on these grounds], the 'consensual amorous relations' that will be banned from our campuses might just be teaching itself."

Power is a zero-sum game in universities, and many of the excesses I have described would not have taken place if university administration still wielded the kind of moral authority deans and provosts once had, the kind that I had seen at its end in James Phinney Baxter at Williams, Whitney Griswold at Yale, and Robert Goheen at Princeton. But as students became activists, staff unionized, faculties politicized, and professors stars, administration became management and education became more and more about economics. By the time it became possible to argue that "good teaching is good sex," presidents and their administrations had become largely fund-raisers, starting ever larger fund drives before the last one ended, and crisis managers trying to satisfy conflicting constituencies (and comply with federal and state regulations) with less and less time for thinking about intellectual issues or shaping education. At Princeton, Bill Bowen had to fight for the large amount of time needed to sort out such complicated intellectual issues as whether to locate microbiology near the chemistry or the physics department. Ill will and distrust covered every disagreement between competing interests with a smog of suspicion. It was a major effort to keep the physical plant from falling down, the endowment from wasting away through inflation and divestments made on political grounds, crime from making the campus uninhabitable. Enormous sums of money were needed to feed the ever louder demands to increase salaries, buy stars, put up new buildings, provide student aid, buy books and journals at madly inflating prices, and on and on. No wonder college presidents more and more were lawyers and economists.

Over the years I had been interviewed for a number of college presidencies, at Carleton College in Minnesota, the University of Colorado, and Swarthmore College, for example. At the last I was thrown into a lecture hall on half an hour's notice and told to describe my conception of a liberal arts education! The experience that made it clear why I was not presidential timber was at Boulder. I was the candidate of a group of science professors at the University of Colorado who wanted to improve the academic status of a large state university that had become more a big-time football team, with a lot of legislative interference, than an educational institution. Boulder is only a hundred miles or so from the ranch where I grew up in Wyoming, and I rather fancied the idea of returning, after all these years, as an apostle of the intellectual life. At first it really did seem like a triumphal return. A state police car met me at the Denver airport and, siren howling, drove at high speed to the capitol, where the chancellor of the university system sat wearing a ten-gallon hat, cowboy boots on the desk, waiting to interview me and make it clear that he ran the show and the vice chancellor at Boulder, which was only the "flagship campus" of the system, did not. Colorado had a huge student body, many of them hikers, climbers, and skiers from out of state. It also had a wonderful campus up against the Rocky Mountains, but intellectually it was what was coming to be known as "the pits." It was also, in keeping with Wild West mythology, as well as the new radicalism, thoroughly democratized, which meant that every interest group on campus had a committee to meet with the presidential candidates. I met with the faculty in the morning, the administrators in the afternoon, the student-body representatives in the evening. The student-body president, who controlled more than a million dollars a year in funds deducted without permission from the students' tuition, took me, along with some members of the football team, to an expensive mountaintop restaurant for dinner, from whence they showed me the political university. The football players got drunk on fancy drinks and grew threatening about Ivy Leaguers. I met with the secretaries and janitors for breakfast, and later with the unions, the scientists, the social scientists, the law school dean, and other professional school deans.

Each group wanted not only to inspect me but also to get my views on their own particular concerns, expecting promises from me as if I were a candidate for political office—which is, of course, just what I was. I tried to remain pleasant but neutral. The only matters where I felt any real competence, faculty appointments and curriculum, were a disappointment. When leading faculty members made it clear to me that they wanted to raise the academic standards of the university across the board, I agreed heartily, gave them my own views, and listened patiently as they explained how full of deadwood the faculty was at the moment. This led me to ask,

> "What is the tenure rate at the present time?"
> "Ninety-seven percent."
> "How do you expect to make any very great
> changes in the faculty when you have only three per-

cent of the positions, plus annual retirements, to work with?"

"Well, we hoped you would be able to work that out."

On the plane back I thought long and hard, and I came to the realization not only that it would be impossible to do what I wanted with the university but that I really did lack in fundamental ways the managerial attitudes and political skills needed to move easily among and get along with all the pressure groups that now had a hand in the political university. I simply had no feel for this kind of thing, and in my fifties, with a risky heart, this was no time to kid myself. I got off the plane in Chicago, called my sponsors in the physics department, and said that I was writing a letter of withdrawal. They didn't like it, but I don't think they would have been able to get me appointed anyway. Shortly afterward, Mary Berry, an African-American professor, was appointed, and she immediately took a leave of absence to work in Washington, placing the administration of the university in the hands of a local nonfaculty administrator, who had probably been the inside candidate all along.

Bart Giamatti was the last hurrah of the old type of college president, more a scholar than a bureaucrat, and his story is a tragic one of how the old ways came to grief in the new university. Bart was a student in the Yale honors program when I was a young teacher. I thought his first paper overwritten, illogical, and generally pompous, and said so. I concluded my lengthy remarks on the paper with the advice: "You must learn to write more simply and directly if you wish to achieve success in any field." Bart was a very cool fellow, popular, exchanging easy jokes with anyone and everyone—"Hey, paisano!"—but within minutes after I had put the paper outside my door he was pounding on it, crushed and angry. Years later, after he had simplified his style and become president of Yale, he would use this story as evidence of how rigorous a Yale education had been in the old days.

It is hard to take your old students as seriously as they deserve in later life. At his inauguration as president of Yale, having driven up from Princeton for the occasion, I looked on, thinking, "What are they doing, making this student president of the university?" His entry into the office was not auspicious. Kingman Brewster, his predecessor, had departed for the Court of St. James's, and the Yale trustees formed a committee headed by Bill Bundy to select his successor, appointing Hanna Gray, the provost, as interim president. The committee decided that Henry Rosovsky, a Yale graduate and now a distinguished economist and dean of the faculty of arts and sciences at Harvard, was just the man. They were so enthusiastic that, instead of sounding him out about whether he would accept the job, they all got on a plane to Boston and rushed into his office to tell him the good news. Henry was not so sure, and he deflated the committee by telling them that he needed a week to think it over, which he did in an airport hotel holed up with Henry Broude, a fellow graduate student in economics at Harvard years before. Broude had also been the assistant to Kingman at Yale, and he knew where all the bodies were buried. At the end of this retreat Rosovsky called in the newspapers to announce publicly that he would rather be dean of Harvard than president of Yale.

At that point the crushed committee should have turned to Hanna Gray, who in truth ought to have been their first candidate anyway. She might well have taken the job, having grown up in New Haven as the daughter of the great German historian Hajo Holborn. Whether they were prejudiced against women, particularly such a no-nonsense woman as Hanna, is an open question, but they passed her over and she went off to the University of Chicago where she had a most successful presidency.

Hurt at having been publicly humiliated, the committee wanted simply to conclude its search as quickly as possible. Giamatti had been a dark horse all along, and now they fastened on him and interviewed him for only half an hour, he told me, before offering him the job. At the inaugural dinner the wife of one of the trustees was asked by another matron who the new president was, and she replied, "Oh, I don't know, some little wop." Bart, who told me this story also, heard the remark and was deeply wounded. His father was a learned professor of Italian at Mount Holyoke College, and his mother was the Bartlett of the middle name he chose to use rather than his given name of Angelo.

No president of Yale entered on his duties, however, with more enthusiastic support from his faculty than A. Bartlett Giamatti. But the real reason Rosovsky had turned the job down, in my opinion, was that Yale had a structural financial deficit and a big backlog of needs. Bart once said sadly that he thought he would be the only president of Yale known for having rewired the campus. The new president had no slush fund from which to reward the faithful; indeed, he had to tighten their collective belts, and faculties do not take well to that kind of thing. ("Why is that man reading books?" asked a distinguished faculty member when he saw the president of Princeton, Harold Shapiro, reading a new scholarly book in the university bookstore. "Why isn't he out raising money for us?") Bart wasn't really cut out for looking Jock Whitneys and Paul Mellons in the eye and casually asking for several million, so he turned in the other direction and began making budget cuts in areas like sports and theater. He found himself locking horns with faculty members who could not understand why so rich a university as Yale always had to be cutting back. "Why not spend out the endowment?" one actually said—an economic historian no less. "The government will never let us go out of business."

PR went no better than finances. A big quarrel with Robert Brustein over personal differences sent the man who had revivified the Yale theater off to Harvard. Bart made a strong appointment when he persuaded the fine lawyer and dean of the law school Abe Goldstein to become provost. He gave Goldstein a fund of $100,000, not so much really, for remodeling the provost's house, a gloomy old Federal pile on Hillhouse Avenue where my family had lived in the Bobby Seale days. The student newspaper, the abominable *Yale Daily News*, found out about the cost of the repairs and spread outrage through the community: "All that paint and wallpaper, those new electrical outlets!" Scenting corruption, the college newshawks were in the president's office in Woodbridge Hall in a flash. "How can you waste money like this when you are cutting back on classes and professors?" Bart had no feel for the delicacy of the matter or the importance of the media, and he faltered about just how much he had authorized: "The decorators probably ran over budget a bit, but it will be corrected." The headlines screamed: "Did the provost spend more than entitled?" Goldstein, stuck in an impossible situation, was properly outraged and resigned, leaving Bart with the difficult job of persuading someone else to take the critical position of provost in those delicate circumstances.

Things came to a crisis in a strike by the clerical and laboratory staff to raise their salaries by a large amount. Social trends had changed the world on all levels by then. Women, who had once been content with low-paying but genteel university jobs because their husbands' salaries could keep the family going, now were often divorced or needed to contribute more to pay the mortgage. Urged on by the perennially ugly union relations at Yale, and by the events of the sixties that had taught everyone how you got what you wanted, the staff turned militant. It was very much a part of Bart's old-fashioned sense of his responsibilities that he did not let himself be pressured into a decision, and in this case when he determined that the university really did not have the several million that were required to meet the demands, he made up his mind to take a strike.

Male and female, town and gown, ethnic and WASP, rich and poor, radical and conservative: it was a witches' brew from the start. The more radical professors furiously flung themselves into the fight on the side of the union, refusing to teach classes on campus and attacking the president viciously wherever they could find him. He was a great football fan, and when he went to a game at the Yale Bowl the pickets gathered to block his path and spat on him as he went by. When I last saw him, after he had announced his resignation, we talked quietly about his student days, and he told me that he was looking for a job. When I assured him that many fine things would come his way, he replied, "Well, they haven't shown up yet." As I left him at the top of the marble stairs outside his office in Woodbridge Hall, he said quietly that he had come to hate much of the university for its hypocritical, self-serving, and cowardly ways.

Of course this was only the prologue to another battle that raised the stakes to a national level. If Woodrow Wilson, another Ivy League president, had his Dean West and his Henry Cabot Lodge, Giamatti had Pete Rose, a relationship detailed in a fascinating study by James Reston, *Collision at Home Plate* (1991). The job that eventually came Bart's way, of course, was commissioner of baseball, and while many in the academic world thought it vulgar for a former president of Yale to take such a position, the man who had always been the most ardent of Boston Red Sox fans and had managed the Yale baseball team considered it his boyhood dream come true. He had the same idealistic view of the purity of baseball that he had of Yale University. His antagonist, however, was the genuine baseball thing, a tough, raunchy, redneck kid who without the skills of a DiMaggio or a Mantle had fought his way to the top of baseball by sheer guts and effort, earning the nickname "Charley Hustle" and becoming the all-time leader in hits in the major leagues. When the drinker and brawler Rose was caught betting on games played by the team he was managing, the Cincinnati Reds, the former college professor and president banned the most popular player in baseball from the game. Charley Hustle didn't take anything lying down, and he fought back; Bart, author of *The Earthly Paradise*, a study of the Garden of Eden in Renaissance literature, would not compromise on the rules that made the game meaningful. Aimed at each other across the years in the manner of Greek tragedy, the two destroyed each other.

They sang "Amazing Grace," his favorite hymn, at Bart's funeral, and the vastness of Woolsey Hall was filled with old friends and enemies. His son Marcus, an actor, spoke fervently of his father, the huge blue "Yale" banner was in the background, the organ brayed "Bright College Years," and the great from far and near praised him as an educator, a man of true principle in a time that had little. One could not help feeling what a totally in-group ceremony it was. Yale was burying one of its own who had done well in a trying life. I may have been alone in thinking that the ritual with all its outsizeness, like the big blue banner and Woolsey Hall itself, exalted a man who had been caught between the old ways of Yale and the new. He was buried across the street in the Grove Street Cemetery, but not in the formal plot for Yale presidents.

It has been argued that relativism and politicization had beneficial effects on the universities, opening up the classroom to the "real world" and clearing away at last the delusions of Enlightenment positivism and the old authoritarianism that in many forms went with it. The record does not, I think, entirely support this sanguine view. The sciences, though they had early along legitimated relativism, were immune from its worst excesses in the universities. Feminist physics ("Newton's *Principia* is a rape manual") and feminist biology ("the laws of nature are patriarchal") were voiced, but they never took hold. Elsewhere, though, it takes an effort to remember the bright hopes of discovering truth that made academic study so lively and so promising in the period after World War II. Margaret Mead's influential study of the American character, *And Keep Your Powder Dry* (1942), may include some boastful remarks ("I leave ideas lying around like pencils"), and her work on growing up in Samoa and reputation were later devastated, but can we help missing her confidence that the social sciences might show us how to "organize a society in which war will have no place? to find the conditions in a culture, in its system of education, in its systems of interpersonal relationships which promote a sense of free will"? How could she have been so certain that the social sciences, particularly anthropology, could "analyze the problems of man's relationships to man as we have analyzed the problems of man's relationship to nature" and that the success of this intellectual venture will "set us free"? B. F. Skinner was no less sure of psychology's power to open up the development of the human mind, Talcott Parsons of sociology's ability to construct a total model of society, and Northrop Frye of literature's capability to reveal the mystical symbolic code that constitutes the human soul. These and many other scholars expressed an enormous optimism that energized the entire academic enterprise. It was possible to do something meaningful, to understand the totality of things.

That feeling of great achievement is gone now, almost without a trace, disappearing into its own impossibility. Relativism and politicization did not destroy it; they filled the vacuum when the old dreams of absolute truth and great learning failed, and the universities they now govern are fragmented, nervous, uncertain, demoralized. Psychology once provided a symbolic center for the whole rationalist enterprise of the old university, the system of the mind, but when the distinguished British psychologist Liam Hudson looked over his subject recently, he saw

> something . . . enduringly melancholy: an academic
> landscape that lacks an adequate foundation in the

truth. . . . While outwardly respectable, like Trollope's Barchester, the self-consciously scientific tradition in psychology emerges as a venue dominated by shabby scholarship and creative scandalmongering; objectivity becomes a slogan, probity a trick of the light. . . . [T]he discipline is not a society of good men and true which harbours the occasional malefactor, but one in which the wilful promotion of one view of reality at the expense of all others is the norm. Psychology is fated, it seems, to serve as one of society's ideological tiltyards. . . . Obviously, it is pointless to pretend that psychology is even a protoscience.

Sociology and anthropology, where grand theories had once attracted scholars the way flames attract moths, have arrived at something like a terminal paralysis. Postmodernist anthropological theories hold that investigators cannot overcome their own biases long enough to say anything objective about different cultures, and that to describe the poverty or ignorance of another culture is to become a collaborator in imperialism. "What right do we have to write about them?" is a question that leaves not much to do except to argue with one another. As one commentator summed up the situation, "Our anthropological Hamlets [are] tortured by doubts about how far one culture could ever really grasp the categories of another."

The "engenderment of history" and "history from the bottom" brought a much fuller sense of the social past, no longer a listing of wars and rulers. But postmodernism also brought to history, at least to some degree, what Gertrude Himmelfarb called "radical skepticism, relativism, and subjectivism that denies not this or that truth about any subject but the very idea of truth—that denies even the *ideal* of truth, truth as something to aspire to even if it can never be fully attained." It became increasingly hard to know what value except disputation the historian could claim for his or her work if facts had become a "fetish" and all methodology "problematic."

It was once again literature, however, that showed the dangers of field disintegration implicit in a relativistic and politically conceived course of study. F. R. Leavis, who had provided the gravity of literary studies a generation earlier, once wrote hopefully that departments of English might come in time to be the "living centres" of universities; but in our time, one writer remarked with clenched teeth that he could read Leavis's words now "only with a sense of pathos and grim mirth." Courses, or centers, or in some cases new departments, appeared for the study of the writings of women, of African-Americans, of Latin Americans, and so on. It was at first argued that these were works of high literary quality that had been unfairly excluded from the traditional canon of literature—Homer, Shakespeare, Goethe—in the interests of maintaining the authority of white European males. In time, however, the aesthetic argument was largely dropped and it was simply said that literature had always been not an aesthetic but a political construct, one way to assert through art the dominance of the masculine power structure. To give the neglected writings of popular culture (or of women or African-Americans or various third-world writers) the status of literature by teaching them in the university was not only to bring their virtues to the attention of the world but to seize—the language was always militant—their rightful place in the power structure for the peoples they represented.

It was argued that the excellence of novels was established not by their formal properties but by the effects they had on society. *Little Women* and *Uncle Tom's Cabin* were by this standard far more important than *The Golden Bowl* or *Huckleberry Finn*. Ideology overwhelmed aesthetics, and the dictum "Read only until you find the victim" ruled. Eugene Goodheart summarizes the kind of questions literature was now raising: "What is the colonialist argument in *The Tempest?* Is Jane Austen complicit with the patriarchy in her celebration of the marriages of her main characters? Is *Heart of Darkness* an imperialist and racist work? Is T. S. Eliot's muse anti-Semitism?" At the extreme, it was denied that there is any meaningful difference between popular culture and high literary art —"logic, linearity, and form are only white, male ideology." The subject itself vaporized, to the point that Houston Baker, professor of English at the University of Pennsylvania and president of the Modern Language Association, could say that the difference between Virginia Woolf and Pearl Buck is no greater than that "between a hoagie and a pizza."

In the end large groups of faculty simply moved out of English to new departments called "cultural studies," and those who remained behind were content to follow their own interests in a fragmented field that no longer had any center or any boundaries. One of the major proponents of the new order, my former student Stephen Greenblatt, spoke candidly of changes that have "called into question the cohesiveness of the field as a whole." Literary study, he went on without regret, can no longer "be comprehended within a single, cohesive frame. What confronts us at the present time in English and American literary studies is not a unified field at all but diverse historical projects and critical idioms that are not organized around a single center but originate from a variety of sources, some of which lie outside the realm of literary study altogether and intersect one another often at strange angles." Old Professor Freeman's question at Oxford a century earlier, "If literature be not about language, what is it about?" would seem to be still waiting for an answer.

14

The Break Between Generations,
Retirement

With powerful centrifugal forces at work, departmental meetings became endlessly divisive and inconclusive. But it was in the classroom that the changes being wrought by new educational philosophies and practices came home most painfully. My undergraduate lecture course on Shakespeare—not helped by the fact that most of the students did not read the plays—was barely sputtering along. As I tried to talk about the way Shakespeare set the tavern off against the palace, or what it meant for an old man like King Lear to have all his traditional beliefs and values disintegrate, a terrible hopelessness would come over me, making it almost impossible to go on as I realized that the students were not in the slightest interested. My voice would deaden and my argument become confused as I tried to skip material and find more vivid ways of making a point. This all made it worse, and the students were ruthless in their comments in the course critique.

Not only had I lost the feel for the students, the classroom itself had changed in fundamental ways. The setting I took for normal was I suppose that described by Jim Maddox in his earlier recollections of the first day in class with me. But different attitudes had by now created a classroom scene that had given up, as Janet Malcolm describes it, its search for solid understanding:

> Modern American pedagogy is poised on the fiction that there is no "greater man" or "lesser man" in the teacher/student dyad. Although the socratizing lecture course is still offered, the action in American higher (no less than lower) education is in the democratizing discussion class. Here any idiotic thing the student says is listened to as if it was brilliant, and here our national vice of talking for the sake of hearing ourselves talk is cultivated as if it was a virtue. A good teacher is some-one who can somehow transform this discouraging gathering of babblers into an inspiring community of minds working together.

So much for the days when teachers said things like "What d'ya mean you don't know? Are you stupid or something?" These leveling undercurrents were not helped by the huge increases in tuition that became normal in this period and changed the relationship of teacher and student to a cash nexus. Average tuition in four-year colleges increased 90 percent between 1970 and 1995, to $12,800 in private schools and $3,000 in public ones. During the same time median family income increased only 9 percent. At the elite schools increases were much higher. When I went to Williams in 1946 the yearly tuition was $450 and my room and board $550. At these prices, the college was giving you out of generosity something in value far in excess of what you were paying. But in 1996–1997 the combined cost at Williams was $28,050 per year, at a time when the median U.S. income before taxes was $35,000. And though aid per full-time student had increased, students could only feel that they were dealing with a marketplace situation. Paying so much, they inevitably demanded economic value in return: entertainment, high grades, relevance, job preparation, certification for admission to professional schools. The trend was laid out precisely in a letter by Mason Lowance to the *Princeton Alumni Magazine* in 1997: "The alarming facts are that between 1980 and 1994, household incomes went up 90 percent, inflation went up 84 percent, and college costs went up 234 percent. Meanwhile, the academic year—the actual time most teachers spend in the classroom—contracted from 36 weeks to 28 weeks."

Probably no single consequence of the expensive classroom was so hard on a teacher's morale as the grade inflation that had begun during the Vietnam War and by the 1980s was built into the system. At Princeton between 1960 and the late 1980s As rose from 16.9 percent of the grades given to 41.2 percent, while Cs dropped from 19.6 percent to 9.4 percent, with almost all of the lowest grades in the sciences and engineering. But how could you penalize your students when they applied for jobs and professional school when other schools were still handing out ever higher grades? At Cornell the percentage of As had doubled, and at Harvard the average grade rose to an A−/B+ from a B/B− average in 1965. At Stanford, "the grade F does not exist. . . . The C is fast becoming extinct. If a B looms, a student can parachute out of a course on the day of the final exam with no consequences. The median grade for undergraduates last year was an A minus" (Michelle Quinn, *New York Times,* May 31, 1994). At Penn, 20 percent of graduating seniors received highest honors, where only 3 percent had done so twenty-five years earlier.

Why do professors go along with grade inflation, which so clearly undercuts their authority and violates their sense of their own integrity? One professor wrote the *New York Times* that "the chairman of my department changed a student's F (32 out of a possible 105 points) to a passing grade. The justification? 'Both of his parents are lawyers' " (July 7, 1995). But fear of being sued is only a secondary concern in a more general breakdown of the authority that a realistic grading system once conferred on teachers and institutions. When the certainty in truth goes it becomes impossible to fail anyone. Gone were the days when Goey Franciscus protested but laughed when I refused to change his ludicrous but instructive grade of minus 40. Now, a famous movie star's daughter came to complain about a grade of C that I had given her terrible essay, on the grounds that "There is no such grade as C." I showed her the registrar's official list of grades, and she still didn't believe it.

I managed to hold my graduate teaching together by offering a course on literature as a social institution, but only a few students were any longer working with me on dissertations. Directing graduate dissertations is the labor of the mine and the galley, and I was grateful for no longer having ten going at a time, as I had at Yale in the early seventies. But I remembered Bill Wimsatt complaining that no students came around to work with him anymore, and I could not help realizing that the same thing was happening to me. The absence of dissertations was a signal that my interests no longer coincided with those of the students, that I was "out of it." Just how far out became clear one day in midsummer when I noticed a new dissertation, titled "What's in a Name?" on Shakespeare's *Romeo and Juliet* on the departmental secretary's desk. My subject, so I sat down to look at it and, as if it had come from some literary Unabomber, it blew up in my hands. Its purpose, the author said, was to "provide astrological identification indicating how Romeo's and Juliet's stars are crossed, as well as which stars. In addition, the other planets ('stars') known to the Renaissance are also onomastically [by the use of names] indicated, and, when combined with the crossed stars of Romeo and Juliet, delineate a complete astrological chart that Shakespeare uses as a structural framework for the play."

So OK, I thought, many things are possible. There was nothing absolutely wrong with an astrological reading of the play: astrology was very much alive in Shakespeare's time, as it was still in the Reagan White House in ours, and the play does speak in astrological terms of the lovers as being "star crossed." But the evidence used to prove the argument that *Romeo and Juliet* was a coded horoscope of the lovers gave big trouble.

The key to the code was said to be located in the names of various characters, which were then racked to force them to yield certain signs of the zodiac and the names of stars or planets. The unpacking began with the four servants, Shakespeare's additions to the story that was the play's source, who appear in the opening scene of the play. Gregory the servant = Gregory the Great, the pope who Christianized Britain = baptism = water used in the sacrament of baptism = Aquarius. Sampson, his mate, yielded in turn the sign of Leo, for the young lion who roared at the biblical Samson and was torn apart for his trouble. Balthasar was not the wise man who followed the star to the manger at Bethlehem, which would have been too easy, but the Chaldean king in the time of the biblical Daniel, Belshazzar, whose name "in time became associated with death," and the house of death is Scorpio. Scorpio also rules the genitalia, which are referred to in the line "Draw thy tool" spoken by Gregory when Balthasar enters in the first scene. The patriarch Abram, or Abraham—the form of the name was considered important and led to a long, learned discussion—came at the beginning of the third of the six ages of the world, the first two being those of Adam and Noah, but he lived in the second age, which "might possibly point to Taurus, the second sign of the zodiac."

The ruling signs of the zodiac, Aquarius, Leo, Scorpio, and Taurus, established, it appeared that they were "fixed qualities," representations of the four elements of earth, air, fire, and water. Using them it was possible to construct a "chaplet" (Capulet) or Fixed Grand Cross, "an astrological configuration having four planets equally distributed through the zodiac."

Other characters of the play were then deciphered as the planets that move through the zodiacal signs. Romeo is Venus because he walks in "a grove of sycamore," and some ancient authority had said that the sycamore is dedicated to Venus. Old Capulet is Saturn, and Mercutio is of course Mercury. The actions of the plot are said to correspond to the movements of stars through the heavens. Since Tybalt, "the king of cats" (= Leo the lion), and Mercutio are "united in death in their duel, we could also say that Leo and Mercury are united." Death is near whenever Balthasar (Scorpio = death) appears. There are death scenes in which he is not present, but these are ignored.

All of this was constructed with the utmost surety and in straightforward prose. When the two Capulet servants, Sampson and Gregory, say that they are glad they are not "colliers," or coal miners who dig in the earth, punning at the same time on "collar"—usually said to be a reference to hanging, or death—the author analyzes their speech with calm certainty in her pseudoscience:

Inasmuch as each sign of the zodiac rules over a part of the body (see Diagram 9), Taurus ruling over the neck, we could say [this putatory kind of construction is frequent] that Samson and Gregory are specifically glad not to be of the earth sign which rules the neck, i.e. Taurus. We have already conjectured that Taurus might also be indicated by the name of Abram, a servant in the House of Montague. Now, the one thing we would expect Samson and Gregory, as loyal members of the House of Capulet, to be glad they are not is that they are not of the House of Montague. Since they are also glad not to be of the sign of Taurus, we can confirm [supposition has now become fact] the conjecture that Shakespeare used Abram rather than Abraham (since Abram would indicate Taurus but Abraham would not).

The author was herself a magus-astrologer. Her faculty mentor was pursuing numerological readings of Spenser. Neither of them seemed to have ever considered what the effect for literature would be of reducing some of its major works to secret codes. This was very much a hush-hush project, being hurried through in the middle of the summer when few people were around, an orals board of three or four sympathetic people could be assembled late on some quiet day, a few words exchanged, the dissertation certified as passed, and a recommendation for the doctorate sent to the graduate school. Some of the reasons why such an outrageous piece of nonsense was being pushed through were to be found in the tangled undergrowth of the history of the Princeton English department. Although this particular dissertation was not characteristic of what was being produced in the Princeton English department, it was an indication of what could get through in the eighties with the ascendancy of the view that one reading is as good as any other.

To give someone a Princeton Ph.D. for this kind of rubbish was unthinkable to me; it seemed to signal the end of the rational tradition, at least in literature, its disappearance back into the darkness from which the Enlightenment had freed us. I set out to derail the train by urging the few professors still around to read—not to fail, but only to read—the dissertation and attend the oral; by going to visit the new graduate dean; and by calling the chairman of the English department, John Fleming, who was teaching in Vermont. Fleming told me that he thought this was the only dissertation of this kind still out there in the dark, but he wouldn't swear to it, and that he was going to do absolutely nothing to prevent this particular student from leaving the graduate school as soon as possible. The graduate dean, Ted Ziolkowski, a man of far sterner scholarly standards than my own, promised to look into the case but found that he could do nothing this far along in the process. "Earlier?" "Perhaps." I persuaded only two junior faculty members I found in the library to look at the dissertation and attend the oral exam. One of them voted with me against passing the dissertation, while the other abstained. Three others present, including the director, voted yes, thus passing the dissertation and in effect awarding the degree.

I protested, I wrote letters, but to no avail. The department was simply annoyed by my intensity. I was not only intellectually outraged, I was humiliated that I was unable to stop this travesty of scholarship. But I was forced to realize my powerlessness, not only in the face of the growing irrationality in the academy, of which astrology seemed the appropriate symbol, but of the crafty old Princeton politics that settled things by going for a walk after lunch. I extracted a few concessions from the department in the fall about the way oral defenses were to be handled publicly in the future, but after voting these changes the professors promptly ignored them.

Well, if teaching in the present seemed to have gone to hell, you could always take comfort from teaching past. Or so I thought. Nothing should please a teacher more than to see his former students mature into fine scholars and teachers, as many of mine had. But I should have known that it was not this simple from my own earlier experiences with Clay Hunt and Charles Prouty.

I got to know Stephen Greenblatt when he took undergraduate courses with me at Yale in the early sixties, and I supervised his undergraduate essay, which won all the prizes and was published as *Three Modern Satirists: Waugh, Orwell, and Huxley* in 1965, just after he received his bachelor's degree. Steve and I were sympathetic, and we corresponded when he went off to Cambridge to study with F. R. Leavis and win more prizes; and when he hesitated between the law and literary studies, I offered long letters arguing for the latter. I can't remember what the attractions I offered were, but they must have helped, for in time he came back to Yale to earn his doctorate, and we saw each other frequently in class and out. I remember particularly, because it took on a good deal of significance later, a long discussion about the need for a truly social theory of literature, as opposed to the still reigning formalistic New Criticism. Neither of us could know the political direction a social criticism would eventually take, nor how large a part Steve and his New Historicism would have in defining one branch of it. But he decided to explore the question at a basic level in his dissertation, "Sir Walter Raleigh: The Functions of Art in the Life of the Courtier and the Adventurer," which I directed and which also won all the prizes and was soon published.

I never tried to write dissertations for my students or tell them in detail what to do, only to criticize what they had written in rough drafts, suggesting possibilities for elaboration and for deletion. I did not imprint them with any methodology or ideology; I had none, except for the standard New Critical emphasis on the formal properties of the actual text. I was also somewhat reserved in manner, and, though we got along well usually, students never became "mine" in some intense master-pupil relationship, either personally or intellectually, as they did in, say, Harold Bloom's case. Openness of mind and precise observation were all I hoped to encourage, so I never felt patriarchal about students whose dissertations I directed.

I was therefore a bit startled when, some years later, without naming me, Steve, who by then was a professor at Berkeley and had progressed mightily in the academic world, wrote a piece in a prominent journal in which he expounded an oedipal theory of intellectual development, making it clear that it was very important for him to feel that he was entirely the author of his own achievements. I had no interest in playing Laius in this drama—Jocasta was, I suppose, Wisdom or Athena—but once this particular play was mentioned I developed certain sensitivities that I had earlier thought not to exist. I noticed that my name appeared seldom in the indexes of his books, for example, and on one occasion he sent a soft-cover copy of a book he had dedicated to me and to Martin Price, another of his mentors, with an inscription to the effect that the dedication had inadvertently been left out of the original hard-cover edition. Well now, literary professors can turn a fact into a symbol with the flick of a cigar. "Hard-cover?" "soft-cover?" You could make a fifty-minute lecture out of either term, a course out of both of them together. And what is this business about "dedication" and "inscription"?

By then the very size and extent—how to get clear of this oedipal language?—of Steve's accomplishments shone with a brightness that cast my own more modest achievements into shadow. He had published a series of books—including *Renaissance Self-Fashioning* (1980) and *Shakespearean Negotiations* (1987)—that made him known as one of our primary literary critics. He had founded a school of criticism, New Historicism, that swept the field, and he had given prestigious lecture series at Montevallo, Tel Aviv, Yale, Tokyo, Harvard, Chicago, Oxford, Princeton. He had held fellowships from Cornell, the National Endowment for the Humanities, the Guggenheim Foundation, the American Council of Learned Societies, the Fulbright fund, and on and on. He had taught at Florence, Trieste, Paris, Chicago, Bologna, Peking, and Harvard, where he eventually settled. His essay "Invisible Bullets: Renaissance Authority and Its Subversion" was often said to be the most influential in Renaissance studies in recent years, and he was proclaimed "the greatest Renaissance scholar of our time." He founded and edits a magazine, *Representations*, that has established a new way of looking at culture and its artifacts. He discussed deconstruction with East German commissars on trains rocketing through the mid-European winter, he exculpated presidents and taught Shakespeare to the admiring Chinese, he summered near Florence and wintered in Morocco.

How to react to this rather overwhelming success? Smiling modestly in the back row of the photograph, identified as a former teacher in the key to the picture, is the standard placement, but it comes not so easily, I was finding. Steve and I maintained a warm if sporadic friendship over the years, helping each other as the opportunity for a review or a letter occurred. Sue and I danced at his wedding to Ellen and went with them on trips when we were both in London at the same time.

When I heard him lecture he always referred warmly to the presence of his old teacher. But we seldom talked about literary matters. The method Steve called New Historicism had real problems, I thought. His idea was to start with interpreting some curious piece of sensational lore from deep in the historical records of the Renaissance— a hermaphrodite, a man who thought that the world was made of a piece of rotting cheese, torturing Indians, how to identify a witch— and then to assert that it was a universal subtext of the time, circulating through all texts, and that it provided the key to understanding some major literary work, usually a Shakespearean play. "Truffle hunting" one critic called the concentration on "vaginal friction" in Twelfth Night, and my own formalist view was that the primary meaning of any literary work was best found by going right down the middle of a text, noting and synthesizing its major, not its marginal, themes. Then too, the New Historicists assume that all writers are politically subversive, as they themselves are to some degree, while my own view is that the artist versus society became the norm only after the Romantic revolution in the late eighteenth century, and that some kind of close relationship with a powerful patron was the usual situation in earlier ages.

But whatever objections I might have, Steve had clearly found an answer to the question we had discussed so long ago, a way of putting literary works in their historical context in ways that made both more interesting, and in doing so gave literature a significant part in social and individual life. Where earlier Renaissance theater historians put their audiences to sleep with background talk about the year the Thames froze over, Banks the horse who counted with his hoof, and Kindheart the toothdrawer, Steve dug up the Catholic conception of Purgatory, the way it related the living and the dead, and the key it offered to the various "maimed rites" of Hamlet.

A pinch of reverse schadenfreude, I am afraid, colored my intellectual reservations about New Historicism, but I was pleased to discover in time that mine was not merely the envy of a master for a student who outdoes him so much as it was the disappointment that comes when a student makes clear where you fell short, where you might have done better if only you had worked harder, let your imagination play more freely over your material, taken more intellectual risks, really thought

hard about what kind of criticism would best serve the cause of literature. Too bad, but a brilliant student inevitably adds to a master's sense
that the world has passed him by, a bit before he thought it was his
time to leave the stage.

Some of the academics I most admired were far less willing to
make their peace with the changes that came to the universities than I
was. My old model Maynard Mack, the man who had shown me what a
teacher of literature might hope to be, violently denounced postmodernism as a serious moral failure: "We are narrowing, not enlarging
our horizons. We are shucking, not assuming our responsibilities. And
we communicate with fewer and fewer because it is easier to jabber in
a jargon than to explain a complicated matter in the real language of
men. How long can a democratic nation afford to support a narcissistic
minority so transfixed by its own image?" (*Prose and Cons*, 1989).

The absolute intransigence of the old guard to the coming of
the new order was acted out in the English department at Harvard,
where I was given a front-row seat when I was appointed chairman
of the standing visiting committee to the department, reporting to the
Board of Overseers. I was given the chance to appoint an all-new committee, and I tried to increase its potential effectiveness by naming
some of the most distinguished professors of literature in the country,
people whom, I thought, the department would have to listen to: Henry
Nash Smith, Donald Davie, Fred Crews, Barbara Herrnstein-Smith, and
Maynard Mack, among others.

By 1980 the Harvard department of English and American literature was still exclusively male in the senior ranks, and the average age
of the professors was over sixty. What had been one of the premier
departments in the country had dwindled over time into a competent
but rather dull and self-satisfied group, dominated by a great scholar,
Walter Jackson Bate. Senior members of the department, distinguished
elderly professors, would look nervously at Jack after they had made
a perfectly commonplace remark to determine whether or not he approved. He was an interesting man, pleasant and powerfully intelligent,
an unmarried midwesterner who had made the department his life, the
kind who could be found in the departmental office, the Hawthornian
Warren House, on Saturdays and Sundays, at Christmas and the Fourth

of July, and since he knew everything and would do all the jobs that no one else wanted he gradually came to own the place. He was also the preeminent scholar in the department, with perhaps the exception of the comparatist Harry Levin, of whom he once remarked, "I thought we rolled a stone in front of that grave years ago." Bate controlled the appointments in the department, and around the time I was made chairman of the visiting committee there was a scandal after he rammed through the promotion to tenure of one of his favorites against the will of the department and the university, and then, just to thumb his nose at timid convention, glowingly reviewed the young man's first book in the New York Review of Books.

Bate was a traditional scholar, a biographer mostly, noted for the standard modern life of Samuel Johnson, with whom he felt great psychological kinship, and he abhorred the structuralism and deconstructive criticism that were making inroads elsewhere, and which, of course, had all the attractions of forbidden fruit to the Harvard students. He taught the criticism course to graduate students out of his own textbook, which contained only traditional criticism. In 1982 he wrote a virulent attack on the new order in Harvard Magazine, charging that overproduction of undereducated Ph.D.s was destroying the great tradition of classical and European letters out of ignorance of the past: "Scarcely one approach to the arts has been advanced in the last twenty years that—in its essential premises—has not been examined and answered (often profoundly) in the previous two thousand years." The humanities, he went on, "seem bent on a self-destructive course, through a combination of anger, fear, and purblind defensiveness; the strongest help from enlightened administration in universities and colleges is indispensable to prevent the suicide (or at least, the self-trivialization) that will result."

The Harvard department had all the usual problems: the undergraduates complained that they never saw the senior staff, the graduate students felt alienated and unwanted, the junior faculty resented having their offices a mile away from their seniors, and they also knew that they were all going to be fired sooner or later, in the usual Harvard manner. The administration was angry at a department that it felt had allowed itself to fall below the standards expected at Harvard, the professors complained about their heavy teaching and administrative responsibilities, and their lack of time for research, and said that the administration had made it impossible for them to make good outside appointments by offering piddling salaries to distinguished people. There were no women or minority members on full tenure. Helen Vendler had just been hired but still spent half her time at Boston University in the hope that she might manage to do some grievous harm to her archenemy, the BU president, John Silber, before departure. The graduate students pointed out that they did most of the undergraduate teaching, which was true, and everyone felt the lack of decent office space. In other words, the usual mess, everyone unhappy, an old-fashioned department blocked and unable to move toward the future.

The visiting committee felt that if the Harvard professors recognized their problems and moved, while they still had control of the situation, to solve them, they might have a chance to meet the revolutionary social and philosophical pressures of deconstruction and feminism in a rational and sensible way. Perhaps, we suggested in our final report, it would help if they scheduled graduate classes on five days of the week instead of the three middle days, which made for uninterrupted long weekends for the professors but meant that scheduling conflicts made it impossible for the students to take courses they needed. Beyond such small but important matters we also tried to impress the professors with the importance of appointing some younger people, certainly some women, of promoting to tenure one or more junior faculty who were not perceived as anyone's favorite, and of offering courses in which recent critical theories were seriously discussed.

In the spring I was summoned to Harvard to meet with a committee on the humanities of the overseers board and with the English department chairman to discuss the report, which by then had been circulated to all, and perhaps even read by some. The chairman was Larry Benson, a very good Chaucer scholar and a staunch Harvard man. We arrived together in the elegant surroundings of the old president's house, and it was easy to see that he was angry and deeply disturbed, barely greeting me. We went into the room where the overseers were gathered, and I was asked to elaborate on my report, which I did, stressing how obvious the need for some of the changes was. When I finished, they thanked me and turned to Professor Benson to ask what he thought of the report. His only answer was that the Harvard English department was the best English department in the country and that no very large changes were needed. When pressed by the overseers, he stayed with it: "No, sir, the Harvard department is absolutely the best department in the country." He would not debate any of my points, he simply wasn't having any of it, and he wasn't going to waste any time on arguing with the opinions of a bunch of outsiders.

The overseers seemed quite content with the chairman's answer, and after a short time they explained to me that they had now received my report and that I was free to leave while they discussed the matter with the Harvard chairman. I got up and went to the airport, more astounded than angry, and that was the end of it. After I left, Harvard closed ranks and got on with being the foremost university in the world. They sent me a nice morocco leather case in Harvard red, "In Gratitude For Service to Harvard" stamped in gold letters on the cover, but not a single one of the visiting committee's recommendations was ever acted on; probably the report was never looked at again. The administration, which had urged me to write a strong, critical report, found it impossible to enforce any of our recommendations, and so let the matter drop. In time the English department changed, not by any master plan, but in response to opportunities and problems as they arose.

More and more, like many other older scholars, I stayed in my study in the library, surrounded by millions of books in the stacks and by the isolation of a place where faculty and students, working at home on their word processors, came less and less. What a pleasure to walk from floor to floor of Firestone, seeing only a librarian here and there or another of the library rats like myself: Tony Grafton reading some obscure Renaissance text held close to his face as he walked along, John Fleming searching out some medieval manual on prayer, Merrill Knapp cataloguing Handel's operas, Sam Hynes editing the many variants for his Oxford edition of Hardy's poems. The books printed since about 1875 on acid paper may have been disintegrating, the backs falling off volumes that had been glued rather than sewn, the pages scribbled on and highlighted by students writing papers, but it was a great research library, with eighteenth-century books and first editions of American and British novels still on the open shelves. When I needed Johnson's *Dictionary* (second printing) or the eighteenth-century *Journal of the House of Commons*, they were in the stacks, not the rare book library, the leather covers shabby and dried but the rag paper, the ink, and the printing perfect still.

Almost any book I required was there, and anything that was not would be ordered or gotten through interlibrary loan. Libraries may be a dying institution, the ziggurats of the old universities, but Firestone still worked, and the surroundings were sensuous in the varied colors of the faded bindings, the order of the shelving system, the smell of old paper, glue, leather, and ink. To step inside the cool of the building on a hot, sticky summer day, go to the card catalogue, or for books published since 1980 to the electronic catalogue, and then walk through one empty floor after another past the rows on rows of books was a genuinely reassuring experience.

But what to do with it all? You could go on doing the things literary scholars had always done, ignoring all that had happened and publishing still another interpretation of *Hamlet*, putting the life and works of another author, say, Richard Savage, in the context of his times, editing the poetry of John Dryden in a sumptuous definitive edition, or tracing some theme like family life or imagination through several diverse works. But all these turns of the literary prayer wheel, worthy though they might be, took for granted the old assumptions about the absolute value of literature. And even if you had profound doubts, as I did, about the nihilistic tendencies and radical political agendas of the avant-garde during the past twenty years in literary studies, they had made the old high-culture assumptions—about canonical perfect works, imaginative geniuses, single, fixed meanings in texts—doubtful at best, no longer even tenable at the extreme. Within limits, the deconstructionists and special-interest groups were right. Texts *do* lend themselves to more than a single legitimate interpretation, large chunks of language *do* rest not on substantial reality but on a void, the concerns of women and minorities *have* been largely excluded from critical consideration, and works of art *are* shaped to accord with dominant political and social interests. In the effort to make their point, and their careers, the deconstructors and ideologues had regularly gone to scandalous extremes, but their inflammatory rhetoric had dramatized, melodramatized really, the reality that the old high literature and the fine arts, like other cultural institutions, are not absolutes based on solid, unchanging facts. They are social constructions, filled with contradictions and logical gaps, put together historically out of available beliefs and technologies to satisfy the needs of those who use them. What emerged from the theorization and politicization of literature, however, was not the establishment of new truths about literature, sweeping away old "truths" to make room for a new Truth, but the relativization of all views. For a time we thought that, but now we believe this, and in time others will think something else. Literature, recent events had demonstrated, is not a monolithic, unchanging product of nature or culture, as the New Critics had posited, but a social institution with a history. And with this understanding, rather than clinging to the past or arguing rancorously with the forces of change, as many of my colleagues did, I thought it might be productive to try to write about how and why literature, like other fields of knowledge, is socially constructed. Rather than trying to write a continuous history of literature's paradigm changes, I began to explore in three volumes (though not in chronological order) the careers of a few writers so deeply involved in great literary shifts that their lives and works offered an explanation of what was happening and why it did.

Shakespeare, the official playwright for King James I, offered a definitive image of a great writer functioning in a court setting under the social arrangements of patronage, which I described in *Shakespeare, the King's Playwright* (1995). From the time of Petrarch until that of Alexander Pope, and even as late as Goethe at Weimar, patronage was almost the only means of support for writers and the only way of locating them in the social order. In ages when there was no author's copyright and no large audience of educated, book-buying readers, professional writers (many of them masquerading as gentlemen amateurs) had survived by practicing an art of service for wealthy and powerful patrons. Shakespeare was among the most interesting of these patronage poets, not only because he was simultaneously involved in a public theater that was breaking the hold of patronage on the arts, but because he himself worked in a patronage relationship with the English king. Though little attention had been paid to the fact, James I, after taking the throne in 1603, made the playwright and his playing company the royal troupe, known as the King's Men. The Shakespeare plays written for performance at court, as well as for the public theater after 1603, constitute a patronage oeuvre in size and importance matched only by other master works of patronage like Michelangelo's Sistine Chapel, Palladio's villas, and Bach's Brandenburg Concertos. Works of genius all, these monuments show how art at its best served the noble patron and at the same time moved toward its own autonomy.

During the eighteenth century, writing evolved from manuscripts exchanged among patrons and friends into a form established in print and geared toward market consumption. The literary system took a new shape that conformed to the new modes of production. Which led me in *Printing Technology, Letters, and Samuel Johnson* (1987) to study how the print business and the market for print commodities in the eighteenth century changed the lives of writers and their conceptions of what was then only beginning to be called literature. Lacking other means of making his way in the world, Johnson led a Grub Street life in all respects—trying to interest the "common reader," meeting printers' deadlines, writing for money. But rather than simply accepting his lot like other hacks, he made himself into the "Great Cham of Literature." He did so not by rejecting the new scene of writing created by the printing business—it is, I believe, impossible for a writer to reject the realities of his technological and financial condition—but by maximizing their opportunities, translating even failure to meet deadlines into the moodiness of a temperamental genius, and elevating the public that bought his books to the status of the sought-after "common readers." In time, Boswell completed the work of making Johnson the writer into a heroic figure, the first Romantic *poète maudit*, by portraying his struggles with illness and depression as the true marks of a great writer overcoming in life and art the emptiness and pain of everyday experience.

As early as the 1960s, the older Romantic–Victorian–fin de siècle conception of literature was disintegrating in ways that I tried to describe in *The Death of Literature* (1990). This book was widely interpreted as arguing that people would no longer write novels and poetry, or teach these kinds of writing in the university, or read fiction. Because these activities were obviously continuing, such an argument would have been nonsense—if I had made it, but I did not. My point was that literature was not a universal feature of cultural life but only the name of the particular literary system that had developed in the print circumstances of the late eighteenth century, when it replaced poetry and belles lettres, and that it had dominated our conception of the literary scene since then. But now, I went on, it was dying as belief in its sustaining pillars—the canonical Great Books, the pure and perfect work of art, its profound benefits to persons and the culture, the transcendental power of the imagination—broke up under the pressures of various new forces: electronic communication technology that was replacing print, deconstructive philosophies, and the radical democratization of the universities.

I sat for years up on the third floor in Firestone Library, six days a week, winter and summer, in a small corner office with gray metal walls and no name on the door, writing these books one after the other. I educated myself in areas I had never ventured into before: the history of the Stuart monarchy, court patronage in the Renaissance, early print-house practices, Grub Street, technology and culture, copyright law, and on and on. As I worked I moved from yellow pads of paper and a typewriter to a computer, a small Macintosh with two floppy-disk drives, each having a capacity of 80 kilobytes, which meant constantly changing disks and sometimes getting caught up in that maddening circle of the Mac demanding Disk A and then Disk B time after time.

Princeton University seemed to feel no regret for the passing of the old order, for it offered professors of my age an increased pension if at sixty we would agree to put more money into our retirement funds and guarantee to retire at sixty-five, instead of the usual sixty-eight or seventy. Presumably this was intended to save money on high salaries, but it conveyed very effectively to me and many others that it was time for our generation to go. In fact there was plenty of money, and the real reason had to be to get the fossils out of the way so that younger people, women and minorities in particular, could be appointed in our places. In time a young black woman took over my office, a distinguished feminist assumed the chair I had held, and a female deconstructionist was assigned my budget slot and my responsibility for teaching the

Renaissance. There was no real antipathy, at least so I believe, between me and my younger colleagues, but neither was there the sense of affinity, of a shared, continuing search for truth, that had made me one with my own elders in an earlier time. Feelings of a break in the continuity of generations were particularly deep in literary studies, where what the older generation had written was no longer considered useful, where professional disagreements were exacerbated by the tensions of gender, race, and class, and where the search for truth had largely been replaced by teaching and publication as careerism and political action.

Something of this sense of loss comes, I suppose, to every teacher in the end—except for those charismatic princes of the lecture hall like Lane Faison, who taught generations of students at Williams the meaning of painting and shaped many of the museum directors in the country. Or the classicist and master of Eliot House at Harvard, John Finley. Both of their retirements were reported in long articles in the *New York Times*. Finley, who had begun teaching in 1933, gave his last lecture in 1976 in his famous course "The Great Age of Athens." It was attended by a thousand students and the president of the university. They gave him two standing ovations, and the president praised him as "the embodiment of Harvard." When I gave my last lecture, on Shakespeare's *Tempest*, I don't think any of the students knew it (though I thought I saw Smithers smirking in the back row). "These our Revels now are ended."

Epilogue

the dogs bark, the caravan passes on

The dogs have barked themselves hoarse in the previous pages, and it is good to be able to report, ten years after the end of my story, that the educational caravan, with some faster camels and some more exotic burdens, still moves along its way. The colleges and universities, at least most of them, get bigger and richer every year, and only occasionally do the coals flare up brightly enough to remind us that a radical democratic spirit is not yet entirely burned out in the academy: another sit-in occupies an administrator's office; the teaching graduate students strike and refuse to turn in their grades; there is yet another attempt to remove SAT scores from consideration in college admissions on the grounds that the tests favor white males and discriminate against women, blacks, and ethnic minorities, all except the Asians who consistently score higher than everyone else.

Ten years have passed since I retired from the university and settled in the reassuring surroundings of the Andrew W. Mellon Foundation (nothing makes people more agreeable than being given money). So quiet are things that I find myself considering that I may, personally and professionally, have taken the events described in earlier chapters too much to heart. To me, as to many of my friends and colleagues, the years from the late 1960s on looked and felt like an academic apocalypse. They clearly were not so catastrophic as all that, but my concern and that of many of my colleagues was not, I think, entirely unjustified, for we were living through a time of structural change in a major social institution. Such times of transition, which always go too far too soon, deeply disturbed those who, like myself, were trained in and attached to the old and passing order. It was not easy to live through, day by working day, the shift from an old university removed from the hurly-burly of money and politics, built on a scientific conception of knowledge, meritocratic, positivistic, authoritarian, private in its decision-making, to a new, more public type of higher education—accessible to everyone, relativistic in its conception of knowledge, consumer oriented, functioning openly—in short, user-friendly. In place of the ancien régime of old elitist institutions grew a new, what shall I call it? Clark Kerr's "multiversity"? Or a "demoversity"?

Looking back, the change seems to have been inevitable. Many factors, great and small, contributed to it—more people going to college, information becoming more widely available, letters of recommendation becoming public, women and minorities demanding and getting equality, grade inflation, authority of all kinds weakening. The leading theme of our society is, after all, democracy, and in a time of social ferment it should not have been surprising that education moved quickly and forcefully in that direction. It had been fitfully moving that way for a long time, going back to the land-grant colleges, the elective curriculum at Harvard, and the G.I. Bill. But in times when democracy was threatened by a very dangerous Cold War, and in times of great prosperity, the process speeded up. Grading systems, teaching philosophies, political attitudes, admissions standards, scholarship, government regulations, electronic technology, the campus ethos—all moved in remarkable concert in a democratic direction, weakening authority and strengthening individual freedom.

The gyroscope at the center of any educational system, if it is not to be just a gymnasium or a fraternity row, is its dominant conception of knowledge, and even this was reoriented toward a more democratic relativism in which there are no absolute authorities and everyone shares to some degree what can be known and how to know it. Even in the sciences a certain amount of undecidability now reigns, while at the other end of the educational spectrum in literature there are no facts, only interpretations.

The democratization of the universities is not yet complete, and a totally democratic system of higher education is probably as unattainable, and as undesirable, as a totally democratic society. Education by its very nature—the transfer of knowledge from those who know to those who don't—is ineradicably authoritarian to some degree, even in community colleges and proprietary schools. And a few elite universities and colleges continue to occupy the top of an educational hierarchy that stubbornly will not altogether level out. The money, the research, the publication, and the most promising students still tend to concentrate in these schools, and their huge increases in tuition, even with generous financial aid, help to maintain them as places mainly for the rich and the very smart. But even these places have been deeply affected by such radical democratic practices as affirmative action, grade inflation, politicization of the softer subjects of instruction, relativistic standards of knowledge, and increasingly nonresident, careerist faculties. Even their high tuitions encourage democratic tendencies in students whose parents pay them, raising expectations of high grades, amusement, and helpful placement services.

Democratization in higher education is irreversible, in ways that, for example, recent failed attempts by elite colleges to reverse grade inflation demonstrate. One school can't do it alone, since to do so would penalize its graduates in the competition for admission to graduate and professional schools. But beyond this, the students won't have it, and the faculty won't cooperate either. Their tenure, promotion, and pay raises are indexed to their popularity with students, a much more potent force for the new gypsy scholar and the non-tenure-track lecturer than for the old tenured professors.

For most Americans there can never be too much democracy, and the democratic changes in higher education over the past fifty years therefore seem to be all to the good. And with this judgment, at least in large part, which American can disagree? It is surely better that people who want a college education can have one. Why should women not be educated, hired, paid, and promoted at the same rate, and in the same schools, as men? Absolute and universal truth does seem increasingly a will-o'-the-wisp, and certainly there is no such thing as one, exactly right, way to interpret a text. Words *are* tricky, and good sense requires that each of us question their authority and the motives of those who use them to construct ideologies that masquerade as truth. Increased availability of information by electronic means can only contribute to the development of an informed citizenry.

But after these obvious goods have been praised, the democratization of American higher education still leaves us with a number of troubling questions. American democracy, as Tocqueville told us long ago, is not always and in all ways the very best kind of thing. It regularly goes too far, and when it does it has a tendency to pervert the very values it tries to further. Open admissions sounds promising, until we hear of arguments about whether entering college students should read at seventh-grade or eighth-grade level, or when the average time spent earning a bachelor's degree expands from four years to seven. More than three-quarters of American colleges and universities, we are told, offered remedial courses in 1996. Grade inflation and pass/fail options move toward the elimination of any distinction based on quality of work. Faculty in the demoversity is composed more and more (40 percent in 1998) of part-time gypsy scholars, lacking employment benefits and the possibility of promotion. The widening division between stars and a teaching underclass might not seem particularly democratic in its workings, but a free, uncontrolled marketplace for labor has traditionally accompanied American democracy, which has historically prized equality of opportunity over equality of income. Paulo Freire's criticism of the banking model of education and the "pedagogy of the oppressed" notwithstanding, capitalism is the economic system democracy chooses to live with, and that an increasingly democratic academy should reject professionalism in favor of the inequities of the market-place was inevitable.

Everyone is entitled to his or her opinion, and there are many right ways of interpreting a text or assembling a history; but there are clearly some wrong ones as well, and dangerous confusion surely re-sults from the leveling view that all interpretations are equal. No doubt the perfection of even the greatest work is overstated, in copyright laws and in theories of the creative imagination; but does it not fly in the face of obvious, undeniable fact to say that there is no such thing as plagia-rism, no such person as an author, and no works that rise, in what they have to say and how they say it, above run-of-the-mill writing? There are many histories, but can we accept one in which the Holocaust is a fiction? There are many readings of a novel, but where are we when every closed door conceals a masturbating girl—"Marianne's shudder-ing sobs . . ."—or anything else the reader wants to put there? Perhaps all activities are touched with personal bias and ideological politics, but is it really true that some degree of objectivity is impossible?

I could go on this way, but the point is clear by now, I hope, that the democratic tendencies in higher education, while praiseworthy in many ways, have gone too far. When we begin to say things like "words can have *no* meaning," "*all* the great books of the past were written by men to put women down," "*every* person is so locked in the self that he or she cannot possibly understand any other person or society in a relatively unbiased way," and "there are *no* facts, or even approxima-tions of facts, only endless fictions," then we have clearly slipped into one more of the kind of unproductive ideologies that have caused so much destruction in our time. But history never runs backward, and to reverse the democratization of American higher education is neither desirable nor possible. What is possible is to realize that we have passed through not just some evolutionary modifications of an old academic order but a structural change in higher education—the description of which I take to be the main point of this book—and that it has brought with it, in the heat of the change, some extreme and harmful politi-cal and theoretical assumptions. But it would be a waste of time and patience to keep on wrangling with one another about whether the old ways were right and the new ways are wrong. What we can do is accept that we have a new, democratic kind of higher education, one that will fit the interests and values of twenty-first-century America in many fundamental and important ways. But it has arrived with some very rough edges and a strident ideology, both of which need considerable smoothing against the grindstone of accumulated knowledge from the past and the real, present needs of an effective educational system.

Index

St. Patrick's Day parade riot (1959), 134–35, 168
Samuelson, Paul, 66
Santayana, George, 15
Sapir, Edward, 22
Sartre, Jean-Paul, 98, 181, 257
Satire, 78, 125–27, 135
SAT scores, 239, 240, 295
Savage, Richard, 290
Schama, Simon, 195–96
Schmidt, Benno, 148
Schuman, Fred, 17
Schwartz, Delmore, 184, 226
Science, 112, 114, 147; government support of, 212, 216; linguistic, 55; and literature, 32, 108–10, 114; Milgram's obedience experiment and, 101; and relativity, xvi, 271, 297; resistance to change, 247, 249, 278
Scoble, Harry, 37, 73
Scribner, Charles, 227, 234
Scully, Vincent, 163, 172
Seale, Bobby, 167–69, 171–73, 174, 176–77
Secret Life (Ryan), 263
Sexual Behavior in the Human Male (Kinsey), 23–25, 31
Shakespeare, William, 44, 67, 75, 140–43, 156, 174, 187, 228, 276, 291; authorship of, 92–93; editing, 95–96, 291; First Folio, 76; Julius Caesar, 95; King Lear, 139; Love's Labours Lost, 187; Measure for Measure, 56; Merchant of Venice, 95; Othello, 33, 95, 117, 135; Rape of Lucrece, 94; Romeo and Juliet, 279–81; Tempest, 94, 294; Twelfth Night, 285
Shakespearean Negotiations (Greenblatt), 284
Shapiro, Harold, 269
Shaw, George Bernard, 68, 223
Shelley, Percy Bysshe, 19–20, 110
Short-Title Catalogue, The (Wing), 79
Showalter, Elaine, 247, 251
Simpson, Alan, 152, 154
Simpson, Eileen, 226
Simpson, Hartley, 82
Sinister Street (Mackenzie), 40
Skinner, B. F., 272
Small World (Lodge), 242, 258
Snow, Sir Charles, 109–10

Sontag, Susan, 116–17
Sophocles, 60, 113, 187, 189
Spitzer, Lyman, 218
Stanford University, 173, 278
Stevens, Holly, 148
Stevens, Wallace, 18, 148
Stone, Lawrence, 218
Structuralism, 112–16, 241, 287
Students, xiii, 89, 99, 101, 166, 193–94, 213, 277; abilities of, 34, 68, 141, 227, 240, 276, 298; activism, 134, 160–63, 168, 175; demographics, 14, 73, 86, 170, 216, 217; female, 68, 74, 209; and grades, 173, 278–79, 297; graduate, 67–68, 77, 129, 140, 207, 211, 215–16; and the law, 90, 208, 210; married, 4–5, 72; part time, 80; and politics, 13, 67, 160, 164, 169, 205; relations with faculty, 90, 106, 124–25, 143, 209, 218, 251, 262–64, 275, 282; and religion, 18, 41, 66; and sex, 22–24, 31, 33, 69, 161, 251–54, 262–64; and wealth and poverty, 17, 40, 50, 74, 88, 91–92, 158, 216, 277
Swift, Jonathan, 79, 127, 135, 159
Sylvester, Richard, 135, 136
Szaz, Thomas, 180

Tate, Allen, 61, 64, 226
Tater, Mrs. Samuel, 73
Taylor, A. J. P., 49
Taylor, Charles, 144, 147, 148, 155, 163, 166
Teaching, 17, 71–72, 97–98, 99, 140–43, 186, 197, 218–19, 253, 277, 282; and grading, 278–79, 281–82; of history, 15; of literature, 14, 45, 157, 256; Milgram's obedience experiment, 99–101; politicized, xv, 66–67, 173, 214, 256, 258, 274, 277; schedule, 16, 80, 278; for sex, 262–65; and skepticism, 22, 108; student reports on, 124, 280; and technology, 242; at two colleges, 71; and writing, 34, 240. See also Faculty
Technology, xvi, 235, 241–45, 292, 293
Television, 122, 191, 230–34, 244, 246
Tenner, Edward, 235
Tenure, 119, 123, 130–34, 135–36, 195, 214,